THE SCO**_____ _____ __**
UNIVERSITY EDUCATION

JOHN HENRY NEWMAN was born in London in 1801 and was educated at Trinity College, Oxford. Ordained a priest in the Church of England in 1825, Newman was appointed to the vicarage of St. Mary the Virgin, Oxford, in 1828. With others he initiated the Oxford Movement in 1833. Newman was received into the Catholic Church in 1845 and became Rector of the Catholic University, Dublin, in 1854. He was created a cardinal in 1879. Newman died at Edgbaston (where he founded the Oratory School in 1859) and was buried at Rednal in 1890.

THE SCOPE AND NATURE
OF
UNIVERSITY EDUCATION

By

JOHN HENRY CARDINAL NEWMAN

Introduction by WILFRID WARD

A Dutton  *Paperback*

Everyman

NEW YORK

E. P. DUTTON & CO., INC.

1958

This paperback edition of
"The Scope and Nature of University Education"
Published 1958 by E. P. Dutton & Co., Inc.

INTRODUCTION

CARDINAL NEWMAN's lectures on the 'Scope and Nature of University Education' have quite special interest as a turning-point in his mental history. At Oxford he was regarded as the head of the reactionaries, the unflinching opponent of all liberalism in theology. In later life he was called by many a liberal Catholic, and though he most strongly repudiated that epithet he did admit in 1866 his 'enthusiastic agreement' with the general line of thought of Montalembert and Lacordaire, who gloried in the title of liberal Catholic. Later on came a phenomenon yet more surprising on the surface. Such advocates of Modernism as Abbé Loisy and M. Leroy claimed Newman's philosophical thought as being in line with their own speculations. The fact is that labels and watchwords are constantly so inadequate as to be quite misleading. Not all opponents of liberalism have been illiberal. All Newman's earlier career emphasized his opposition to liberalism. His later years brought in evidence his true liberality. Newman was never a Modernist, but he was keenly alive to the changes of outlook wrought by the thought and research of modern days. One side of his thought was emphasized at Oxford, another was developed in his later Catholic life. And the change was brought about by the circumstances in which these lectures were written.

The inadequacy of popular watchwords explains in other cases also the gradual fusion of schools of thought which had been at first simply opposed to one another. While liberal thinkers have claimed as their ally a man whose opposition to liberalism was the very keynote of his mission at Oxford, we have seen a similar alliance in later times between the descendants within the Church of England of the two opposite schools which divided Oxford in the forties. The High Church party which long carried on the traditions of Tractarianism startled the world in 1889 by a manifesto on behalf of breadth in theology—the famous *Lux Mundi*. The writers I allude to singled out especially the subject of biblical inspiration and the historical treatment of dogma, both of which had been exclusively associated in earlier years with those implacable foes of Tractarianism, the disciples of Dr Arnold. The old opposition in matters theological was between the High Church and the Broad Church, though the phrase 'Broad Church' was subsequent to Newman's day. But *Lux Mundi*, whose authors all claimed to be High Churchmen, was as broad as it was high in its theology. It differed from Broad Church theology in retaining the idea of the Catholic Church, which the Oxford Movement had brought into evidence, as of paramount importance both in theology and in the philosophy of belief.

Newman never exhibited the highly speculative vein apparent in *Lux Mundi*. But throughout his opposition to unrestrained theological liberalism, a liberalism which threw overboard the idea of a corporate Church and the sacredness of tradition, he had been alive to the necessity of facing fearlessly the new outlook presented by advancing science and research. We can see this clearly in the first of the Oxford University Sermons, preached when he was only twenty-five years old. In the days of the Oxford Movement no doubt he was a party man and his party was in a sense reactionary. But to careful readers of the University Sermons and the Essay on Development the width of his outlook was quite apparent. His conception of the development of Christian doctrine as gradually bringing into view fresh aspects of truth really made room for the advancement of secular knowledge, its gradual reconciliation with the essence of traditional Catholic truth, and the necessary modifications in the analysis of that truth. What changed with him was, as I have said, not so much his views as his party and his emphasis. He had opposite dangers to face in the earlier and the later period. At Oxford he feared that Christianity would be swept away by the tide of rationalistic liberalism which lost sight of the profound truths contained in the Christian tradition and derived from revelation. In later years his fear was exactly the opposite. He was alive to the danger lest theological narrowness might be an equally dangerous opponent to Christianity by bringing about an apparent alliance between orthodoxy and obscurantism. The lectures here published mark the point at which this change of emphasis began. They are one long plea for the compatibility of a complete culture of mind and all the frankness it entails with adherence to the Catholic faith. He was, as rector of a Catholic university, face to face with the necessity of marking out for sharp-witted young men an attitude towards science and theology which was entirely reasonable. The task before him was the formation in the undergraduate of a mentality which should be at once thoroughly educated and thoroughly religious. He declares in his own preface to these lectures that he does not regard a university as concerned with research, only with teaching and education. But when he began the duties of his office he saw that this hard and fast line could not be drawn. A thoughtful Catholic must take account of problems which every other thoughtful man was discussing. It was impossible in a time of constant scientific movement to disregard or be indifferent to the results of research.

The lectures on the Scope and Nature of University Education, therefore, led up to his great plea for intellectual liberty in a university. That plea is contained in the lecture on Christianity and Scientific Investigation which is published in the larger volume known as *The Idea of a University*, and is given at the end of the present book. In the face of constantly advancing science and criticism the attitude of the thoughtful Catholic in their regard was an urgent question, and he hoped gradually to define that attitude in a university which should contain experts in all the sciences, and which being a learned body might consent to allow the complete freedom of discussion which is indispensable to true scientific progress. The danger of scandal and of upsetting the popular mind by novel views would be reduced to a *minimum* in discussions conducted not by a mixed body of learned and unlearned in the periodical press, but among specialists in a university. Thus the conception of a university as a place in which young men should form habits of frank, cultivated, and accurate thought was enlarged in the lecture on Christianity and Scientific Investigation so as to include the fuller idea of a great institution which should gradually define the attitude of a cultivated Catholic towards scientific investigation and work out some approach to a synthesis between all the sciences, including the science of theology. Undoubtedly the medieval universities had in a very different state of the scientific world performed this function, and his ambition was that a Catholic university might once again perform a similar work in the nineteenth century.

'What an empire is in political history,' he writes in the lecture of which I speak, 'such is a university in the sphere of philosophy and research. It is, as I have said, the high protecting power of all knowledge and science, of fact and principle, of inquiry and discovery, of experiment and speculation; it maps out the territory of the intellect, and sees that the boundaries of each province are religiously respected, and that there is neither encroachment nor surrender on any side. It acts as umpire between truth and truth, and, taking into account the nature and importance of each, assigns to all their due order of precedence. It maintains no one department of thought exclusively, however ample and noble; and it sacrifices none. It is deferential and loyal, according to their respective weight, to the claims of literature, of physical research, of history, of metaphysics, of theological science. It is impartial towards them all, and promotes each in its own place and for its own object. It is ancillary certainly, and of necessity, to the Catholic Church; but in the same way that one of the Queen's judges is an officer of the Queen's, and nevertheless determines certain legal proceedings between the Queen and her subjects. . . . Its immediate end (with which alone we have here to do) is to secure the due disposition, according to one sovereign order, and the cultivation in that order, of all the provinces and methods of thought which the human intellect has created. In this point of view, its several professors are like the ministers of various political powers at one court or conference. They represent their respective sciences, and attend to the private interests of those sciences respectively; and, should dispute arise between those sciences, they are the persons to talk over and arrange it, without risk of extravagant pretensions on any side, of angry collision, or of popular commotion. A liberal philosophy becomes the habit of minds thus exercised; a breadth and spaciousness of thought, in which lines, seemingly parallel, may converge at leisure, and principles, recognized as incommensurable, may be safely antagonistic.'

Whether Newman's idea will ever be practicable it is hard to say; this must largely depend on the readiness of Rome to accord to universities something of the weight and influence which they had in the Middle Ages. The idea, however, was well worth suggesting, and if it could be realized its importance can hardly be exaggerated. Such an institution as he conceived would constitute a reliable authority where mere private judgment might in most cases be hopelessly at fault—for individuals cannot be specialists all round. In the ever-shifting intellectual scene wrought by the active thought and research of our day Christians fall chiefly into two parties. There are on the one hand the independent intellectual freelances who—with inevitably inadequate knowledge—judge entirely for themselves on these complex questions, and on the other hand there are the more anxious and narrow spirits who adhere to traditionary views and shrink from change. This latter class includes many who are little alive to facts brought to light by modern research which are to frank minds simply undeniable. This general division holds good outside the Roman Catholic body, but it is that body which Newman had especially in his mind. In the Catholic Church itself authority normally acts, as Newman points out in the 'Apologia,' as a check on the developments which are desired by eager intellectual reformers who are generally somewhat undiscriminating and one-sided, though they may be pioneers of true advance. Thus in appearance, at all events, authority and enlightened thought are ranged on opposite sides. But Newman sought to institute a subordinate authority which should represent simply and solely genuine knowledge and thought exercised in the interests of truth. Such an authority might inspire the freelances with respect. The supreme tribunals in Rome itself are quite inevitably influenced not solely by the interests of scientific truth, but to a great extent by considerations of ecclesiastical expediency. And in cases where the interests of truth are urgently pressing, a temporizing policy on their part might exasperate the intellectual minority. Truth is, as Newman points out in his preface to the 'Via Media,' only one of the three interests which the Church safeguards. She has to consider also the interests of devotion, and the interests of rule; and, as he adds, the guiding principle of the ruler is expediency. Such a university as Newman contemplated, on the other hand, would reach its synthesis or its practical *modus vivendi* between theology and modern research guided solely by scientific interests—theology, of course, being included among the sciences. The results thus reached would place at the disposal of Rome a body of probable conclusions which must command the respect of scholars and thoughtful men. A letter written by Newman to myself only two years before he died showed that this idea never deserted him. If it could be achieved it would make this great difference in the situation, that Rome, instead of feeling that the immediate alternative lay between taking sides in these controversies either with theologians of excessively conservative tendencies or else with some of the highly speculative theories of Abbé Loisy, would have a third course ready marked out; Roman tribunals could utilize in their decisions the results of the discussions between the learned men in the Catholic university.

The bearing of this on matters which have anxiously interested the public in recent years is obvious. The history of Modernism would have been widely different had Newman's ideal been fully realized. Highly sensitive and easily overwrought intellectual natures may be driven to extremes by a lack of understanding in authoritative quarters of the problems which exercise them intensely. It was a sense of this danger which led many of us so eagerly to desire the formation of a biblical commission which should fulfil in the department of biblical exegesis the functions of Newman's ideal university. But such a commission, seated in Rome itself, becomes of its nature official. Being official, considerations of expediency are sure to prevail at times over considerations of intellectual truth, and it tends to conform to the law which Newman recognized, that Rome must be conservative; that Rome's normal function is to be a brake on development. The less responsible and less final authority of a university would be in quite a different position. Constant pressure would be exercised on the teaching body by the inquiring minds of thoughtful young men which needed reasonable satisfaction. Such young men desire to be at once religious and rational. Cheap apologetics which do not carry genuine conviction would inevitably be set aside, and it would be impossible to ignore patent facts in the early history of the Church or the text of the Bible. If the presence of first-rate experts were secured, a rational and coherent body of thought must gradually be wrought out by the intercourse between them. The larger-minded theologians and the Christian men of science would find a *modus vivendi*. This was the ideal of Cardinal Mercier in founding the Institut de St Thomas at Louvain, and it lay at the root of his saying that every theologian should be in our day also a man of science.

If such a body were habitually tolerated by Roman authority men like Loisy and Tyrrell, instead of being goaded to extremes by total lack of sympathy in authoritative quarters, might conceivably have taken their place in the good work, content to bear a part in it and contributing their conclusions to the common stock of discussion, but ready to refrain from insisting on them in instances where no interpretation of Catholic theology could admit them. Such scholars, living in the society of other learned men who understood them, would not improbably have become genuinely more moderate from the presence of an opposition which was really scientific. There is much in Tyrrell's history which points to this possibility, but anyhow, even assuming that he and Loisy were men who would inevitably have broken with Catholic teaching however interpreted,

there are beyond question many whom the existence of such
a university as Newman desired and its respectful recognition by authority would have affected in the way I have
described. It is hardly too much to say that the encyclical
'Pascendi' would not have been written had Newman's
ideal been realized, for the policy marked out by that
encyclical might easily lead to the almost indiscriminate
proscription of novelty as dangerous. I am not denying
that theologians by collating this encyclical with other
documents equally authoritative may find that a satisfactory *via media* has sanction from Rome. Indeed,
shortly after its publication the Professor of Biblical
Exegesis at the Institut Catholique in Paris pointed this
out in a remarkable lecture. But the encyclical 'Pascendi'
read by itself is an eloquent witness to just that state of
things I have spoken of which Newman desired to remedy,
namely, that Rome felt herself to be solicited by opposite
extreme parties; that she felt the practical alternative to lie
between sanctioning unbridled liberty and taking measures
of the utmost severity against innovation. This arose
from the absence of a recognized body of discriminating
thought in these complex questions. The work of discriminating is arduous, and can only be done by learned
men. It must be a work of time, it cannot be extemporized
to meet an emergency. A university with its continuous
life of thought and learning is just the machinery that is
required. It is not a court which is called upon to hear
evidence and decide at a moment of crisis; it is an ever-
living, ever-working machine which is constantly at work
on these problems and has first-rate experts at its disposal.

In point of fact, Newman's exposition of the functions of
the ideal Catholic university was an integral portion of his
vindication of the claims of authority against the claims of
private judgment. His early quarrel with the liberals was
that they strove to enforce the speculation of the hour

against the gradually accumulating knowledge due to the experience of the race. They ignored those grounds of belief which had their roots in experience and were beyond the access of the individual reason. This view is apparent in a remarkable letter to his mother written as early as 1829. The contest became primarily ecclesiastical and theological when the Oxford Movement began in 1833. But the philosophy which underlay his views was the philosophy of Coleridge. Like Coleridge he vindicated the claims of tradition as representing the thought of great minds and the revelation of Christ Himself. Tradition thus supplies the human race with knowledge not provable by the individual reason. The mind of the ages was an authority which the individual thinker had no right to set aside because he could not establish by his own demonstration what was really based on the experience and insight of many minds in the past. The corporate conviction which had its roots in past experience, and had stood the test of later experience, was an authoritative basis on which the individual thinker could work. It was only when later experience was at variance with traditional beliefs that their interpretation must be modified. The business of the individual was to continue the work of his predecessors and correct it in detail, not to wreck it. But he was to continue this work, as his ancestors had wrought it out, by co-operative reasoning which should issue in a body of more or less authoritative conclusions. While he opposed 'reason' when it meant the individual's private judgment when it presumed to set aside the acquisitions of the race, he regarded 'reason' as absolutely supreme in the domain of science. For science was itself organized experience. And he contemplated the erection of a fresh authority which should represent contemporary thought and science and should correct and enlarge, but not set aside, the legacy we have received from the past.

Hence the apparently opposite language he uses at different times in regard to human 'reason,' which seems at first sight so perplexing. He seems at once to be the critic of reason and its staunch supporter. The 'usurpations of reason' were a favourite theme in Oxford days. These usurpations are dwelt on even in the 'Apologia.' The tendency of the human reason freely exercised is, he there maintains, to destroy religious belief. That he used such language in 1864 is a fact which should give pause to any idea that there was a real change in Newman's fundamental views. What he had said in 1839 he repeated in 1864. On the other hand, in the lecture I am considering he regards human reason as supreme. If it really reaches a demonstration which is at variance with received religious opinions it means, he contends, that those opinions, though they may have been even supposed to be part of revealed truth, are really only opinions which have become confused by Christians with revelation. But grave innovations on received views cannot wisely be allowed to prevail on the strength of the *ipse dixit* of a private individual. The ideal university which welcomes discussion among experts is the terrain in which such conclusions gradually become corporate and authoritative. It is the intellectual authority of the day which at once uses and controls private judgment, as the accumulations of past experience themselves are the outcome of co-operation among many minds which have mutually corrected each other. The Essay on Development in its early chapters describes this co-operation in the past in the domain of theology itself. The lecture on Christianity and Scientific Investigation describes it in the present in the field of all the sciences, theology included.

'. . . I am making no outrageous request,' he writes, 'when, in the name of a university, I ask religious writers, jurists, anatomists, physiologists, chemists, geologists, and historians to go on quietly, and in a neighbourly way, in their own respective lines of speculation, research, and experiment, with full faith in the consistency of that multiform truth which they share between them, in a generous confidence that they will be ultimately consistent, one and all, in their combined results, though there may be momentary collisions, awkward appearances, and many forebodings and prophecies of contrariety, and at all times things hard to the imagination, though not, I repeat, to the reason. It surely is not asking them a great deal to beg of them— since they are forced to admit mysteries in the truths of revelation, taken by themselves, and in the truths of reason, taken by themselves—to beg of them, I say, to keep the peace, to live in goodwill, and to exercise equanimity if, when nature and revelation are compared with each other, there be, as I have said, discrepancies—not in the issue, but in the reasonings, the circumstances, the associations, the anticipations, the accidents, proper to their respective teachings. ... He who believes revelation with that absolute faith which is the prerogative of a Catholic is not the nervous creature who startles at every sudden sound, and is fluttered by every strange or novel appearance which meets his eyes. He has no sort of apprehension, he laughs at the idea, that anything can be discovered by any other scientific method which can contradict any one of the dogmas of his religion. He knows full well there is no science whatever but in the course of its extension runs the risk of infringing, without any meaning of offence on its own part, the path of other sciences: and he knows also that, if there be any one science which, from its sovereign and unassailable position, can calmly bear such unintentional collisions on the part of the children of earth, it is theology. He is sure, and nothing shall make him doubt, that, if anything seems to be proved by astronomer, or geologist, or chronologist, or antiquarian, or ethnologist, in contradiction to the dogmas of faith, that point will eventually turn out, first, *not* to be proved, or secondly, not *contradictory*, or thirdly, not contradictory to anything *really revealed*, but to something which has been confused with revelation.'

I have already alluded to the famous passage in the 'Apologia' in which Newman maintains that the human reason where it has a free career practically issues in infidelity in matters of religious belief, and on the other hand I have noted the absolute trust in the human reason shown in the lectures of which I am speaking. A further word of explanation must be given as to this contrast. In the 'Apologia' he expressly says that he is not considering the human reason lawfully exercised—so considered he admits that it leads to truth. He is regarding the reason as it is practically exercised in fallen man, as tainted by original sin, as perverted by passion, and as exceeding its lawful limits and professing to judge of the truths of revelation, which belong really to a sphere above its competence. In the Dublin lecture, on the contrary, he is dealing with lawful exercise of the reason in the terrain of science. Here the vices of the reason referred to in the 'Apologia' have practically no place. It is a sphere in which the reason is competent to come to its own conclusions. In such a sphere reason is not confused by an atmosphere of human passion, but works in the dry light of scientific inquiry. No passage in the lecture on Christianity and Scientific Investigation is more memorable than that in which he exhorts the scientific specialists in his ideal university to be confident that those free discussions which he advocates will find their issue in truth.

'What I would urge upon everyone, whatever may be his particular line of research—what I would urge upon men of science in their thoughts of theology—what I would venture to recommend to theologians, when their attention is drawn to the subject of scientific investigations—is a great and firm belief in the sovereignty of truth. Error may flourish for a time, but truth will prevail in the end. The only effect of error ultimately is to promote truth. Theories, speculations, hypotheses, are started; perhaps they are to die, still not before they have suggested ideas better than themselves. These better ideas are taken up in turn by other men and, if they do not lead to truth, nevertheless they lead to what is still nearer the truth than themselves; and thus knowledge on the whole makes progress. The errors of some minds in scientific investigation are more fruitful than the truths of others. A science seems making no progress, but to abound in failures, yet imperceptibly all the time it is advancing.'

The remarkable contrast in Newman's language concerning reason in the two contexts I am considering is completed and further explained in the last lecture he ever gave at Dublin, delivered before the Dublin Medical School. In that lecture he points out that the phenomena which are the basis of morals and religion may be obscured in the human mind by passion or moral fault or other causes. Reason then becomes powerless in dealing with them, for we cannot reason on elements of knowledge of which we have lost sight. Physical nature on the other hand, which is the subject-matter of scientific reasoning, is always unmistakably present. Hence the wide contrast between the functions of reason in the two cases. Here again it is important to give his own words, as the point is too subtle to risk a summary.

'The physical nature lies before us, patent to the sight, ready to the touch, appealing to the senses in so unequivocal a way that the science which is founded upon it is as real to us as the fact of our personal existence. But the phenomena which are the basis of morals and religion have nothing of this luminous evidence. Instead of being obtruded upon our notice, so that we cannot possibly overlook them, they are dictates either of conscience or of faith. They are faint shadows and tracings, certain indeed, but delicate, fragile, and almost evanescent, which the mind recognizes at one time, not at another, discerns when it is calm, loses when it is in agitation. The reflection of sky and mountains in the lake is a proof that sky and mountains are around it; but the twilight, or the mist, or the sudden storm hurries away the beautiful image, which leaves behind it no memorial of what it was. Something like this are the moral law and the informations of faith, as they present themselves to individual minds. Who can deny the existence of conscience? Who does not feel the force of its injunctions? But how dim is the illumination in which it is invested, and how feeble its influence, compared with that evidence of sight and touch which is the foundation of physical science! How easily can we be talked out of our clearest views of duty, how does this or that moral precept crumble into nothing when we rudely handle it, how does the fear of sin pass off from us as quickly as the glow of modesty dies away from the countenance, and then we say: "It is all superstition!" However, after a time we look round, and then to our surprise we see, as before, the same law of duty, the same moral precepts, the same protests against sin, appearing over against us, in their old places, as if they never had been brushed away, like the divine handwriting upon the wall at the banquet. Then perhaps we approach them rudely, and inspect them irreverently, and accost them sceptically, and away they go again, like so many spectres, shining in their cold beauty, but not presenting themselves bodily to us, for our inspection, so to say, of their hands and feet. And thus these awful, supernatural, bright, majestic, delicate apparitions, much as we may in our heart acknowledge their sovereignty, are no match as a foundation of science for the hard, palpable, material facts which make up the province of physics.'

He goes on to claim as among the most important functions of the Catholic Church that it guards and keeps before men those religious truths of which human nature left to itself may so easily lose sight. The Church is, as he expresses it in the 'Apologia,' 'the concrete representative of things invisible.'

I have now, I think, taken a fairly complete view of the lines of thought worked out by Newman in his lectures at the Catholic University of Dublin. The problem before him was to make men good Catholics and thoroughly educated men. And he had to outline their attitude towards the modern world of thought and research and to erect an authority which would enable them to take a reasonable view (in the rough) of questions whose exact solution could only be reached by the co-operation of specialists. While in his early career he had vindicated the Catholic Church as an authority preserving and enforcing religious truth against the speculations of private judgment, in Dublin he urged the value of a standing board of experts as an authority which should set aside the vagaries of private judgment in the scientific domain, theology entering into his scheme as one of the sciences. In each case he sought to control private judgment by corporate judgment to which individuals should minister. In the first period the authority he invoked told for conservatism, in the last it told for progress. These opposite roles arose from the widely different circumstances in which he found himself, but nevertheless they revealed fundamental unity of thought. At Oxford his mission was to overthrow individualistic liberalism which was tantamount to rationalism, and to vindicate against it the traditions of the corporate Church.

Hence he was conservative. In Dublin he strove to counteract the influence of those who failed to look frankly at the trend of science owing to their extreme conservatism in theology. He desired to build up in the rising generation minds which should be at once sensitively alive to the world of fact, and Catholic in religious belief. Consequently he was at this period on the whole an opponent of the conservative theologians. At Oxford he had deprecated free discussion of the truths of revelation as rationalistic; at Dublin he advocated the freest discussion as indispensable in the terrain of science, including scientific theology. At Oxford his object had been to vindicate the corporate Church as a standing witness to religious truth. In Dublin his object was to erect a standing committee of experts as an intellectual guide for educated Catholics. At both periods he was the friend of reason, the opponent of private judgment and of rationalism. The wide difference between the two periods in his rhetoric involved no difference of logic. The animus was different, for at Oxford the liberal school aroused his apprehensions for the safety of Christianity, while at Dublin he feared lest Cardinal Cullen might promote a system of education which should be frankly obscurantist. The writings of the Oxford period gave the basis of his faith, notably the University Sermons, and portions of the Essay on Development. The Dublin period indicated the lines of the superstructure, that is to say the intellectual position, faith being supposed, which an educated Christian ought to entertain towards the thought and science of his day.

I have in this Introduction travelled far from the immediate argument of the lectures on the Scope and Nature of University Education, because their interest is so greatly enhanced by the lines of thought to which they led Newman under pressure of his experience in the university. They need the supplement which they led him to write in order that we may understand their significance. This fact, I think, explains a remark in his prefatory note. He says that the lectures satisfied him less than anything he had published. I venture to think that the cause of this was just what I am pointing out, that they could not stand by themselves as satisfactory without the development of those further considerations which I have attempted to exhibit in this Introduction. Taken in conjunction with the essay on Christianity and Scientific Investigation, the lectures on the Scope and Nature of University Education are second in importance to none of Newman's writings.

WILFRID WARD.

SELECT BIBLIOGRAPHY

COMPLETE WORKS. 40 volumes, 1874–81.

THEOLOGICAL WORKS. *Arians of the Fourth Century*, 1833; 5th ed. edited by G. H. Forbes, 1876; *Tracts for the Times* (twenty-four by Newman, including the celebrated No. 90), 6 vols., 1834–41; last ed. edited by A. W. Evans, 1933; *Parochial Sermons*, 6 vols., 1834–42; *Restoration of Suffragan Bishops*, 1835; *Letter to Parishioners . . . at Littlemore*, 1835; *Elucidation of Dr Hampden's Theological Statements*, 1836; *Letter to the Margaret Professor of Divinity*, 1836; *Make Ventures for Christ's Sake* (a sermon), 1836; *Lectures on the Prophetical Office of the Church*, 1837; *A Letter . . . on Certain Points of Faith and Practice*, 1838; *Lectures on Justification*, 1838; 4th ed., 1885; *The Church of the Fathers*, 1840; 4th ed., 1868; *The Tamwood Reading Room*, 1841; *Letter to the Rev. R. W. Jelf on Tract 90*, 1841; *Sermon on the Theory of Religious Belief*, 1842; *Plain Sermons*, vol. v, 1843; *Sermons on Subjects of the Day*, 1843; 5th ed. edited by W. J. Copeland, 1885; *Essay on the Development of Christian Doctrine*, 1845; 3rd ed., 1878; *Dissertatiunculae*, 1847; *Discourses to Mixed Congregations*, 1849; *Christ upon the Waters* (a sermon), 1850; *Lectures on Certain Difficulties felt by Anglicans*, 1850; *Lectures on the Present Position of Catholics in England*, 1851; 5th ed., 1880; *Remarks on the Oratorian Vocation* (privately printed), 1856; *Sermons on Various Occasions*, 1857; 5th ed., 1881; *Mr Kingsley and Dr Newman*, 1864; *Apologia pro Vita Sua*, 1864; last ed. edited by C. Sarolea (Everyman's Library), 1912; *A Letter to Pusey on his 'Eirenicon,'* 1866; *The Pope and the Revolution* (a sermon), 1866; *An Essay in Aid of a Grammar of Assent*, 1870; 5th ed., 1881; *Two Essays on Miracles*, 1870; *Causes of the Rise and Success of Arianism*, 1872; *Discussions and Arguments*, 1872; *The Heresy of Apollinaris*, 1874; *Tracts, Theological and Ecclesiastical*, 1874; *Letter to the Duke of Norfolk on occasion of Gladstone's Expostulation*, 1875; *The Via-Media of the Anglican Church*, 2 vols., 1877; *Two Sermons preached . . . on Trinity Sunday 1880* (privately printed), 1880; *Inspiration of the Canonical Scripture*, 1884; *Meditations and Devotions*, 1893.

[Posthumous publications: *The Mission of St Philip Neri*, 1901; *The Fitness of the Glories of Mary*, 1904; *The Glories of Mary for the Sake of her Son*, 1904; *Addresses to Cardinal Newman with his Replies* (edited by W. P. Neville), 1905; *The Mission of the Benedictine Order*, 1908; *Sermon Notes* (edited by the Fathers of the Birmingham Oratory), 1913; *Cardinal Newman on the Benedictine Order* (two essays reprinted from *Atlantis*), edited by Dom Norbert Birt, 1914.]

EDUCATIONAL AND MISCELLANEOUS BOOKS. *Loss and Gain*, 1848; *Discourses on the Scope and Nature of University Education*, 1852; revised ed. *The Scope and Nature of University Education*, 1859; enlarged with ten essays and called *The Idea of a University Education*, 1873; *Lectures on the History of the Turks*, 1854; *Callista: a Sketch of the Third Century*, 1856; last ed., 1906; *The Office and the Work of the Universities*, 1856; *Lectures and Essays on University Subjects*, 1859; *Essays Critical and Historical*, 2 vols., 1872; *Historical Sketches*, 3 vols., 1872–3.

POEMS AND HYMNS. *St Bartholomew's Eve* (with J. W. Bowden), 1821; *Memorials of the Past*, 1832; *Lyra Apostolica* (with J. W. Bowden and others), 1836; *Verses on Religious Subjects*, 1853; *Hymns for the Use of the Birmingham Oratory*, 1854; *Hymn Tunes of the Oratory*, Birmingham (privately printed), 1860; *Verses for Penitents* (privately printed), 1863; *The Dream of Gerontius*, 1866; 23rd ed., 1888; last ed. edited by W. F. P. Stockley, 1923; *Verses on Various Occasions*, 1868.

LETTERS. *Letters and Correspondence of John Henry Newman during his Life in the English Church*, edited by Anne Mozley, 2 vols., 1891; *Correspondence of John Henry Newman with John Keble and Others, 1839–45*, 1917; A set of unpublished letters in F. L. Cross's *John Henry Newman*, 1933; *Cardinal Newman and Edward Froude, F.R.S.: a Correspondence*, edited by G. H. Hargrave, 1933.

TRANSLATIONS. *The Devotions of Bishop Andrewes, 1842–4*, 1920; *Select Treatises of St Athanasius*, 2 vols., 1842–4; the *Ecclesiastical History* of M. L'Abbé Fleury, 1842–4.

Newman contributed to the *Encyclopaedia Metropolitana* and to numerous periodicals.

BIOGRAPHICAL AND CRITICAL. F. W. Newman: *The Early History of Cardinal Newman*, 1891; E. A. Abbott: *The Anglican Career of Cardinal Newman*, 1892; W. Ward: *The Life of Cardinal Newman* 1912; J. J. Reilly: *Newman as a Man of Letters*, 1925; J. L. May: *Cardinal Newman*, 1929; F. L. Cross: *John Henry Newman*, 1933; J. M. Flood: *Cardinal Newman and Oxford*, 1933; J. E. Ross: *John Henry Newman*, 1933; H. Tristram: *Newman and his Friends*, 1933; S. Dark: *Newman*, 1934; J. F. Cronin: *Cardinal Newman: his Theory of Knowledge*, 1935.

CONTENTS

PREFACE

THE view which these discourses take of a university is of the following kind: that it is a place of *teaching* universal *knowledge*. This implies that its object is, on the one hand, intellectual, not moral; and, on the other, that it is the diffusion and extension of knowledge rather than the advancement. If its object were scientific and philosophical discovery, I do not see why a university should have students; if religious training, I do not see how it can be the seat of literature and science.

Such is a university in its *essence*, and independently of its relation to the Church. But, practically speaking, it cannot fulfil its object duly, such as I have described it, without the Church's assistance; or, to use the theological term, the Church is necessary for its *integrity*. Not that its main characters are changed by this incorporation: it still has the office of intellectual education; but the Church steadies it in the performance of that office.

Such are the main principles of the discourses which follow; though it would be unreasonable for me to expect that I have treated so large and important a field of thought with the fullness and precision necessary to secure me from incidental misconceptions of my meaning on the part of the reader. It is true there is nothing novel or singular in the argument which I have been pursuing, but this does not protect me from such misconceptions; for the very circumstance that the views I have been delineating are not original with me may lead to false notions as to my relations in opinion towards those from whom I happened in the first instance to learn them, and may cause me to be interpreted by the objects or sentiments of schools to which I should be simply opposed.

For instance, some persons may be tempted to complain that I have servilely followed the English idea of a university, to the disparagement of that knowledge which I profess to be so strenuously upholding; and they may anticipate that an academical system, formed upon my model, will result in nothing better or higher than in the production of that antiquated variety of human nature and remnant of feudalism called 'a gentleman.'[1] Now I have anticipated this charge in various parts of my discussion; if, however, any Catholic is found to prefer it (and to Catholics of course this volume is addressed), I would have him first of all ask himself the previous question, *what* he conceives to be the reason contemplated by the Holy See in recommending just now to the Irish Church the establishment of a Catholic university? Has the Supreme Pontiff recommended it for the sake of the sciences, which are to be the matter, or rather of the students, who are to be the subjects, of its teaching? Has he any obligation or duty at all towards secular knowledge as such? Would it become his apostolical ministry, and his descent from the Fisherman, to have a zeal for the Baconian or other philosophy of man for its own sake? Is the Vicar of Christ bound by office or by vow to be the preacher of the theory of gravitation, or a martyr for electro-magnetism? Would he be acquitting himself of the dispensation committed to him if he were smitten with an abstract love of these matters, however true, or beautiful, or ingenious, or useful? Or rather, does he not contemplate such achievements of the intellect, as far as he contemplates them, solely and simply in their relation to the interests of revealed truth? Surely, what he does he does for the sake of religion; if he looks with satisfaction on strong temporal governments, which promise perpetuity, it is for the sake of religion; and if he

---

[1] *Vide* Huber's *English Universities*, London, 1843, vol. ii., part I, pp. 321, etc.

encourages and patronizes art and science, it is for the sake of religion. He rejoices in the widest and most philosophical systems of intellectual education, from an intimate conviction that truth is his real ally, as it is his profession; and that knowledge and reason are sure ministers to faith.

This being undeniable, it is plain that, when he suggests to the Irish Hierarchy the establishment of a university, his first and chief and direct object is, not science, art, professional skill, literature, the discovery of knowledge, but some benefit or other, by means of literature and science, to his own children; not indeed their formation on any narrow or fantastic type, as, for instance, that of an 'English gentleman' may be called, but their exercise and growth in certain habits, moral or intellectual. Nothing short of this can be his aim if, as becomes the successor of the Apostles, he is to be able to say with St Paul: 'Non judicavi me scire aliquid inter vos, nisi Jesum Christum, et hunc crucifixum.' Just as a commander wishes to have tall and well-formed and vigorous soldiers, not from any abstract devotion to the military standard of height or age, but for the purposes of war, and no one thinks it anything but natural and praiseworthy in him to be contemplating, not abstract qualities, but his own living and breathing men; so, in like manner, when the Church founds a university, she is not cherishing talent, genius, or knowledge for their own sake, but for the sake of her children, with a view to their spiritual welfare and their religious influence and usefulness, with the object of training them to fill their respective posts in life better, and of making them more intelligent, capable, active members of society.

Nor can it justly be said that in thus acting she sacrifices science, and under a pretence of fulfilling the duties of her mission perverts a university from its proper end, as soon as it is taken into account that there are other institutions far more suited to act as instruments of stimulating philosophical inquiry, and extending the boundaries of our knowledge, than a university. Such, for instance, are the literary and scientific 'academies,' which are so celebrated in Italy and France, and which have frequently been connected with universities, as committees, or, as it were, congregations or delegacies subordinate to them. Thus the present Royal Society originated in Charles II's time, in Oxford; such just now are the Ashmolean and Architectural Societies in the same seat of learning, which have risen in our own time. Such, too, is the British Association, a migratory body, which at least at times is found in the halls of the Protestant universities of the United Kingdom, and the faults of which lie, not in its exclusive devotion to science, but in graver matters which it is irrelevant here to enter upon. Such again is the Antiquarian Society, the Royal Academy for the Fine Arts, and others which might be mentioned. This then is the sort of institution which primarily contemplates science itself, and not students; and, in thus speaking, I am saying nothing of my own, being supported by no less an authority than Cardinal Gerdil. 'Ce n'est pas,' he says, 'qu'il y ait aucune véritable opposition entre l'esprit des académies et celui des universités; ce sont seulement des vues différentes. Les universités sont établies pour *enseigner* les sciences *aux élèves* qui veulent s'y former; les académies se proposent *de nouvelles recherches* à faire dans la carrière des sciences. Les universités d'Italie ont fourni des sujets qui ont fait honneur aux académies; et celles-ci ont donné aux universités des professeurs, qui ont rempli les chaires avec la plus grande distinction.' [1]

The nature of the case and the history of philosophy combine to recommend to us this 'division of' intellectual 'labour' between academies and universities. To discover and to teach are distinct functions; they are also

[1] *Opere*, vol. iii, p. 353.

distinct gifts, and are not commonly found united in the same person. He too who spends his day in dispensing his existing knowledge to all comers is unlikely to have either leisure or energy to acquire new. The common sense of mankind has associated the search after truth with seclusion and quiet. The greatest thinkers have been too intent on their subject to admit of interruption; they have been men of absent minds and idiosyncratic habits, and have, more or less, shunned the lecture room and the public school. Pythagoras, the light of Magna Graecia, lived for a time in a cave. Thales, the light of Ionia, lived unmarried and in private, and refused the invitations of princes. Plato withdrew from Athens to the groves of Academus. Aristotle gave twenty years to a studious discipleship under him. Friar Bacon lived in his tower upon the Isis. Newton indulged in an intense severity of meditation which almost shook his reason. The great discoveries in chemistry and electricity were not made in universities. Observatories are more frequently out of universities than in them, and even when within their bounds need have no moral connection with them. Porson had no classes; Elmsley lived a good part of his life in the country. I do not say that there are not great examples the other way, perhaps Socrates, certainly Lord Bacon; still, I think it must be allowed on the whole that, while teaching involves external engagements, the natural home for experiment and speculation is retirement.

Returning, then, to the consideration of the question, from which I may seem to have digressed, thus much we have made good—that, whether or no a Catholic university should put before it, as its great object, to make its students 'gentlemen,' still to make them something or other *is* its great object, and not simply to protect the interests and advance the dominion of Science. If then this may be taken for granted, as I think it may, the only point which remains to be settled is, whether I have formed a probable conception of the *sort of benefit* which the Holy See has intended to confer on Catholics who speak the English tongue by recommending to the Irish Hierarchy the establishment of a university; and this I now proceed to consider.

Here, then, it is natural to ask those who are interested in the question whether any better interpretation of the recommendation of the Holy See can be given than that which I have suggested in this volume. Certainly it does not seem to me rash to pronounce that, whereas Protestants have great advantages of education in the schools, colleges, and universities of the United Kingdom, our ecclesiastical rulers have it in purpose that Catholics should enjoy the like advantages, whatever they are, to the full. I conceive they view it as prejudicial to the interests of religion that there should be any cultivation of mind bestowed upon Protestants which is not given to their own youth also. As they wish their schools for the poorer and middle classes to be at least on a par with those of Protestants, they contemplate the same object also as regards that higher education which is given to comparatively the few. Protestant youths who can spare the time continue their studies till the age of twenty-one or twenty-two; thus they employ a time of life all-important and especially favourable to mental culture. I conceive that our prelates are impressed with the fact and its consequences, that a youth who ends his education at seventeen is no match (*caeteris paribus*) for one who ends it at twenty-one.

All classes indeed of the community are impressed with a fact so obvious as this. The consequence is that Catholics who aspire to be on a level with Protestants in discipline and refinement of intellect have recourse to Protestant universities to obtain what they cannot find at home. Assuming (as the Rescripts from Propaganda allow me to do) that Protestant education is inexpedient for our youth, we see here an additional reason why those advantages, whatever they are, which Protestant communities dispense through the medium of Protestantism should be accessible to Catholics in a Catholic form.

What are these advantages? I repeat, they are in one word the culture of the intellect. Robbed, oppressed, and thrust aside, Catholics in these islands have not been in a condition for centuries to attempt the sort of education which is necessary for the man of the world, the statesman, the landholder, or the opulent gentleman. Their legitimate stations, duties, employments, have been taken from them, and the qualifications withal, social and intellectual, which are necessary both for reversing the forfeiture and for availing themselves of the reversal. The time is come when this moral disability must be removed. Our desideratum is, not the manners and habits of gentlemen—these can be, and are, acquired in various other ways, by good society, by foreign travel, by the innate grace and dignity of the Catholic mind—but the force, the steadiness, the comprehensiveness, and the versatility of intellect, the command over our own powers, the instinctive just estimate of things as they pass before us, which sometimes indeed is a natural gift, but commonly is not gained without much effort and the exercise of years.

This is real cultivation of mind; and I do not deny that the characteristic excellences of a gentleman are included in it. Nor need we be ashamed that they should be, since the poet long ago wrote that 'Ingenuas didicisse fideliter artes, Emollit mores.' Certainly a liberal education does manifest itself in a courtesy, propriety, and polish of word and action, which is beautiful in itself and acceptable to others; but it does much more. It brings the mind into form—for the mind is like the body. Boys outgrow their shape and their strength; their limbs have to be knit together, and their constitution needs tone. Mistaking

animal spirits for nerve, and over-confident in their health,
ignorant what they can bear and how to manage themselves, they are immoderate and extravagant, and fall into
sharp sicknesses. This is an emblem of their minds; at
first they have no principles laid down within them as a
foundation for the intellect to build upon; they have no
discriminating convictions and no grasp of consequences.
In consequence they talk at random, if they talk much, and
cannot help being flippant, or what is emphatically called
young. They are merely dazzled by phenomena, instead of
perceiving things as they are.

It were well if none remained boys all their lives; but
what is more common than the sight of grown men talking
on political or moral or religious subjects in that offhand,
idle way, which we signify by the word *unreal*? 'That
they simply do not know what they are talking about' is
the spontaneous silent remark of any man of sense who
hears them. Hence such persons have no difficulty in
contradicting themselves in successive sentences, without
being conscious of it. Hence others, whose defect in
intellectual training is more latent, have their most unfortunate crotchets, as they are called, or hobbies, which
deprive them of the influence which their estimable qualities
would otherwise secure. Hence others can never look
straight before them, never see the point, and have no
difficulties in the most difficult subjects. Others are
hopelessly obstinate and prejudiced, and return the next
moment to their old opinions, after they have been driven
from them, without even an attempt to explain why.
Others are so intemperate and intractable that there is no
greater calamity for a good cause than that they should
get hold of it. It is very plain from the very particulars I
have mentioned that, in this delineation of intellectual
infirmities, I am drawing, not from Catholics, but from
the world at large; I am referring to an evil which is forced

upon us in every railway carriage, in every coffee-room or table-d'hôte, in every mixed company, an evil, however, to which Catholics are not less exposed than the rest of mankind.

When the intellect has once been properly trained and formed to have a connected view or grasp of things, it will display its powers with more or less effect according to its particular quality and measure in the individual. In the case of most men it makes itself felt in the good sense, sobriety of thought, reasonableness, candour, self-command, and steadiness of view which characterize it. In some it will have developed habits of business, power of influencing others, and sagacity. In others it will elicit the talent of philosophical speculation, and lead the mind forward to eminence in this or that intellectual department. In all it will be a faculty of entering with comparative ease into any subject of thought, and of taking up with aptitude any science or profession. All this it will be and will do in a measure, even when the mental formation be made after a model but partially true; for, as far as effectiveness goes, even false views of things have more influence and inspire more respect than no views at all. Men who fancy they see what is not are more energetic, and make their way better, than those who see nothing; and so the undoubting infidel, the fanatic, the bigot, are able to do much, while the mere hereditary Christian, who has never realized the truths which he holds, is unable to do anything. But, if consistency of view can add so much strength even to error, what may it not be expected to furnish to the dignity, the energy, and the influence of truth!

Someone, however, will perhaps object that I am but advocating that spurious philosophism which shows itself in what, for want of a word, I may call 'viewiness,' when I speak so much of the formation, and consequent grasp, of the intellect. It may be said that the theory of university education which I have been delineating, if acted upon, would teach youths nothing soundly or thoroughly, and would dismiss them with nothing better than brilliant general views about all things whatever.

This indeed would be a most serious objection, if well founded, to what I have advanced in this volume, and would gain my immediate attention, had I any reason to think that I could not remove it at once, by a simple explanation of what I consider the true *mode* of educating, were this the place to do so. But these discourses are directed simply to the consideration of the *aims* and *principles* of education. Suffice it then to say here that I hold very strongly that the first step in intellectual training is to impress upon a boy's mind the idea of science, method, order, principle, and system; of rule and exception, of richness and harmony. This is commonly and excellently done by making him begin with grammar; nor can too great accuracy, or minuteness and subtlety of teaching, be used towards him, as his faculties expand, with this simple view. Hence it is that critical scholarship is so important a discipline for him when he is leaving school for the university. A second science is the mathematics; this should follow grammar, still with the same object, viz. to give him a conception of development and arrangement from and around a common centre. Hence it is that chronology and geography are so necessary for him, when he reads history, which is otherwise little better than a story-book. Hence, too, metrical composition, when he reads poetry, in order to stimulate his powers into action in every practicable way, and to prevent a merely passive reception of images and ideas which in that case are likely to pass out of mind as soon as they have entered it. Let him once gain this habit of method, of starting from fixed points, of making his ground good as he goes, of distinguishing what he knows from what he does not know, and I conceive he will be gradually initiated into the largest and truest philosophical views, and will feel nothing but impatience and disgust at the random theories and imposing sophistries and dashing paradoxes, which carry away half-formed and superficial intellects.

Such particoloured ingenuities are indeed one of the chief evils of the day, and men of real talent are not slow to minister to them. An intellectual man, as the world now conceives of him, is one who is full of 'views' on all subjects of philosophy, on all matters of the day. It is almost thought a disgrace not to have a view at a moment's notice on any question from the Personal Advent to the cholera or mesmerism. This is owing in great measure to the necessities of periodical literature, now so much in request. Every quarter of a year, every month, every day, there must be a supply, for the gratification of the public, of new and luminous theories on the subjects of religion, foreign politics, home politics, civil economy, finance, trade, agriculture, emigration, and the colonies. Slavery, the gold-fields, German philosophy, the French Empire, Wellington, Peel, Ireland, must all be practised on, day after day, by what are called original thinkers. As the great man's guest must produce his good stories or songs at the evening banquet, as the platform orator exhibits his telling facts at midday, so the journalist lies under the stern obligation of extemporizing his lucid views, leading ideas, and nutshell truths for the breakfast table. The very nature of periodical literature, broken into small wholes, and demanded punctually to an hour, involves this extempore philosophy. 'Almost all the *Ramblers*,' says Boswell of Johnson, 'were written just as they were wanted for the press; he sent a certain portion of the copy for an essay, and wrote the remainder while the former part of it was printing.' Few men have the gifts of Johnson, who to great vigour and resource of intellect, when it was fairly roused, united a rare common-sense and a conscientious regard for veracity, which preserved him from flippancy or extravagance in writing. Few men are Johnsons; yet how many men at this day are assailed by incessant demands on their mental powers, which only a productiveness like his could suitably supply! There is a demand for a reckless originality of thought, and a sparkling plausibility of argument, which he would have despised, even if he could have displayed; a demand for crude theory and unsound philosophy, rather than none at all. It is a sort of repetition of the 'Quid novi?' of the Areopagus, and it must have an answer. Men must be found who can treat, where it is necessary, like the Athenian sophist, *de omni scibili*:

> Grammaticus, Rhetor, Geometres, Pictor, Aliptes,
> Augur, Schoenobates, Medicus, Magus, omnia novit.

I am speaking of such writers with a feeling of real sympathy for men who are under the rod of a cruel slavery. I have never indeed been in such circumstances myself, nor in the temptations which they involve; but most men who have had to do with composition must know the distress which at times it occasions them to have to write— a distress sometimes so keen and so specific that it re-sembles nothing else than bodily pain. That pain is the token of the wear and tear of mind; and, if works done comparatively at leisure involve such mental fatigue and exhaustion, what must be the toil of those whose intellects are to be flaunted daily before the public in full dress, and that dress ever new and varied, and spun, like the silk-worm's, out of themselves! Still, whatever true sympathy we may feel for the ministers of this dearly purchased luxury, and whatever sense we may have of the great intellectual power which the literature in question displays, we cannot honestly close our eyes to the evil.

One other remark suggests itself, which is the last I shall think it necessary to make. The authority, which in former times was lodged in universities, now resides in very great measure in that literary world, as it is called, to which I have been alluding. This is not satisfactory if, as no one can deny, its teaching be so offhand, so ambitious, so changeable. It increases the seriousness of the mischief that so very large a portion of its writers are anonymous, for irresponsible power can never be anything but a great evil; and, moreover, that, even when they are known, they can give no better guarantee for the philosophical truth of their principles than their popularity at the moment, and their happy conformity in ethical character to the age which admires them. Protestants, however, may do as they will: it is a matter for their own consideration; but at least it concerns us that our own literary tribunals and oracles of moral duty should bear a graver character. At least it is a matter of deep solicitude to Catholic prelates that their people should be taught a wisdom safe from the excesses and vagaries of individuals, embodied in institutions which have stood the trial and received the sanction of ages, and administered by men who have no need to be anonymous, as being supported by their consistency with their predecessors and with each other.

21st November 1852.

DISCOURSE I

IN addressing myself, gentlemen, to the consideration of a question which has excited so much interest, and elicited so much discussion at the present day, as that of university education, I feel some explanation is due from me for supposing, after such high ability and wide experience have been brought to bear upon it, that any field remains for the additional labours either of a disputant or of an inquirer. If, nevertheless, I still venture to ask permission to continue the discussion, already so protracted, it is because the subject of liberal education, and of the principles on which it must be conducted, has ever had a hold upon my own mind; and because I have lived the greater part of my life in a place which has all that time been occupied in a series of controversies among its inmates and with strangers, and of measures, experimental or definitive, bearing upon it. About fifty years since, the Protestant university of which I was so long a member, after a century of inactivity, at length was roused, at a time when (as I may say) it was giving no education at all to the youth committed to its keeping, to a sense of the responsibilities which its profession and its station involved, and it presents to us the singular example of an heterogeneous and an independent body of men setting about a work of self-reformation, not from any pressure of public opinion, but because it was fitting and right to undertake it. Its initial efforts, begun and carried on amid many obstacles, were met from without, as often happens in such cases, by ungenerous and jealous criticisms, which, at the very moment that they were urged,

1

were beginning to be unjust. Controversy did but bring out more clearly to its own apprehension the views on which its reformation was proceeding, and throw them into a philosophical form. The course of beneficial change made progress, and what was at first but the result of individual energy, and an act of the academical corporation, gradually became popular, and was taken up and carried out by the separate collegiate bodies of which the university is composed. This was the first stage of the controversy. Years passed away, and then political adversaries arose against it, and the system of education which it had established was a second time assailed; but still, since that contest was conducted for the most part through the medium, not of political acts, but of treatises and pamphlets, it happened as before that the threatened dangers, in the course of their repulse, did but afford fuller development and more exact delineation to the principles of which the university was the representative.

In the former of these two controversies the charge brought against its studies was their remoteness from the occupations and duties of life, to which they are the formal introduction, or, in other words, their *inutility*; in the latter, it was their connection with a particular form of belief, or, in other words, their *religious exclusiveness*.

Living then so long as a witness, though hardly as an actor, in these scenes of intellectual conflict, I am able, gentlemen, to bear witness to views of university education, without authority indeed in themselves, but not without value to a Catholic, and less familiar to him, as I conceive, than they deserve to be. And, while an argument originating in the controversies to which I have referred may be serviceable at this season to that great cause in which we are here so especially interested, to me personally it will afford satisfaction of a peculiar kind; for, though it has been my lot for many years to take a prominent, sometimes a presumptuous, part in theological discussions, yet the natural turn of my mind carries me off to trains of thought like those which I am now about to open, which, important though they be for Catholic objects, and admitting of a Catholic treatment, are sheltered from the extreme delicacy and peril which attach to disputations directly bearing on the subject-matter of divine revelation.

There are several reasons why I should open the discussion with a reference to the lessons with which past years have supplied me. One reason is this: It would concern me, gentlemen, were I supposed to have got up my opinions for the occasion. This, indeed, would have been no reflection on me personally, supposing I were persuaded of their truth, when at length addressing myself to the inquiry; but it would have destroyed, of course, the force of my testimony, and deprived such arguments as I might adduce of that moral persuasiveness which attends on tried and sustained conviction. It would have made me seem the advocate, rather than the cordial and deliberate maintainer and witness, of the doctrines which I was to support; and, though it might be said to evidence the faith I reposed in the practical judgment of the Church, and the intimate concurrence of my own reason with the course she had authoritatively sanctioned, and the devotion with which I could promptly put myself at her disposal, it would have cast suspicion on the validity of reasonings and conclusions which rested on no independent inquiry, and appealed to no past experience. In that case it might have been plausibly objected by opponents that I was the serviceable expedient of an emergency, and never could be more than ingenious and adroit in the management of an argument which was not my own, and which I was sure to forget again as readily as I had mastered it. But this is not so. The views to which I have referred have grown into my whole system of thought, and are, as it were, part of myself.

Many changes has my mind gone through: here it has known no variation or vacillation of opinion, and though this by itself is no proof of truth, it puts a seal upon conviction and is a justification of earnestness and zeal. The principles which I am now to set forth under the sanction of the Catholic Church were my profession at that early period of my life, when religion was to me more a matter of feeling and experience than of faith. They did but take greater hold upon me as I was introduced to the records of Christian antiquity, and approached in sentiment and desire to Catholicism; and my sense of their truth has been increased with the events of every year since I have been brought within its pale.

And here I am brought to a second and more important reason for referring, on this occasion, to the conclusions at which Protestants have arrived on the subject of liberal education; and it is as follows: Let it be observed, then, that the principles on which I would conduct it are attainable, as I have already implied, by the mere experience of life. They do not come simply of theology; they imply no supernatural discernment; they have no special connection with revelation; they almost arise out of the nature of the case; they are dictated by merely human prudence and wisdom, though a divine illumination be absent, and they are recognized by common sense, even where self-interest is not present to quicken it; and, therefore, though true and just and good in themselves, they imply nothing whatever as to the religious profession of those who maintain them. They may be held by Protestants as well as by Catholics; nay, there is reason to anticipate that in certain times and places they will be more thoroughly investigated, and better understood, and held more firmly by Protestants than by ourselves.

It is natural to expect this from the very circumstance that the philosophy of education is founded on truths in the natural order. Where the sun shines bright, in the warm climate of the south, the natives of the place know little of safeguards against cold and wet. They have, indeed, bleak and piercing blasts; they have chill and pouring rain, but only now and then, for a day or a week; they bear the inconvenience as they best may, but they have not made it an art to repel it; it is not worth their while; the science of calefaction and ventilation is reserved for the north. It is in this way that Catholics stand relatively to Protestants in the science of education; Protestants depending on human means solely are led to make the most of them: their sole resource is to use what they have; 'Knowledge' is their 'power' and nothing else; they are the anxious cultivators of a rugged soil. It is otherwise with us; 'funes ceciderunt mihi in praeclaris.' We have a goodly inheritance. This is apt to cause us (I do not mean to rely too much on prayer and the divine blessing, for that is impossible; but) we sometimes forget that we shall please Him best, and get most from Him, when, according to the fable, we 'put our shoulder to the wheel,' when we use what we have by nature to the utmost, at the same time that we look out for what is beyond nature in the confidence of faith and hope. However, we are sometimes tempted to let things take their course, as if they would in one way or another turn up right at last for certain; and so we go on, living from hand to mouth, getting into difficulties and getting out of them, succeeding certainly on the whole, but with failure in detail which might be avoided, and with much of imperfection or inferiority in our appointments and plans, and much disappointment, discouragement, and collision of opinion in consequence. If this be in any measure the state of the case, there is certainly so far a reason for availing ourselves of the investigations and experience of those who are not Catholics, when we have to address ourselves to the subjects of liberal education.

Nor is there surely anything derogatory to the position of a Catholic in such a proceeding. The Church has ever appealed and deferred to witnesses and authorities external to herself in those matters in which she thought they had means of forming a judgment: and that on the principle, Cuique in sua arte credendum. She has even used unbelievers and pagans in evidence of her truth, as far as their testimony went. She avails herself of scholars, critics, and antiquarians who are not of her communion. She has worded her theological teaching in the phraseology of Aristotle; Aquila, Symmachus, Theodotion, Origen, Eusebius, and Apollinaris, all more or less heterodox, have supplied materials for primitive exegetics. St Cyprian called Tertullian his master; St Augustine refers to Ticonius; Bossuet, in modern times, complimented the labours of the Anglican Bull; the Benedictine editors of the fathers are familiar with the labours of Fell, Ussher, Pearson, and Beveridge. Pope Benedict XIV cites according to the occasion the works of Protestants without reserve, and the late French collection of Christian apologists contains the writings of Locke, Burnet, Tillotson, and Paley. If, then, I come forward in any degree as borrowing the views of certain Protestant schools on the point which is to be discussed, I do so, gentlemen, as believing, first, that the Catholic Church has ever, in the plenitude of her divine illumination, made use of whatever truth or wisdom she has found in their teaching or their measures; and next, that in particular times or places her children are likely to profit from external suggestions or lessons, which cannot be considered necessary for herself.

And here I may mention a third reason for appealing at the outset to the proceedings of Protestant bodies in regard to liberal education. It will serve to intimate the mode in which I propose to handle my subject altogether. Observe then, gentlemen, I have no intention, in anything I shall say, of bringing into the argument the authority of the Church, or any authority at all; but I shall consider the question simply on the grounds of human reason and human wisdom. I am investigating in the abstract, and am determining what is in itself right and true. For the moment I know nothing, so to say, of history. I take things as I find them; I have no concern with the past; I find myself here; I set myself to the duties I find here; I set myself to further, by every means in my power, doctrines and views true in themselves, recognized by Catholics as such, familiar to my own mind; and to do this quite apart from the consideration of questions which have been determined without me and before me. I am here the advocate and the minister of a certain great principle; yet not merely advocate and minister, else had I not been here at all. It has been my previous keen sense and hearty reception of that principle that has been at once the cause, as I must suppose, of my selection, and the ground of my acquiescence. I am told on authority that a principle is necessary, which I have ever felt to be true. And I argue in its behalf on its own merits, the authority which brings me here being my reason for arguing, but not the ground of my argument itself.

And a fourth reason is here suggested for consulting the history of Protestant institutions, when I am going to speak of the object and nature of university education. It will serve to remind you, gentlemen, that I am concerned with questions, not of immutable truth, but of practice and expedience. It would ill have become me to undertake a subject on which points of dispute have arisen among persons so far above me in authority and name, in relation to a state of society about which I have so much to learn, if it involved an appeal to sacred truths, or the determination of some imperative rule of conduct. It would have been presumptuous in me so to have acted, nor am I so acting. Even the question of the union of theology with the secular sciences, which is its religious side, simple as it is of solution in the abstract, has, according to difference of circumstances, been at different times differently decided. Necessity has no law, and expedience is often one form of necessity. It is no principle with sensible men, of whatever cast of opinion, to do always what is abstractedly best. Where no direct duty forbids, we may be obliged to do, as being best under circumstances, what we murmur and rise against while we do it. We see that to attempt more is to effect less; that we must accept so much, or gain nothing; and so perforce we reconcile ourselves to what we would have far otherwise, if we could. Thus a system of what is called mixed education, in which theology and the sciences are taught separately, may, in a particular place or time, be the least of evils; it may be of long standing; it may be dangerous to meddle with; it may be professedly a temporary arrangement; it may be under a process of improvement; its disadvantages may be neutralized by the persons by whom, or the provisions under which, it is administered.

Hence it was that in the early ages the Church allowed her children to attend the heathen schools for the acquisition of secular accomplishments, where, as no one can doubt, evils existed at least as great as can attend on mixed education now. The gravest fathers recommended for Christian youth the use of pagan masters; the most saintly bishops and most authoritative doctors had been sent in their adolescence by Christian parents to pagan lecture halls.[1] And, not to take other instances, at this very time, and in this very country, as regards at least the poorer classes of the community, whose secular acquirements ever must be limited, it has seemed best to the Irish bishops, under the circumstances, to suffer the introduction into the country of a system of mixed education in the schools called national. Such a state of things, however, is passing

[1] *Vide* M. L'Abbé Lalanne's recent work.

away; as regards university education at least, the highest authority has now decided that the plan which is abstractedly best is in this time and country also most expedient.

This is the branch of my subject on which I propose first to enter, and I do so without further delay. It is one of the two questions on which the Protestant controversies turned to which I have alluded. The earlier of them was the *inutility* of Oxford education, the latter was its *exclusiveness*; in the former it was debated whether liberal knowledge should have the foremost place in university teaching; in the latter, whether theology should be excluded. I am to begin with the latter.

It is the fashion just now, gentlemen, as you very well know, to erect so-called universities without making any provision in them at all for theological chairs. Institutions of this kind exist both here and in England. Such a procedure, though defended by writers of the generation just past with much plausible argument and not a little wit, seems to me an intellectual absurdity; and my reason for saying so runs, with whatever abruptness, into the form of a syllogism: A university, I should lay down, by its very name professes to teach universal knowledge: theology is surely a branch of knowledge: how then is it possible to profess all branches of knowledge, and yet to exclude not the meanest, nor the narrowest of the number? I do not see that either premiss of this argument is open to exception.

As to the range of university teaching, certainly the very name is inconsistent with restrictions of any kind. Whatever was the original reason of its adoption, which is unknown,[1] I am only putting on it its popular, its recognized sense, when I say that a university should teach universal knowledge. That there is a real necessity for this universal teaching in the highest schools of intellect I will show by

[1] In Roman law it means a corporation. *Vide* Keuffel, *de Scholis.*

and by; here it is sufficient to say that such universality is considered by writers on the subject as the very characteristic of a university, as contrasted with other seats of learning. Thus Johnson, in his dictionary, defines it to be 'a school where all arts and faculties are taught'; and Mosheim, writing as an historian, says that, before the rise of the university of Paris—for instance, at Padua, or Salamanca, or Cologne—'the whole circle of sciences then known was not taught'; but that the school of Paris, 'which exceeded all others in various respects, as well as in the number of teachers and students, was the first to embrace all the arts and sciences, and therefore first became a university.'[1]

If, with other authors, we consider the word to be derived from the invitation which is held out by a university to students of every kind, the result is the same; for, if certain branches of knowledge were excluded, those students of course would be excluded also who desired to pursue them.

Is it then logically consistent in a seat of learning to call itself a university, and to exclude theology from the number of its studies? And again, is it wonderful that Catholics, even in the view of reason, putting aside faith or religious duty, should be dissatisfied with existing institutions which profess to be universities, and refuse to teach theology; and that they should in consequence desire to possess seats of learning which are, not only more Christian, but more philosophical in their construction, and larger and deeper in their provisions?

But this, of course, is to assume that theology *is* a science, and an important one: so I will throw my argument into another form. I say, then, that if a university be, from the nature of the case, a place of instruction, where universal knowledge is professed, and if in a certain university, so-called, the subject of religion is excluded, one of two

[1] Hist., vol. ii, p. 529. London, 1841.

conclusions is inevitable—either, on the one hand, that the province of religion is very barren of real knowledge, or, on the other hand, that in such university one special and important branch of knowledge is omitted. I say the advocate of such an institution must say *this*, or he must say *that*; he must own, either that little or nothing is known about the Supreme Being, or that his seat of learning calls itself what it is not. This is the thesis which I lay down, and on which I shall insist in the remainder of this discourse. I repeat, such a compromise between religious parties as is involved in the establishment of a university which makes no religious profession implies that those parties severally consider—not indeed that their own respective opinions are trifles in a moral and practical point of view—of course not; but certainly as much as this, that they are not knowledge. Did they in their hearts believe that their private views of religion, whatever they are, were absolutely and objectively true, it is inconceivable that they would so insult them as to consent to their omission in an institution which is bound, from the nature of the case—from its very idea and its name—to make a profession of all sorts of knowledge whatever.

I think this will be found to be no matter of words. I allow then fully that, when men combine together for any common object, they are obliged, as a matter of course, in order to secure the advantages accruing from united action, to sacrifice many of their private opinions and wishes and to drop the minor differences, as they are commonly called, which exist between man and man. No two persons perhaps are to be found, however intimate, however congenial in tastes and judgments, however eager to have one heart and one soul, but must deny themselves, for the sake of each other, much which they like or desire, if they are to live together happily. Compromise, in a large sense of the word, is the first principle of combination; and anyone who

insists on enjoying his rights to the full, and his opinions
without toleration for his neighbour's, and his own way in
all things, will soon have all things altogether to himself,
and no one to share them with him. But most true as
this confessedly is, still there is an obvious limit, on the
other hand, to these compromises, necessary as they are;
and this is found in the proviso that the differences surrendered should be *but* 'minor,' or that there should be no
sacrifice of the main object of the combination, in the concessions which are mutually made. Any sacrifice which
compromises that object is destructive of the principle of
the combination, and no one who would be consistent can
be a party to it.

Thus, for instance, if men of various religious denomi-
nations join together for the dissemination of what are
called 'evangelical' tracts, it is under the belief that, the
object of their uniting, as recognized on all hands, being
the spiritual benefit of their neighbours, no religious
exhortation, whatever be its character, can essentially
interfere with that benefit, which is founded upon the
Lutheran doctrine of justification. If, again, they agree
together in printing and circulating the Protestant Bible,
it is because they, one and all, hold to the principle that,
however serious be their differences of religious sentiment,
such differences fade away before the one great principle
which that circulation symbolizes—that the Bible, the
whole Bible, and nothing but the Bible is the religion of
Protestants. On the contrary, if the committee of some
such association inserted tracts into the copies of the said
Bible which they sold, and tracts in recommendation of the
Athanasian Creed or the merit of good works, I conceive
any subscribing member would have a just right to complain of a proceeding which compromised both the principle
of private judgment and the doctrine of justification by
faith only. These instances are sufficient to illustrate my

general position, that coalitions and comprehensions for an object have their life in the prosecution of that object, and cease to have any meaning as soon as that object is compromised or disparaged.

When, then, a number of persons come forward, not as politicians, not as diplomatists, lawyers, traders, or speculators, but with the one object of advancing universal knowledge, much we may allow them to sacrifice—ambition, reputation, leisure, comfort, gold; one thing they may not sacrifice—knowledge itself. Knowledge being their object, they need not of course insist on their own private views about ancient or modern history, or national prosperity, or the balance of power; they need not of course shrink from the co-operation of those who hold the opposite views; but stipulate they must that knowledge itself is not compromised—and as to those views, of whatever kind, which they do allow to be dropped, it is plain they consider such to be opinions, and nothing more, however dear, however important to themselves personally; opinions ingenious, admirable, pleasurable, beneficial, expedient, but not worthy the name of knowledge or science. Thus no one would insist on the Malthusian teaching being a *sine qua non* in a seat of learning who did not think it simply ignorance not to be a Malthusian; and no one would consent to drop the Newtonian theory who thought it to be proved true, in the same sense as the existence of the sun and moon is true. If, then, in an institution which professes all knowledge, nothing is professed, nothing is taught about the Supreme Being, it is fair to infer that every individual in the number of those who advocate that institution, supposing him consistent, distinctly holds that nothing is known for certain about the Supreme Being; nothing such as to have any claim to be regarded as an accession to the stock of general knowledge existing in the world. If, on the other hand, it turns out that something considerable is

known about the Supreme Being, whether from reason or
revelation, then the institution in question professes every
science, and yet leaves out the foremost of them. In a
word, strong as may appear the assertion, I do not see how
I can avoid making it, and bear with me, gentlemen, while
I do so, viz. such an institution cannot be what it professes, if there be a God. I do not wish to declaim; but
by the very force of the terms it is very plain that a Divine
Being and such a university cannot coexist.

Still, however, this may seem to many an abrupt conclusion, and will not be acquiesced in: what answer, gentlemen, will be made to it? Perhaps this: it will be said that
there are different kinds or spheres of knowledge, human,
divine, sensible, intellectual, and the like; and that a
university certainly takes in all varieties of knowledge in its
own line, but still that it has a line of its own. It contemplates, it occupies a certain order, a certain platform, of
knowledge. I understand the remark; but I own to you,
gentlemen, I do not understand how it can be made to
apply to the matter in hand. I cannot so construct my
definition of the subject-matter of university knowledge,
and so draw my boundary lines around it, as to include
therein the other sciences commonly studied at universities,
and to exclude the science of religion. Are we to limit our
idea of university knowledge by the evidence of our senses?
then we exclude history; by testimony? we exclude metaphysics; by abstract reasoning? we exclude physics. Is not
the being of a God reported to us by testimony, handed
down by history, inferred by an inductive process, brought
home to us by metaphysical necessity, urged on us by the
suggestions of our conscience? It is a truth in the natural
order, as well as in the supernatural. So much for its
origin; and, when obtained, what is it worth? Is it a great
truth or a small one? Is it a comprehensive truth? Say

that no other religious idea whatever were given but it, and you have enough to fill the mind; you have at once a whole dogmatic system. The word God is a theology in itself, indivisibly one, inexhaustibly various, from the vastness and the simplicity of its meaning. Admit a God, and you introduce among the subjects of your knowledge a fact encompassing, closing in upon, absorbing every other fact conceivable. How can we investigate any part of any order of knowledge, and stop short of that which enters into every order? All true principles run over with it, all phenomena converge to it; it is truly the first and the last. In word indeed, and in idea, it is easy enough to divide knowledge into human and divine, secular and religious, and to lay down that we will address ourselves to the one without interfering with the other; but it is impossible in fact. Granting that divine truth differs in kind from human, so do human truths differ in kind one from another. If the knowledge of the Creator is in a different order from knowledge of the creature, so, in like manner, metaphysical science is in a different order from physical, physics from history, history from ethics. You will soon break up into fragments the whole circle of secular knowledge, if you begin the mutilation with divine.

I have been speaking simply of natural theology; my argument of course is stronger when I go on to revelation. Let the doctrine of the Incarnation be true: is it not at once of the nature of an historical fact, and of a metaphysical? Let it be true that there are angels: how is this not a point of knowledge in the same sense as the naturalist's asseveration that there are myriads of living things on the point of a needle? That the earth is to be burned by fire is, if true, as large a fact as that huge monsters once played amid its depths; that antichrist is to come is as categorical a heading to a chapter of history as that Nero or Julian was Emperor of Rome; that a divine influence moves the will is a subject of thought not more mysterious than the result of volition on the animal frame, which we admit as a fact in metaphysics.

I do not see how it is possible for a philosophical mind, first, to believe these religious facts to be true; next, to consent to put them aside; and thirdly, in spite of this, to go on to profess to be teaching all the while *de omni scibili*. No; if a man thinks in his heart that these religious facts are short of truth, are not true in the sense in which the fall of a stone to the earth is true, I understand his excluding religion from his university, though his professes other reasons for its exclusion. In that case the varieties of religious opinion under which he shelters his conduct are not only his apology for publicly ignoring religion, but a cause of his privately disbelieving it. He does not think that anything is known or can be known for certain about the origin of the world or the end of man.

This, I fear, is the conclusion to which intellects, clear, logical, and consistent, have come, or are coming, from the nature of the case; and, alas! in addition to this *prima facie* suspicion, there are actual tendencies in the same direction in Protestantism, viewed whether in its original idea, or again in the so-called evangelical movement in these islands during the last century. The religious world, as it is styled, holds, generally speaking, that religion consists, not in knowledge, but in feeling or sentiment. The old Catholic notion, which still lingers in the Established Church, was that faith was an intellectual act, its object truth, and its result knowledge. Thus, if you look into the Anglican Prayer Book, you will find definite *credenda*, as well as definite *agenda*; but in proportion as the Lutheran leaven spread, it became fashionable to say that faith was, not an acceptance of revealed doctrine, not an act of the intellect, but a feeling, an emotion, an affection, an appetency; and, as this view of faith obtained, so was the connection of faith with truth and knowledge more and more either forgotten or denied. At length the identity of this (so-called) spirituality of heart and the virtue of faith was acknowledged on all hands. Some men indeed disapproved the pietism in question, others admired it; but whether they admired or disapproved, both the one party and the other found themselves in agreement on the main point, viz. in considering that this really was in substance religion, and nothing else; that religion was based, not on argument, but on taste and sentiment, that nothing was objective, everything subjective, in doctrine. I say, even those who saw through the affectation in which the religious school of which I am speaking clad itself still came to that religion, as such, consisted in something short of intellectual exercises, viz. in the affections, in the imagination, in inward persuasions and consolations, in pleasurable sensations, sudden changes, and sublime fancies. They learned to believe, and to take it for granted, that religion was nothing beyond a *supply* of the wants of human nature, not an external fact and a work of God. There was, it appeared, a demand for religion, and therefore there was a supply; human nature could not do without religion, any more than it could do without bread; a supply was absolutely necessary, good or bad, and, as in the case of the articles of daily sustenance, an article which was really inferior was better than none at all. Thus religion was useful, venerable, beautiful, the sanction of order, the stay of government, the curb of self-will and self-indulgence, which the laws cannot reach: but, after all, on what was it based? Why, that was a question delicate to ask, and imprudent to answer; but if the truth must be spoken, however reluctantly, the long and the short of the matter was this, that religion was based on custom, on prejudice, on law, on education, on habit, on loyalty, on feudalism, on enlightened expedience, on many, many things, but not at all on reason; reason was neither its warrant nor its instrument, and science had as little connection with it as with the fashions, or the state of the weather.

You see, gentlemen, how a theory or philosophy which began with the religious changes of the sixteenth century has led to conclusions which the authors of those changes would be the first to denounce, and has been taken up by that large and influential body which goes by the name of liberal or latitudinarian; and how, where it prevails, it is as unreasonable of course to demand for religion a chair in a university, as to demand one for fine feeling, sense of honour, patriotism, gratitude, maternal affection, or good companionship, proposals which would be simply unmeaning.

Now in illustration of what I have been saying I will appeal, in the first place, to a statesman, but not merely so, to no mere politician, no trader in places, or votes, or the stock market, but to a philosopher, to an orator, to one whose profession, whose aim, has ever been to cultivate the fair, the noble, and the generous. I cannot forget the celebrated discourse of the celebrated man to whom I am alluding; a man who is first in his peculiar walk; and who, moreover (which is much to my purpose), has had a share, as much as anyone alive, in effecting the public recognition in these islands of the principle of separating secular and religious knowledge. This brilliant thinker, during the years in which he was exerting himself in its behalf, made a speech, or discourse, on occasion of a public solemnity; and in reference to the bearing of general knowledge upon religious belief, he spoke as follows:

'As men,' he said, 'will no longer suffer themselves to be led blindfold in ignorance, so will they no more yield to the vile principle of judging and treating their fellow creatures, not according to the intrinsic merit of their actions, but according to the accidental and involuntary coincidence of their opinions. The great truth has finally gone forth to all the ends of the earth,' and he prints it in capital letters, 'that man shall no more render account to man for his belief, over which he has himself no control. Henceforward, nothing shall prevail upon us to praise or to blame anyone for that which he can no more change than he can the hue of his skin or the height of his stature.' [1] You see, gentlemen, if this philosopher is to decide the matter, religious ideas are just as far from being real, or representing anything beyond themselves, are as truly peculiarities, idiosyncrasies, accidents of the individual, as his having the stature of a Patagonian, or the features of a Negro.

But perhaps this was the rhetoric of an excited moment. Far from it, gentlemen, or I should not have fastened on the words of a fertile mind, uttered so long ago. What Mr Brougham laid down as a principle in 1825 resounds on all sides of us, with ever-growing confidence and success, in 1852. I open the Minutes of the Committee of Council on Education for the years 1848–50, presented to both Houses of Parliament by command of Her Majesty, and I find one of Her Majesty's Inspectors of Schools, at page 467 of the second volume, dividing 'the topics usually embraced in the better class of primary schools' into four: the knowledge of *signs*, as reading and writing; of *facts*, as geography and astronomy; of *relations and laws*, as mathematics; and lastly *sentiment*, such as poetry and music. Now on first catching sight of this division it occurred to me to ask myself, before ascertaining the writer's own resolution of the matter, under which of these four heads would fall religion, or whether it fell under any of them. Did he put it aside as a thing too delicate and sacred to be enumerated with earthly studies? Or did he distinctly contemplate it when he made his division? Anyhow, I could really find a place for it under the first head, or the second, or the third; for it has to

[1] Mr Brougham's Glasgow discourse.

do with facts, since it tells of the Self-subsisting; it has to do with relations, for it tells of the Creator; it has to do with signs, for it tells of the due manner of speaking of Him. There was just one head of the division to which I could not refer it, viz. to *sentiment*; for, I suppose, music and poetry, which are the writer's own examples of sentiment, have not much to do with truth, which is the main object of religion. Judge then my surprise, gentlemen, when I found the fourth was the very head selected by the writer of the report in question as the special receptacle of religious topics. 'The inculcation of *sentiment*,' he says, 'embraces reading in its higher sense, poetry, music, together with moral and religious education.' What can be clearer than that, in this writer's idea (whom I am far from introducing for his own sake, because I have no wish to hurt the feelings of a gentleman who is but exerting himself zealously in the discharge of anxious duties; I do but introduce him as an illustration of the wide-spreading school of thought to which he belongs), what, I say, can more clearly prove than a candid avowal like this that, in the view of that school, religion is not knowledge, has nothing whatever to do with knowledge, and is excluded from a university course of instruction, not simply because the exclusion cannot be helped, from political or social obstacles, but because it has no business there at all, because it is to be considered a mere taste, sentiment, opinion, and nothing more?

The writer avows this conclusion himself in the explanation into which he presently enters, in which he says: 'According to the classification proposed, the *essential idea* of all religious education will consist in the direct cultivation of the *feelings*.' What we contemplate, then, what we aim at, when we give a religious education, is, it seems, not to impart any knowledge whatever, but to satisfy any-how desires which will arise after the Unseen in spite of us, to provide the mind with a means of self-command, to impress on it the beautiful ideas which saints and sages have struck out, to embellish it with the bright hues of a celestial piety, to teach it the poetry of devotion, the music of well-ordered affections, and the luxury of doing good. As for the intellect, its exercise happens to be unavoidable, whenever moral impressions are made, from the constitution of the human mind, and it varies in its conclusions with the peculiarities of the individual. Something like this seems to be the writer's meaning, but we need not pry into its finer issues in order to gain a distinct view of its general bearing; and taking it, as I think we fairly may take it, as a specimen of the philosophy of the day, as adopted by those who are not conscious unbelievers, or open scoffers, I consider it amply explains how it comes to pass that this day's philosophy sets up a system of universal knowledge, and teaches of plants, and earths, and creeping things, and beasts, and gases, about the crust of the earth and the changes of the atmosphere, about sun, moon, and stars, about man and his doings, about the history of the world, about sensation, memory, and the passions, about duty, about cause and effect, about all things imaginable except one—and that is, about Him that made all these things, about God. I say the reason is plain because they consider knowledge, as regards the creature, is illimitable, but impossible or hopeless as regards the being and attributes and works of the Creator.

Here, however, it may be objected to me that this representation is certainly extreme, for the school in question does, in fact, lay great stress on the evidence afforded by the creation to the being and attributes of the Creator. I may be referred, for instance, to the words of one of the speakers on a memorable occasion. At the very time of laying the first stone of the University of London, I confess it, a learned person, since elevated to the Protestant see of Durham, which he still fills, opened the proceedings with prayer. He addressed the Diety, as the authoritative report informs us, 'the whole surrounding assembly standing uncovered in solemn silence.' 'Thou,' he said, in the name of all present, 'Thou hast constructed the vast fabric of the universe in so wonderful a manner, so arranged its motions, and so formed its productions, that the contemplation and study of Thy works exercise at once the mind in the pursuit of human science, and lead it onwards to *divine truth.*' Here is apparently a distinct recognition that there is such a thing as truth in the province of religion; and, did the passage stand by itself, and were it the only means we possessed of ascertaining the sentiments of the powerful body whom this distinguished person there represented, it would, as far as it goes, be satisfactory. I admit it; and I admit also the recognition of the being and certain attributes of the Deity contained in the writings of the gifted person whom I have already quoted, whose genius, versatile and multiform as it is, in nothing has been so constant as in its devotion to the advancement of knowledge, scientific and literary. He then, in his 'Discourse of the objects, advantages, and pleasures of science,' after variously illustrating what he terms its 'gratifying treats,' crowns the catalogue with mention of 'the *highest* of *all* our gratifications in the contemplation of science,' which he proceeds to explain thus:

'We are raised by them,' says he, 'to an understanding of the infinite wisdom and goodness which the Creator has displayed in all His works. Not a step can be taken in any direction,' he continues, 'without perceiving the most extraordinary traces of design; and the skill, everywhere conspicuous, is calculated in so vast a proportion of instances to promote the happiness of living creatures, and especially of ourselves, that we can feel no hesitation in concluding that, if we knew the whole scheme of Providence, every part would be in harmony with a plan of absolute benevolence. Independent, however, of this most consoling inference, the delight is inexpressible of being able to follow, as it were, with our eyes the marvellous works of the Great Architect of Nature, to trace the unbounded power and exquisite skill which are exhibited in the most minute, as well as the mightiest parts of His system. The pleasure derived from this study is unceasing, and so various that it never tires the appetite. But it is unlike the low gratifications of sense in another respect: it elevates and refines our nature, while those hurt the health, debase the understanding, and corrupt the feelings; it teaches us to look upon all earthly objects as insignificant and below our notice, except the pursuit of knowledge and the cultivation of virtue, that is to say the strict performance of our duty in every relation of society; and it gives a dignity and importance to the enjoyment of life, which the frivolous and the grovelling cannot even comprehend.'

Such are the words of this prominent champion of mixed education. If logical inference be, as it undoubtedly is, an instrument of truth, surely, it may be answered to me, in admitting the possibility of inferring the Divine Being and attributes *from* the phenomena of nature, he distinctly admits a basis of truth for the doctrines of religion.

I wish, gentlemen, to give these representations their full weight, both from the gravity of the question, and the consideration due to the persons whom I am arraigning; but, before I can feel sure I understand them, I must ask an abrupt question. When I am told, then, by the partisans of universities without theological teaching, that human science leads to belief in a Supreme Being, without denying the fact, nay, as a Catholic, with full conviction of it, nevertheless I am obliged to ask what the statement means in *their* mouths, what they, the speakers, understand by the word God. Let me not be thought offensive if I question whether it means the same thing on the two sides of the controversy. With us Catholics, as with the first race of Protestants, as with Mohammedans, and all theists, the word contains, as I have already said, a theology in itself. At the risk of anticipating what I shall have occasion to insist upon in my next discourse, let me say that, according to the teaching of monotheism, God is an individual, self-dependent, all-perfect, unchangeable Being; intelligent, living, personal, and present; almighty, all-seeing, all-remembering; between whom and His creatures there is an infinite gulf; who has no origin, who is all-sufficient for Himself; who created and upholds the universe; who will judge every one of us, sooner or later, according to that law of right and wrong which He has written on our hearts. He is One who is sovereign over, operative amidst, independent of, the appointments which He has made; One in whose hands are all things, who has a purpose in every event, and a standard for every deed, and thus has relations of His own towards the subject-matter of each particular science which the book of knowledge unfolds; who has with an adorable, never-ceasing energy mixed Himself up with all the history of creation, the constitution of nature, the course of the world, the origin of society, the fortunes of nations, the action of the human mind; and who thereby necessarily becomes the subject-matter of a science far wider and more noble than any of those which are included in the circle of secular education.

This is the doctrine which belief in a God implies: if it means anything, it means all this, and cannot keep from meaning all this, and a great deal more; and, even though there were nothing in the religious tenets of the last three centuries to disparage dogmatic truth, still, even then, I should have difficulty in believing that a doctrine so mysterious, so peremptory, approved itself as a matter of course to educated men of this day who gave their minds attentively to consider it. Rather, in a state of society such as ours, in which authority, prescription, tradition, habit, moral instinct, and the divine influences go for nothing, in which patience of thought, and depth and consistency of view, are scorned as subtle and scholastic, in which free discussion and fallible judgment are prized as the birthright of each individual, I must be excused if I exercise towards this age, as regards its belief in this doctrine, some portion of that scepticism which it exercises itself towards every received but unscrutinized assertion whatever. I cannot take it for granted, I must have it brought home to me by tangible evidence, that the spirit of the age means by the Supreme Being what Catholics mean. Nay, it would be a relief to my mind to gain some ground of assurance that the parties influenced by that spirit had, I will not say a true apprehension of God, but even so much as the idea of what a true apprehension is.

Nothing is easier than to use the word, and mean nothing by it. The heathens used to say: 'God wills' when they meant 'fate'; 'God provides' when they meant 'chance'; 'God acts' when they meant 'instinct' or 'sense'; and 'God is everywhere' when they meant 'the soul of nature.' The Almighty is something infinitely different from a principle, or a centre of action, or a quality, or a generalization of phenomena. If then by the word you do but mean a Being who has contrived the world and keeps it in order, who acts in it, but only in the way of general Providence, who acts towards us but only through what are called laws of nature, who is more certain not to act at all than to act independent of those laws, who is known and approached indeed, but only through the medium of those laws; such a God it is not difficult for anyone to conceive, not difficult for anyone to endure. If, I say, as you would revolutionize society, so you would revolutionize heaven, if you have changed the divine sovereignty into a sort of constitutional monarchy, in which the throne has honour and ceremonial enough, but cannot issue the most ordinary command except through legal forms and precedents, and with the countersignature of a minister, then belief in a God is no more than an acknowledgment of existing, sensible powers and phenomena, which none but an idiot can deny. If the Supreme Being is powerful or skilful, just so far forth as the telescope shows power, and the microscope shows skill, if His moral law is to be ascertained simply by the physical processes of the animal frame, or His will gathered from the immediate issues of human affairs, if His Essence is just as high and deep and broad and long as the universe, and no more; if this be the fact, then will I confess that there is no specific science about God, that theology is but a name, and a protest in its behalf an hypocrisy. Then is He but coincident with the laws of the universe; then is He but a function, or correlative, or subjective reflection and mental impression of each phenomenon of the material or moral world, as it flits before us. Then, pious as it is to think of Him, while the pageant of experiment or abstract reasoning passes by, still, such piety is nothing more than a poetry of thought or an ornament of language, and has not even an infinitesimal influence upon philosophy or science, of which it is rather the parasitical production. I understand, in that case, why theology should require no specific teaching, for there is nothing to mistake about; why it is powerless against scientific anticipations, for it merely is one of them; why it is simply absurd in its denunciations of heresy, for heresy does not lie in the region of fact and experiment. I understand, in that case, how it is that the religious sense is but a 'sentiment,' and its exercise a 'gratifying treat,' for it is like the sense of the beautiful or the sublime. I understand how the contemplation of the universe 'leads onwards to *divine* truth,' for divine truth is not something separate from nature, but it is nature with a divine glow upon it. I understand the zeal expressed for natural theology, for this study is but a mode of looking at nature, a certain view taken of nature, private and personal, which one man has, and another has not, which gifted minds strike out, which others see to be admirable and ingenious, and which all would be the better for adopting. It is but the theology of nature, just as we talk of the *philosophy* or the *romance* of history, or the *poetry* of childhood, or the picturesque, or the sentimental, or the humorous, or any other abstract quality, which the genius or the caprice of the individual, or the fashion of the day, or the consent of the world, recognizes in any set of objects which are subjected to its contemplation.

Such ideas of religion seem to me short of monotheism; I do not impute them to this or that individual who belongs to the school which gives them currency; but what I read about the 'gratification' of keeping pace in our scientific researches with 'the Architect of Nature'; about the said gratification 'giving a dignity and importance to the enjoyment of life,' and teaching us that knowledge and our duties to society are the only earthly objects worth our notice, all this, I own it, gentlemen, frightens me; nor is Dr Maltby's address to the Deity sufficient to reassure me. I do not see much difference between avowing that there is no God, and implying that nothing definite can for certain be known about Him; and when I find religious education treated as the cultivation of sentiment, and religious belief as the accidental hue or posture of the mind, I am reluctantly but forcibly reminded of a very unpleasant page of metaphysics, viz. of the relations between God and nature insinuated by such philosophers as Hume. This acute though most low-minded of speculators, in his inquiry concerning the human understanding, introduces, as is well known, Epicurus, that is, a teacher of atheism, delivering an harangue to the Athenian people, not indeed in defence, but in extenuation of that opinion. His object is to show that, whereas the atheistic view is nothing else than the repudiation of theory, and an accurate representation of phenomenon and fact, it cannot be dangerous, unless phenomenon and fact be dangerous. Epicurus is made to say that the paralogism of philosophy has ever been that of arguing from nature in behalf of something beyond nature, greater than nature; whereas God, as he maintains, being known only through the visible world, our knowledge of Him is absolutely commensurate with our knowledge of it— is nothing distinct from it—is but a mode of viewing it. Hence it follows that, provided we admit, as we cannot help admitting, the phenomena of nature and the world, it is only a question of words whether or not we go on to the hypothesis of a second Being, not visible but immaterial, parallel and coincident with nature, to whom we give the name of God. 'Allowing,' he says, 'the gods to be the authors of the existence or order of the universe, it follows that they possess that precise degree of power, intelligence, and benevolence which appears in their workmanship; but nothing further can be proved, except we call in the assistance of exaggeration and flattery to supply the defects of argument and reasoning. So far as the traces of any attributes, at present, appear, so far may we conclude these attributes to exist. The supposition of further attributes is mere hypothesis; much more the supposition that, in distant periods of place and time, there has been, or will be, a more magnificent display of these attributes, and a scheme of administration more suitable to such imaginary virtues.'

Here is a reasoner who would not hesitate to deny that there is any distinct science or philosophy possible concerning the Supreme Being; since every single thing we know of Him is this or that or the other phenomenon, material or moral, which already falls under this or that natural science. In him then it would be only consistent to drop theology in a course of university education: but how is it consistent in anyone who shrinks from his companionship? I am glad to see that the author, several times mentioned, is in opposition to Hume in one sentence of the quotation I have made from his discourse upon science, deciding, as he does, that the phenomena of the material world are insufficient for the full exhibition of the divine attributes, and implying that they require a supplemental process to complete and harmonize their evidence. But is not this supplemental process a science? and if so, why not acknowledge its existence! If God is more than nature, theology claims a place among the sciences: but, on the other hand, if you are not sure of as much as this, how do you differ from Hume or Epicurus?

I end then as I began: religious doctrine is knowledge. This is the important truth, little entered into at this day, which I wish that all who have honoured me with their presence here would allow me to beg them to take away with them. I am not catching at sharp arguments, but laying down grave principles. Religious doctrine is knowledge, in as full a sense as Newton's doctrine is knowledge. University education without theology is simply unphilosophical. Theology has at least as good a right to claim a place there as astronomy.

In my next discourse it will be my object to show that its omission from the list of recognized sciences is not only indefensible in itself, but prejudicial to all the rest.

DISCOURSE II

WHEN men of great intellect, who have long and intently
and exclusively given themselves to the study or investigation of some one particular branch of secular knowledge,
whose mental life is concentrated and hidden in their
chosen pursuit, and who have neither eyes nor ears for
anything which does not immediately bear upon it, when
such men are at length made to realize that there is a clamour
all around them, which must be heard, for what they have
been so little accustomed to place in the category of knowledge as religion, and that they themselves are accused of
disaffection to it, they are impatient at the interruption;
they call the demand tyrannical, and the requisitionists
bigots or fanatics. They are tempted to say that their only
wish is to be let alone; for themselves, they are not dreaming
of offending anyone, or interfering with anyone; they are
pursuing their own particular line, they have never spoken
a word against anyone's religion, whoever he may be, and
never mean to do so. It does not follow that they deny
the existence of a God because they are not found talking
of it, when the topic would be utterly irrelevant. All they
say is that there are other beings in the world besides the
Supreme Being; their business is with them. After all, the
creation is not the Creator, nor things secular religious.
Theology and human science are two things, not one, and
have their respective provinces, contiguous it may be and
cognate to each other, but not identical. When we are
contemplating earth, we are not contemplating heaven;

30

and when we are contemplating heaven, we are not contemplating earth.   Separate subjects should be treated
separately.   As division of labour, so division of thought
is the only means of successful application.   'Let us go our
own way,' they say, 'and you go yours.   We do not pretend
to lecture on theology, and you have no claim to pronounce
upon science.'

With this feeling they attempt a sort of compromise,
between their opponents who claim for theology a free
introduction into the schools of science, and themselves
who would exclude it altogether, and it is this: viz. that it
should remain indeed excluded from the public schools, but
that it should be permitted in private, wherever a sufficient
number of persons is found to desire it.   Such persons,
they seem to say, may have it all their own way, when they
are by themselves, so that they do not attempt to disturb a
comprehensive system of instruction, acceptable and useful
to all, by the intrusion of opinions peculiar to their own
minds.

I am now going to attempt a philosophical answer to this
representation, that is, to the project of teaching secular
knowledge in the university lecture room, and remanding
religious knowledge to the parish priest, the catechism, and
the parlour; and in doing so you must pardon me, gentlemen,
if my subject should oblige me to pursue a course of thought
which is wearisome to the hearer; I begin then thus:

Truth is the object of knowledge of whatever kind; and
when we inquire what is meant by truth, I suppose it is
right to answer that truth means facts and their relations,
which stand towards each other pretty much as subjects
and predicates in logic.   All that exists, as contemplated
by the human mind, forms one large system or complex
fact, and this of course resolves itself into an indefinite
number of particular facts, which, as being portions of a
whole, have countless relations of every kind, one towards

another. Knowledge is the apprehension of these facts, whether in themselves or in their mutual positions and bearings. And, as all taken together form one integral subject for contemplation, so there are no natural or real limits between part and part; one is ever running into another; all, as viewed by the mind, are combined together, and possess a correlative character one with another, from the internal mysteries of the Divine Essence down to our own sensations and consciousness, from the most solemn appointments of the Lord of all down to what may be called the accident of the hour, from the most glorious seraph down to the vilest and most noxious of reptiles.

Now it is not wonderful that, with all its capabilities, the human mind cannot take in this whole vast fact at a single glance, or gain possession of it at once. Like a short-sighted reader, its eye pores closely, and travels slowly, over the awful volume which lies open for its inspection. Or again, as we deal with some huge structure of many parts and sides, the mind goes round about it, noting down first one thing, then another, as it best may, and viewing it under different aspects, by way of making progress towards mastering the whole. So by degrees and by circuitous advances does it rise aloft and subject to itself that universe into which it has been born.

These various partial views or abstractions, by means of which the mind looks out upon its object, are called sciences, and embrace respectively larger or smaller portions of the field of knowledge; sometimes extending far and wide, but superficially, sometimes with exactness over particular departments, sometimes occupied together on one and the same portion, sometimes holding one part in common, and then ranging on this side or that in absolute divergence one from the other. Thus optics has for its subject the whole visible creation, so far forth as it is simply visible; mental philosophy has a narrower province, but a richer one.

Astronomy, plane and physical, each has the same subject-matter, but views it or treats it differently; lastly, geology and comparative anatomy have subject-matters partly the same, partly distinct.   Now these views or sciences, as being abstractions, have far more to do with the relations of things than with things themselves.   They tell us what things are only or principally by telling us their relations, or assigning predicates to subjects; and therefore they never tell us all that can be said about a thing, even when they tell something, nor do they bring it before us, as the senses do. They arrange and classify facts; they reduce separate phenomena under a common law; they trace effects to a cause.   Thus they serve to transfer our knowledge from the custody of memory to the surer and more abiding protection of philosophy, thereby providing both for its spread and its advance; for, inasmuch as sciences are forms of knowledge, they enable the intellect to master and increase it; and, inasmuch as they are instruments, to communicate it readily to others.   Still, after all, they proceed on the principle of a division of labour, even though that division is an abstraction, not a literal separation into parts; and, as the maker of a bridle or an epaulet has not, on that account, any idea of the science of tactics or strategy, so in a parallel way it is not every science which equally, nor any one which fully, enlightens the mind in the knowledge of things as they are, or brings home to it the external object on which it wishes to gaze.   Thus they differ in importance; and according to their importance will be their influence, not only on the mass of knowledge to which they all converge and contribute, but on each other.

Since then sciences are the results of mental processes about one and the same subject-matter, viewed under its various aspects, and are true results, as far as they go, yet at the same time separate and partial, it follows that on the one hand they need external assistance, one by one, by reason of their incompleteness, and on the other that they are able to afford it to each other, by reason, first, of their independence in themselves, and then of their connection in their subject-matter. Viewed altogether, they approximate to a representation or subjective reflection of the objective truth, as nearly as is possible to the human mind, which advances towards the accurate apprehension of that object in proportion to the number of sciences which it has mastered; and which, when certain sciences are away, in such a case has but a defective apprehension, in proportion to the value of the sciences which are thus wanting, and the importance of the field on which they are employed.

Let us take, for instance, man himself as our object of contemplation; then at once we shall find we can view him in a variety of relations; and according to those relations are the sciences of which he is the subject-matter, and according to our acquaintance with them is our possession of a true knowledge of him. We may view him in relation to the material elements of his body, or to his mental constitution, or to his household and family, or to the community in which he lives, or to the Being who made him; and in consequence we treat of him respectively as physiologists, or as moral philosophers, or as writers of economics, or of politics, or as theologians. When we think of him in all these relations together, or as the subject at once of all the sciences I have named, then we may be said to reach unto and rest in the idea of man as an object or external fact, similar to that which the eye takes of his outward form. On the other hand, according as we are only physiologists, or only politicians, or only moralists, so is our idea of man more or less unreal; we do not take in the whole of him, and the defect is greater or less in proportion as the relation is or is not important which is omitted, whether his relation to God, or to his king, or to his children, or to his own component parts. And if there be one relation about which we know nothing at all except that it exists, then is our knowledge of him, confessedly and to our own consciousness, deficient and partial, and that, I repeat, in proportion to the importance of the relation.

That therefore is true of sciences in general which we are apt to think applies only to pure mathematics, though to pure mathematics it applies especially, viz. that they cannot be considered as simple representations or informants of things as they are. We are accustomed to say, and say truly, that the conclusions of pure mathematics are applied, corrected, and adapted by mixed; but so too the conclusions of anatomy, chemistry, dynamics, and other sciences are revised and completed by each other. Those several conclusions do not represent whole and substantive things, but views, true so far as they go; and in order to ascertain how far they do go, that is, how far they correspond to the object to which they belong, we must compare them with the views taken out of that object by other sciences. Did we proceed upon the abstract theory of forces we should assign a much more ample range to a projectile than in fact the resistance of the air allows it to accomplish. Let, however, that resistance be made the subject of scientific analysis, and then we shall have a new science, assisting, and to a certain point completing, for the benefit of questions of fact, the science of projection. On the other hand, the science of projection itself, considered as belonging to the forces it contemplates, is not more perfect, as such, by this supplementary investigation. And in like manner as regards the whole circle of sciences, one corrects another for purposes of fact, and one without the other cannot dogmatize, except hypothetically and upon its own abstract principles. For instance, the Newtonian philosophy requires the admission of certain metaphysical postulates, if it is to be more than a theory or an hypothesis; as, for instance, that what happened yesterday will happen to-morrow; that there is such a thing as matter, that our senses are trustworthy, that there is a logic of induction, and so on.   Now to Newton metaphysicians grant all that he asks; but, if so be, they may not prove equally accommodating to another who asks something else, and then all his most logical conclusions in the science of physics would remain hopelessly on the stocks, though finished, and never could be launched into the sphere of fact.

Again, did I know nothing about the passage of bodies, except what the theory of gravitation supplies, were I simply absorbed in that theory so as to make it measure all motion on earth and in the sky, I should indeed come to many right conclusions, I should hit off many important facts, ascertain many existing relations, and correct many popular errors: I should scout and ridicule with great success the old notion that light bodies flew up and heavy bodies fell down; but I should go on with equal confidence to deny the phenomenon of capillary attraction.   Here I should be wrong, but only because I carried out my science irrespectively of other sciences.   In like manner, did I simply give myself to the investigation of the external action of body upon body, I might scoff at the very idea of chemical affinities and combinations, and reject it as simply unintelligible.   Were I a mere chemist, I should deny the influence of mind upon bodily health; and so on as regards the devotees of any science, or family of sciences, to the exclusion of others; they necessarily become bigots and quacks, scorning all principles and reported facts which do not belong to their own pursuit, and thinking to effect everything without aid from any other quarter.   Thus before now chemistry has been substituted for medicine;

and again, political economy, or intellectual enlightenment, or the reading of the Scriptures, has been cried up as a panacea against vice, malevolence, and misery.

Summing up, gentlemen, what I have said, I lay it down that all knowledge forms one whole, because its subject-matter is one; for the universe in its length and breadth is so intimately knit together that we cannot separate off portion from portion, and operation from operation, except by a mental abstraction; and then again, as to its Creator, though He of course in His own Being is infinitely separate from it, yet He has so implicated Himself with it, and taken it into His very bosom by His presence in it, His providence over it, His impressions upon it, and His influences through it, that we cannot truly or fully contemplate it without contemplating Him. Next, sciences are the results of that mental abstraction which I have spoken of, being the logical record of this or that aspect of the whole subject-matter of knowledge. As they all belong to one and the same circle of objects, they are one and all connected together; as they are but aspects of things, they are severally incomplete in their relation to the things themselves, though complete in their own idea and for their own respective purposes; on both accounts they at once need and subserve each other. And further, the comprehension of the bearings of one science on another, and the use of each to each, and the location and limitation and adjustment and due appreciation of them all, one with another, this belongs, I conceive, to a sort of science distinct from all of them, and in some sense a science of sciences, which is my own conception of what is meant by philosophy, in the true sense of the word, and of a philosophical habit of mind, and which in these discourses I shall call by that name. This is what I have to say about knowledge and philosophical knowledge generally; and now I proceed to

apply it to the particular science which has led me to draw
it out.

I say, then, that the systematic omission of any one
science from the catalogue prejudices the accuracy and
completeness of our knowledge altogether, and that in
proportion to its importance. Not even theology itself,
though it comes from heaven, though its truths were given
once for all at the first, though they are more certain on
account of the Giver than those of mathematics, not even
theology do I exclude from the law to which every mental
exercise is subject, viz. from that imperfection which ever
must attend the abstract when it would determine the
concrete. Nor do I speak only of natural religion; for
even the teaching of the Catholic Church is variously influenced by the other sciences. Not to insist on the introduction of the Aristotelic philosophy into its phraseology,
its interpretations of prophecy are directly affected by the
issues of history; its comments upon Scripture by the
conclusions of the astronomer and the geologist; and its
casuistical decisions by the various experience, political,
social, and psychological, with which times and places are
ever supplying it.

What theology gives, it has a right to take; or rather, the
interests of truth oblige it to take. If we would not be
beguiled by dreams, if we would ascertain facts as they are,
then, granting theology is a real science, we cannot exclude
it and still call ourselves philosophers. I have asserted
nothing as yet as to the pre-eminent dignity of religious
truth; I only say, if there be religious truth at all, we cannot
shut our eyes to it without prejudice to truth of every kind,
physical, metaphysical, historical, and moral; for it bears
upon all truth. And thus I answer the objection with which
I opened this discourse. I supposed the question put to

me by a philosopher of the day: 'Why cannot you go your way, and let us go ours?' I answer, in the name of theology: 'When Newton can dispense with the metaphysician, then may you dispense with us.' So much at first sight; now I am going on to claim a little more for theology, by classing it with branches of knowledge which may with greater decency be compared to it.

Let us see, then, how this supercilious treatment of so momentous a science, for momentous it must be if there be a God, runs in a somewhat parallel case. The great philosopher of antiquity, when he would enumerate the causes of the things that take place in the world, after making mention of those which he considered to be physical and material, adds: 'And the mind and everything which is by means of man.'[1] Certainly; it would have been a preposterous course, when he would trace the effects he saw around him to their respective sources, had he directed his exclusive attention upon some one class or order of originating principles, and ascribed to these everything which happened anywhere. It would indeed have been unworthy a genius so curious, so penetrating, so fertile, so analytical, as Aristotle's, to have laid it down that everything on the face of the earth could be accounted for by the material sciences, without the hypothesis of moral agents. It is incredible that in the investigation of physical results he could ignore so influential a being as man, or forget that not only brute force and elemental movement but knowledge also is power. And this so much the more, inasmuch as moral and spiritual agents belong to another, not to say a higher, order than physical; so that the omission supposed would not have been merely an oversight in matters of detail, but a philosophical error, and a fault in division.

[1] Arist., *Ethic. Nicom.*, iii. 3.

However, we live in an age of the world when the career of science and literature is little affected by what was done, or would have been done, by this venerable authority; so we will suppose, in England or Ireland, in the middle of the nineteenth century, a set of persons of name and celebrity to meet together, in spite of Aristotle, to adopt a line of proceeding which they conceive the circumstances of the time render imperative. We will suppose that a difficulty just now besets the enunciation and discussion of all matter of science, in consequence of the extreme sensitiveness of large classes of the community, ministers and laymen, on the subjects of necessity, responsibility, the standard of morals, and the nature of virtue. Parties run so high that the only way of avoiding constant quarrelling in defence of this or that side of the question is, in the judgment of the persons I am supposing, to shut up the subject of anthropology altogether. This is accordingly done. Henceforth man is to be as if he were not, in the general course of education; the moral and mental sciences are to have no professorial chairs, and the treatment of them is to be simply left as a matter of private judgment, which each individual may carry out as he will. I can just fancy such a prohibition abstractedly possible; but one thing I cannot fancy possible, viz. that the parties in question, after this sweeping act of exclusion, should forthwith send out proposals on the basis of such exclusion for publishing an encyclopaedia, or erecting a national university. It is necessary, however, gentlemen, for the sake of the illustration which I am setting before you, to imagine what cannot be. I say, let us imagine a project for organizing a system of scientific teaching, in which the agency of man in the material world cannot allowably be recognized, and may allowably be denied. Physical and mechanical causes are exclusively to be treated of; volition is a forbidden subject. A prospectus is put out, with a list of sciences, we will say astronomy, optics, hydrostatics, galvanism, pneumatics, statics, dynamics, pure mathematics, geology, botany, physiology, anatomy, and so forth; but not a word about the mind and its powers, except what is said in explanation of the omission. That explanation is to the effect that the parties concerned in the undertaking have given long and anxious thought to the subject, and have been reluctantly driven to the conclusion that it is simply impracticable to include in the list of university lectures the philosophy of mind. What relieves, however, their regret is the reflection that domestic feelings and polished manners are best cultivated in the family circle and in good society, in the observance of the sacred ties which unite father, mother, and child, in the correlative claims and duties of citizenship, in the exercise of disinterested loyalty and enlightened patriotism. With this apology, such as it is, they pass over the consideration of the human mind and its powers and works 'in solemn silence,' in their scheme of university education.

Let a charter be obtained for it; let professors be appointed, lectures given, examinations passed, degrees awarded: what sort of exactness or trustworthiness, what philosophical largeness, will attach to views formed in an intellectual atmosphere thus deprived of some of the constituent elements of daylight? What judgment will foreign countries and future times pass on the labours of the most acute and accomplished of the philosophers who have been parties to so portentous an unreality? Here are professors gravely lecturing on medicine, or history, or political economy, who, so far from being bound to acknowledge, are free to scoff at the action of mind upon matter, or of mind upon mind, or the claims of mutual justice and charity. Common sense indeed and public opinion set bounds at first to so intolerable a licence; yet, as time goes on, an omission which was originally but a matter

of expedience commends itself to the reason; and at length
a professor is found, more hardy than his brethren, still
however, as he himself maintains, with sincere respect for
domestic feelings and good manners, who takes on him to
deny psychology *in toto*, to pronounce the influence of mind
in the visible world a superstition, and to account for every
effect which is found in the world by the operation of
physical causes. Hitherto intelligence and volition were
accounted real powers; the muscles act, and their action
cannot be represented by any scientific expression; a stone
flies out of the hand and the propulsive force of the muscle
resides in the will; but there has been a revolution, or at
least a new theory in philosophy, and our professor, I say,
after speaking with the highest admiration of the human intellect, limits its independent action to the region of speculation, and denies that it can be a motive principle, or can
exercise a special interference, in the material world. He
ascribes every work, or external act of man, to the innate
force or soul of the physical universe. He observes that
spiritual agents are so mysterious and unintelligible, so
uncertain in their laws, so vague in their operation, so
sheltered from experience, that a wise man will have nothing
to say to them. They belong to a different order of causes,
which he leaves to those whose profession it is to investigate
them, and he confines himself to the tangible and sure.
Human exploits, human devices, human deeds, human
productions, all that comes under the scholastic terms of
'genius' and 'art,' and the metaphysical ideas of 'duty,'
'right,' and 'heroism,' it is his office to contemplate all
these merely in their place in the eternal system of physical
cause and effect. At length he undertakes to show how the
whole fabric of material civilization has arisen from the
constructive powers of physical elements and physical laws.
He descants upon palaces, castles, temples, exchanges,
bridges, causeways, and shows that they never could have

grown into the imposing dimensions which they present to us, but for the laws of gravitation and the cohesion of part with part. The pillar would come down, the loftier the more speedily, did not the centre of gravity fall within its base; and the most admired dome of Palladio or Sir Christopher would give way, were it not for the happy principle of the arch. He surveys the complicated machinery of a single day's arrangements in a private family: our dress, our furniture, our hospitable board; what would become of them, he asks, but for the laws of physical nature? Firm stitches have a natural power, in proportion to the toughness of the material adopted, to keep together separate portions of cloth; sofas and chairs could not turn upside-down, even if they would; and it is a property of caloric to relax the fibres of animal matter, acting through water in one way, through oil in another, and this is the whole mystery of the most elaborate cuisine—but I should be tedious if I continued the illustration.

Now, gentlemen, pray understand how it is to be here applied. I am not supposing that the principles of theology and psychology are the same, or arguing from the works of man to the works of God, which Paley has done, which Hume has protested against. I am not busying myself to prove the existence and attributes of God, by means of the argument from design. I am not proving anything at all about the Supreme Being. On the contrary, I am assuming His existence, and I do but say this: that, man existing, no university professor who had suppressed in physical lectures the idea of volition, who did not take volition for granted, could escape a one-sided, a radically false view of the things which he discussed; not indeed that his own definitions, principles, and laws would be wrong, or his abstract statements; but his considering his own study to be the key of everything that takes place on the face of the earth, and his passing over anthropology, this would be his error. I say it would not be his science which was untrue, but his so-called knowledge which was unreal. He would be deciding on facts by means of theories. The various busy world, spread out before our eyes, is physical, but it is more than physical; and, in making its actual system identical with his scientific analysis, formed on a particular aspect, such a professor as I have imagined was betraying a want of philosophical depth, and an ignorance of what a university education ought to be. He was no longer a teacher of liberal knowledge, but a narrow-minded bigot. While his doctrines professed to be conclusions formed upon an hypothesis or partial truth, they were undeniable; not if they professed to give results in fact which he could grasp and take possession of. Granting, indeed, that a man's arm is moved by a simple physical cause, then of course we may dispute about the various external influences which, when it changes its position, sway it to and fro, like a scarecrow in a garden; but to assert that the motive cause *is* physical, this is an assumption in a case when our question is about a matter of fact, not about the logical consequences of an assumed premiss. And in like manner, if a people prays, and the wind changes, the rain ceases, the sun shines, and the harvest is safely housed, when no one expected it, our professor may, if he will, consult the barometer, discourse about the atmosphere, and throw what has happened into an equation, ingenious though it be not true; but, should he proceed to rest the phenomenon, in matter of fact, simply upon a physical cause, to the exclusion of a divine, and to say that the given case actually belongs to his science because other like cases do, I must tell him: Ne sutor ultra crepidam: he is making his particular craft usurp and occupy the universe. This then is the drift of my illustration. Our excluding volition from our range of ideas is a denial of the soul, and our ignoring divine agency is a virtual denial of God. Moreover, supposing man can will and act of himself in spite of physics, to shut up this great truth, though one, is to put our whole encyclopaedia of knowledge out of joint; and supposing God can will and act of Himself in this world which He has made, and we deny or slur it over, then we are throwing the circle of universal science into a like, or a far worse confusion.

Worse incomparably, for the idea of God, if there be a God, is infinitely higher than the idea of man, if there be man. If to plot out man's agency is to deface the book of knowledge, on the supposition of that agency existing, what must it be, supposing it exists, to blot out the agency of God? See, gentlemen, I have now run beyond the first portion of the argument to which this discourse is devoted. I have hitherto been engaged in showing that all the sciences come to us as one, that they all relate to one and the same integral subject-matter, that each separately is more or less an abstraction, wholly true as an hypothesis, but not wholly trustworthy in the concrete, conversant with relations more than with facts, with principles more than with agents, needing the support and guarantee of its sister sciences, and giving in turn while it takes—from which it follows that none can safely be omitted if we would obtain the exactest knowledge possible of things as they are, and that the omission is more or less important in proportion to the field which each covers, and the depth to which it penetrates, and the order to which it belongs; for its loss is a positive privation of an influence which exerts itself in the correction and completion of the rest. This general statement is the first branch of my argument, and now comes my second, which is its application, and will not occupy us so long. I say, the second question simply regards the Science of God, or theology, viz. what, in matter of fact, are its pretensions, what its importance, what its influence upon other branches of knowledge, supposing there be a

God, which it would not become me to set about proving? Has it vast dimensions, or does it lie in a nutshell? Will its omission be imperceptible, or will it destroy the equilibrium of the whole system of knowledge? This is the inquiry to which I proceed.

Now what is theology? First, I will tell you what it is not. And here, in the first place (though of course I speak on the subject as a Catholic), observe that, strictly speaking, I am not assuming that Catholicism is true, while I make myself the champion of theology. Catholicism has not formally entered into my argument hitherto, nor shall I just now assume any principle peculiar to it, for reasons which will appear in the sequel, though of course I shall use Catholic language. Neither, secondly, will I fall into the fashion of the day, of identifying natural theology with physical; which said physical theology is a most jejune study, considered as a science and really is no science at all, for it is ordinarily nothing more than a series of pious or polemical remarks upon the physical world viewed religiously, whereas the word natural really comprehends man and society, and all that is involved therein, as the great Protestant writer, Dr Butler, shows us. Nor, in the third place, do I mean by theology polemics of any kind; for instance, what are called 'the evidences of religion' or 'the Christian evidences'; for, though these constitute a science supplemental to theology and are necessary in their place, they are not theology itself, unless an army is synonymous with the body politic. Nor, fourthly, do I mean by theology that vague thing called 'Christianity,' or 'our common Christianity,' or 'Christianity the law of the land,' if there is any man alive who can tell what it is. I discard it, for the very reason that it cannot throw itself into a proposition. Lastly, I do not understand by theology acquaintance with the Scriptures; for, though no person of religious feelings can read Scripture but he will find those feelings roused, and gain much knowledge of history into the bargain, yet historical reading and religious feeling are not science. I mean none of these things by theology, I simply mean the Science of God, or the truths we know about God put into system; just as we have a science of the stars, and call it astronomy, or of the crust of the earth, and call it geology.

For instance, I mean, for this is the main point, that, as in the human frame there is a living principle, acting upon it and through it by means of volition, so, behind the veil of the visible universe, there is an invisible, intelligent Being, acting on and through it, as and when He will. Further, I mean that this invisible Agent is in no sense a soul of the world, after the analogy of human nature, but, on the contrary, is absolutely distinct from the world, as being its Creator, Upholder, Governor, and Sovereign Lord. Here we are at once brought into the circle of doctrines which the idea of God embodies. I mean then by the Supreme Being one who is simply self-dependent, and the only Being who is such; moreover, that He is without beginning or eternal, and the only Eternal; that in consequence He has lived a whole eternity by Himself; and hence that He is all-sufficient, sufficient for His own blessedness, and all-blessed, and ever-blessed. Further, I mean a Being who, having these prerogatives, has the supreme good, or rather is the Supreme Good, or has all the attributes of good in infinite intenseness; all wisdom, all truth, all justice, all love, all holiness, all beautifulness; who is omnipotent, omniscient, omnipresent; ineffably one, absolutely perfect; and such that what we do not know and cannot even imagine of Him is far more wonderful than what we do and can. I mean One who is sovereign over His own will and actions, though always according to the eternal rule of right and wrong, which is Himself. I mean, moreover, that He created all things out of nothing, and preserves them every

moment, and could destroy them as easily as He made
them; and that, in consequence, He is separated from them
by an abyss, and is incommunicable in all His attributes.
And further, He has stamped upon all things, in the hour of
their creation, their respective natures, and has given them
their work and mission and their length of days, greater or
less, in their appointed place. I mean, too, that He is
ever present with His works, one by one, and confronts
everything He has made by His particular and most loving
providence, and manifests Himself to each according to its
needs; and has on rational beings imprinted the moral law,
and given them power to obey it, imposing on them the
duty of worship and service, searching and scanning them
through and through with His omniscient eye, and putting
before them a present trial and a judgment to come.

Such is what theology teaches about God, a doctrine, as
the very idea of its subject-matter presupposes, so mysterious as in its fullness to lie beyond any system, and to seem
in parts even to be irreconcilable with itself, the imagination
being unable to embrace what the reason determines. It
teaches of a Being infinite, yet personal; all-blessed, yet
ever operative; absolutely separate from the creature, yet
in every part of the creation at every moment; above all
things, yet under everything. It teaches of a Being who,
though the highest, yet in the work of creation, conser-
vation, government, retribution, makes Himself, as it were,
the minister and servant of all; who, though inhabiting
eternity, allows Himself to take an interest, and to feel a
sympathy, in the matters of space and time. His are all
beings, visible and invisible, the noblest and the vilest of
them. His are the substance, and the operation, and the
results of that system of physical nature into which we are
born. His, too, are the powers and achievements of the
intellectual essences, on which He has bestowed an independent action and the gift of origination. The laws of

the universe, the principles of truth, the relation of one thing to another, their qualities and virtues, the order and harmony of the whole, all that exists, is from Him; and, if evil is not from Him, as assuredly it is not, this is because evil has no substance of its own, but is only the defect, excess, perversion, or corruption of that which has. All we see, hear, and touch, the remote sidereal firmament, as well as our own sea and land, and the elements which compose them, and the ordinances they obey, are His. The primary atoms of matter, their properties, their mutual action, their disposition and collocation, electricity, magnetism, gravitation, light, and whatever other subtle principles or operations the wit of man is detecting or shall detect, are the work of His hands. From Him has been every movement which has convulsed and refashioned the surface of the earth. The most insignificant or unsightly insect is from Him, and good in its kind; the ever-teeming, inexhaustible swarms of animalculae, the myriads of living motes invisible to the naked eye, the restless ever-spreading vegetation which creeps like a garment over the whole earth, the lofty cedar, the umbrageous banana, are His. His are the tribes and families of birds and beasts, their graceful forms, their wild gestures, and their passionate cries.

And so in the intellectual, moral, social, and political world. Man, with his motives and works, his languages, his propagation, his diffusion, is from Him. Agriculture, medicine, and the arts of life are His gifts. Society, laws, government, He is their sanction. The pageant of earthly royalty has the semblance and the benediction of the Eternal King. Peace and civilization, commerce and adventure, wars when just, conquest when humane and necessary, have His co-operation, and His blessing upon them. The course of events, the revolution of empires, the rise and fall of states, the periods and eras, the progresses and the retrogressions of the world's history, not indeed

the incidental sin, over-abundant as it is, but the great outlines and the results of human affairs, are from His disposition.   The elements and types and seminal principles
and constructive powers of the moral world, in ruins though
it be, are to be referred to Him.   He 'enlighteneth every
man that cometh into this world.'   His are the dictates of
the moral sense, and the retributive reproaches of conscience.   To Him must be ascribed the rich endowments of
the intellect, the radiation of genius, the imagination of the
poet, the sagacity of the politician, the wisdom (as Scripture
calls it) which now rears and decorates the temple, now
manifests itself in proverb or in parable.   The old saws of
nations, the majestic precepts of philosophy, the luminous
maxims of law, the oracles of individual wisdom, the
traditionary rules of truth, justice, and religion, even though
embedded in the corruption or alloyed with the pride, of
the world, betoken His original agency, and His long-suffering presence.   Even where there is habitual rebellion
against Him, or profound far-spreading social depravity,
still the undercurrent, or the heroic outburst, of natural
virtue, as well as the yearnings of the heart after what it has
not, and its presentiment of its true remedies, are to be
ascribed to the Author of all good.   Anticipations or
reminiscences of His glory haunt the mind of the self-
sufficient sage, and of the pagan devotee; His writing is
upon the wall, whether of the Indian fane or of the porticoes
of Greece.   He introduces Himself, He all but concurs,
according to His good pleasure, and in His selected season,
in the issues of unbelief, superstition, and false worship, and
changes the character of acts by His overruling operation.
He condescends, though He gives no sanction, to the
altars and shrines of imposture, and He makes His own
fiat the substitute for its sorceries.   He speaks amid the
incantations of Balaam, raises Samuel's spirit in the witch's
cavern, prophesies of the Messiah by the tongue of the

Sibyl, forces Python to recognize His ministers, and baptizes by the hand of the misbeliever. He is with the heathen dramatist in his denunciations of injustice and tyranny, and his auguries of divine vengeance upon crime. Even on the unseemly legends of a popular mythology He casts His shadow, and is dimly discerned in the ode or the epic, as in troubled water or in fantastic dreams. All that is good, all that is true, all that is beautiful, all that is beneficent, be it great or small, be it perfect or fragmentary, natural as well as supernatural, moral as well as material, comes from Him.

If this be a sketch, accurate in substance and as far as it goes, of the doctrines proper to theology, and especially of the doctrine of a particular Providence, which is the portion of it most on a level with human sciences, I cannot understand at all how, supposing it to be true, it can fail, considered as knowledge, to exert a powerful influence on philosophy, literature, and every intellectual creation or discovery whatever. I cannot understand how it is possible, as the phrase goes, to blink the question of its truth or falsehood. It meets us with a profession and a proffer of the highest truths of which the human mind is capable; it embraces a range of subjects the most diversified and distant from each other. What science will not find one part or other of its province traversed by its path? What results of philosophic speculation are unquestionable, if they have been gained without inquiry as to what theology had to say to them? Does it cast no light upon history? Has it no influence upon the principles of ethics? Is it without any sort of bearing on physics, metaphysics, and political science? Can we drop it out of the circle of knowledge without allowing, either that that circle is thereby mutilated, or on the other hand that theology is no science?

And this dilemma is the more inevitable, because theology is so precise and consistent in its intellectual structure.

When I speak of theism or monotheism, I am not throwing together discordant doctrines; I am not merging belief, opinion, persuasion, of whatever kind, into a shapeless aggregate, by the help of ambiguous words, and dignifying this medley by the name of theology. I speak of one idea unfolded in its just proportions, carried out upon an intelligible method, and issuing in necessary and immutable results; understood indeed at one time and place better than at another, held here and there with more or less of inconsistency, but still, after all, in all times and places, where it is found, the evolution, not of two ideas, but of one.

And here I am led, gentlemen, to another and most important point in the argument for the doctrine—I mean its wide reception. Theology, as I have described it, is no accident of particular minds, as are certain systems, for instance, of prophetical interpretation. It is not the sudden birth of a crisis, as the Lutheran or Wesleyan doctrine. It is not the splendid development of some uprising philosophy, as the Cartesian or Platonic. It is not the fashion of a season, as certain medical treatments may be considered. It has had a place, if not possession, in the intellectual world from time immemorial; it has been received by minds the most various, and in systems of religion the most hostile to each other. It has *prima facie* claims upon us so strong that it can only be rejected on the ground of those claims being nothing more than imposing, that is, false. As to our own countries, it occupies our language, it meets us at every turn in our literature, it is the secret assumption, too axiomatic to be distinctly professed, of all our writers; nor can we help assuming it ourselves, without the most unnatural vigilance. Whoever philosophizes starts with it, and introduces it when he will, without any apology. Bacon, Hooker, Taylor, Cudworth, Locke, Newton, Clarke, Berkeley, Butler, and it would be as easy to find more, as difficult to find greater names among

English authors, inculcate or comment upon it. Men the most opposed, in creed or cast of mind, Addison and Johnson, Shakespeare and Milton, Lord Herbert and Baxter, herald it forth. Nor is it an English or a Protestant notion only; you track it across the Continent, you pursue it into former ages. When was the world without it? Have the systems of atheism or pantheism, as sciences, prevailed in the literature of nations, or received a formation or attained a completeness such as monotheism? We find it in old Greece, and even in Rome, as well as in Judea and the East. We find it in popular literature, in philosophy, in poetry, as a positive and settled teaching, differing not at all in the appearance it presents, whether in Protestant England, or in schismatical Russia, or in the Mohammedan populations, or in the Catholic Church. If ever there was a subject of thought which had earned by prescription to be received among the studies of a university, and which could not be rejected except on the score of convicted imposture, as astrology or alchemy; if there be a science anywhere which at least could claim not to be ignored, but to be entertained, and either distinctly accepted or distinctly reprobated, or rather which cannot be passed over in a scheme of universal instruction, without involving a positive denial of its truth, it is this ancient, this far-spreading philosophy.

And now, gentlemen, I may bring a somewhat tedious discussion to a close. It will not take many words to sum up what I have been urging. I say then, if the various branches of knowledge which are the matter of teaching in a university so hang together that none can be neglected without prejudice to the perfection of the rest, and if theology be a branch of knowledge, of wide reception, of philosophical structure, of unutterable importance, and of supreme influence, to what conclusion are we brought from these two premisses but this? that to withdraw theology from the public schools is to impair the completeness and to invalidate the trustworthiness of all that is actually taught in them.

But I have been insisting simply on natural theology, and that because I wished to carry along with me those who were not Catholics, and, again, as being confident that no one can really set himself to master and to teach the doctrine of an intelligent Creator in its fullness, without going on a great deal further than he at present dreams. I ask, then, secondly: If this science, even as human reason may attain to it, has such claims on the regard, and enters so variously into the objects, of the Professor of Universal Knowledge, how can any Catholic imagine that it is possible for him to cultivate philosophy and science with due attention to their ultimate end, which is truth, supposing that system of revealed facts and principles which constitutes the Catholic faith, which goes so far beyond nature, and which he knows to be most true, be omitted from among the subjects of his teaching?

In a word, religious truth is not only a portion, but a condition of general knowledge. To blot it out is nothing short, if I may so speak, of unravelling the web of university education. It is, according to the Greek proverb, to take the spring from out of the year; it is to imitate the preposterous proceeding of those tragedians who represented a drama with the omission of its principal part.

DISCOURSE III

BEARING OF OTHER BRANCHES OF KNOWLEDGE ON THEOLOGY

NOTHING is more common in the world at large than to consider the resistance made on the part of religious men, especially Catholics, to the separation of secular education from religion as a plain token that there is some real contrariety between human science and revelation. It matters not to the multitude who draw this inference whether the protesting parties avow their belief in this contrariety or not; it is borne in upon the many, so to say, as self-evident that religious men would not thus be jealous and alarmed about science, did they not feel instinctively, though they may not recognize it, that knowledge is their born enemy, and that its progress will be certain to destroy, if it is not arrested, all that they hold venerable and dear. It looks to the world like a misgiving on our part similar to that which is imputed to our refusal to educate by means of the Bible only; why should you dread it, men say, if it be not against you? And in like manner, why should you dread secular education, except that it is against you? Why impede the circulation of books which take religious views opposite to your own? Why forbid your children and scholars the free perusal of poems, or tales, or essays, or other light literature which you fear would unsettle their minds? Why oblige them to know these persons and to shun those, if you think that your friends have reason on their side as fully as your opponents? Truth is bold and unsuspicious; want of self-reliance is the mark of falsehood.

Now, as far as this objection relates to any supposed

opposition between secular science and divine, which is the subject on which I am at present engaged, I made a sufficient answer to it in my foregoing discourse. In it I said that, in order to have possession of truth at all, we must have the whole truth; that no one science, no two sciences, no one family of sciences, nay, not even all secular science, is the whole truth; that revealed truth enters to a very great extent into the province of science, philosophy, and literature, and that to put it on one side, in compliment to secular science, is simply, under colour of a compliment, to do science a great damage. I do not say that every science will be equally affected by the omission; pure mathematics will not suffer at all; chemistry will suffer less than politics, politics than history, ethics, or metaphysics; still, that the various branches of science are intimately connected with each other, and form one whole, which whole is impaired, and to an extent which it is difficult to limit, by any considerable omission of knowledge, of whatever kind, and that revealed knowledge is very far indeed from an inconsiderable department of knowledge, this I consider undeniable. As the written and unwritten word of God make up revelation as a whole, and the written, taken by itself, is but a part of that whole, so in turn revelation itself may be viewed as one of the constituent parts of human knowledge, considered as a whole, and its omission is the omission of one of those constituent parts. Revealed religion furnishes facts to the other sciences, which those sciences, left to themselves, would never reach; and it invalidates apparent facts which, left to themselves, they would imagine. Thus, in the science of history, the preservation of our race in Noah's ark is an historical fact, which history never would arrive at without revelation; and, in the sciences of physiology and moral philosophy, our race's progress and perfectibility is a dream, because revelation contradicts it, whatever may be plausibly argued in its behalf by scientific inquirers. It is not then that Catholics are afraid of human knowledge, but that they are proud of divine knowledge, and that they think the omission of any kind of knowledge whatever, human or divine, to be, as far as it goes, not knowledge, but ignorance.

Thus I anticipated the objection in question last week: now I am going to make it the introduction to a further view of the relation of secular knowledge to divine. I observe, then, that, if you drop any science out of the circle of knowledge, you cannot keep its place vacant for it; that science is forgotten; the other sciences close up, or, in other words, they exceed their proper bounds, and intrude where they have no right. For instance, I suppose if ethics were sent into banishment, its territory would soon disappear, under a treaty of partition, as it may be called, between law, political economy, and physiology; what, again, would become of the province of experimental science, if made over to the Antiquarian Society; or of history, if surrendered out and out to metaphysicians? The case is the same with the subject-matter of theology; it would be the prey of a dozen various sciences, if theology were put out of possession; and not only so, but those sciences would be plainly exceeding their rights and their capacities in seizing upon it. They would be sure to teach wrongly, where they had no mission to teach at all. The enemies of Catholicism ought to be the last to deny this; for they have never been blind to a like usurpation, as they have called it, on the part of theologians; those who accuse us of wishing, in accordance with Scripture language, to make the sun go round the earth are not the men to deny that a science which exceeds its limits falls into error.

I neither then am able nor care to deny, rather I assert the fact, and to-day I am going on to account for it, that any secular science, cultivated exclusively, may become dangerous to religion; and I account for it on this broad principle, that no science whatever, however comprehensive it may be, but will fall largely into error, if it be constituted the sole exponent of all things in heaven and earth, and that for the simple reason that it is encroaching on territory not its own, and undertaking problems which it has no instruments to solve. And I set off thus:

One of the first acts of the human mind is to take hold of and appropriate what meets the senses, and herein lies a chief distinction between man's and a brute's use of them. Brutes gaze on sights, they are arrested by sounds; and what they see and what they hear are sights and sounds only. The intellect of man, on the contrary, energizes as well as his eye or ear, and perceives in sights and sounds something beyond them. It seizes and unites what the senses present to it; it grasps and forms what need not be seen or heard except in detail. It discerns in lines and colours, or in tones, what is beautiful and what is not. It gives them a meaning, and invests them with an idea. It gathers up a succession of notes, as it were, into a point of time, and calls it a melody; it has a keen sensibility toward angles and curves, lights and shadows, tints and contours. It distinguishes between rule and exception, between accident and design. It assigns phenomena to a general law, qualities to a subject, acts to a principle, and effects to a cause. In a word, it philosophizes; for I suppose science and philosophy, in their elementary idea, are nothing else but this habit of *viewing*, as it may be called, the objects which sense conveys to the mind, of throwing them into system, and uniting and stamping them with one form.

This method is so natural to us, as I have said, as to be almost spontaneous; and we are impatient when we cannot exercise it, and in consequence we do not always wait to have the means of exercising it aright, but we often put up with insufficient or absurd views or interpretations of what we meet with, rather than have none at all. We refer the various matters which are brought home to us, material or moral, to causes which we happen to know of, or to such as are simply imaginary, sooner than refer them to nothing; and according to the activity of our intellect do we feel a pain and begin to fret, if we are not able to do so. Here we have an explanation of the multitude of offhand sayings, flippant judgments, and shallow generalizations with which the world abounds. Not from self-will only, nor from malevolence, but from the irritation which suspense occasions is the mind forced on to pronounce, without sufficient data for pronouncing. Who does not form some view or other, for instance, of any public man, or any public event, nay, even so far in some cases as to reach the mental delineation of his appearance or of its scene? Yet how few have a right to form any view. Hence the misconceptions of character, hence the false impressions and reports of words or deeds which are the rule, rather than the exception, in the world at large; hence the extravagances of undisciplined talent, and the narrowness of conceited ignorance; because, though it is no easy matter to view things correctly, yet the busy mind will ever be viewing. We cannot do without a view, and we put up with an illusion when we cannot get a true one.

Now, observe how this impatience acts in matters of research and speculation. What happens to the ignorant and hot-headed will take place in the case of every person whose education or pursuits are contracted, whether they be merely professional, merely scientific, or of whatever other peculiar complexion. Men whose life lies in the cultivation of one science, or the exercise of one method of thought, have no more right, though they have often more ambition, to generalize upon the basis of their own pursuit yet beyond its range, than the schoolboy or the ploughman to judge of a Prime Minister. But they must have something to say on every subject: habit, fashion, the public require it of them; and if so, they can only give sentence according to their knowledge. You might think this ought to make such a person modest in his enunciations; not so: too often it happens that, in proportion as his knowledge is narrow is, not his distrust of it, but the deep hold it has upon him, his absolute conviction of his own conclusions, and his positiveness in maintaining them. He has the obstinacy of the bigot, whom he scorns, without the bigot's apology, that he has been taught, as he thinks, his doctrine from heaven. Thus he becomes what is commonly called a man of one idea; which properly means a man of one science, and of the view, partly true, but subordinate, partly false, which is all that can proceed out of anything so partial. Hence it is that we have the principles of utility, of combination, of progress, of philanthropy or, in material sciences, comparative anatomy, phrenology, electricity, exalted into leading ideas, and keys, if not of all knowledge, at least of many things more than belong to them—principles, all of them true to a certain point, yet all degenerating into error and quackery, because they are carried to excess, at a point where they require interpretation and restraint from other quarters, and because they are employed to do what is simply too much for them, inasmuch as a little science is not deep philosophy.

Lord Bacon has set down the abuse of which I am speaking among the impediments to the advancement of the sciences, when he observes that 'men have used to infect their meditations, opinions, and doctrines with some conceits which they have most admired, or *some sciences which they have most applied*, and give all things else a *tincture* according to them *utterly untrue and improper*. . . . So have the alchemists made a philosophy out of a few experiments of the furnace; and Gilbertus, our countryman, hath made a philosophy out of the observations of a lodestone. So Cicero, when, reciting the several opinions of the nature of the soul, he found a musician that held the soul was but a harmony, saith pleasantly: "Hic ab arte suâ non recessit." (He was true to his art.) But of these conceits Aristotle speaketh seriously and wisely when he saith: "Qui respiciunt ad pauca, de facili pronunciant." (They who contemplate a few things have no difficulty in deciding.)'

And now I have said enough to explain the inconvenience which I conceive necessarily to result from a refusal to recognize theological truth in a course of universal knowledge; it is not only the loss of theology, it is the perversion of other sciences. What it unjustly forfeits, others unjustly seize. They have their own department, and, in going out of it, attempt to do what they really cannot do; and that the more mischievously, because they do teach what in its place is true, though when out of its place, perverted or carried to excess, it is not true. And, as every man has not the capacity of separating truth from falsehood, they persuade the world of what is false by urging upon them what is true. Nor is it open enemies alone who encounter us here, sometimes it is friends, sometimes persons who, if not friends, at least have no wish to oppose religion, and are not conscious they are doing so; and it will carry out my meaning more fully if I give some illustrations of it.

As to friends, I may take as an instance the cultivation of the fine arts, painting, sculpture, architecture, to which I may add music. These high ministers of the beautiful and the noble are, it is plain, special attendants and handmaids of religion; but it is equally plain that they are apt to forget their place, and, unless restrained with a firm hand, instead of being servants will aim at becoming principals. Here lies the advantage, in an ecclesiastical point of view, of their more rudimental state, I mean of the ancient style of architecture, of Gothic sculpture and painting, and of what is called Gregorian music, that these inchoate sciences have so little innate vigour and life in them that they are in no danger of going out of their place, and giving the law to religion. But the case is very different when genius has breathed upon their natural elements, and has developed them into what I may call intellectual powers. When painting, for example, grows into the fullness of its function as a simply imitative art, it at once ceases to be a dependant on the Church. It has an end of its own, and that of earth: nature is its pattern, and the object it pursues is the beauty of nature, even till it becomes an ideal beauty, but a natural beauty still. It cannot imitate that beauty of angels and saints which it has never seen. At first, indeed, by out- lines and emblems it shadowed out the Invisible, and its want of skill became the instrument of reverence and modesty; but as time went on and it attained its full dimen- sions as an art, it rather subjected religion to its own ends than ministered to the ends of religion, and, in its long galleries and stately chambers, adorable figures and sacred histories did but mingle amid the train of earthly, not to say unseemly, forms which it created, borrowing withal a colouring and a character from that bad company. Not content with neutral ground for its development, it was attracted by the sublimity of divine subjects to ambitious and hazardous essays. Without my saying a word more, you will clearly understand, gentlemen, that under these circumstances religion was bound to exert itself, that the world might not gain an advantage over it. Put out of sight the severe teaching of Catholicism in the schools of painting, as men now would put it aside in their philo- sophical studies, and in no long time you would have had the hierarchy of the Church, the Anchorite and Virgin- martyr, the Confessor and the Doctor, the Angelic Hosts, the Mother of God, the Crucifix, the Eternal Trinity, supplanted by a sort of pagan mythology in the guise of sacred names, by a creation indeed of high genius, of intense, and dazzling, and soul-absorbing beauty, in which, however, there was nothing which subserved the cause of religion, nothing on the other hand which did not directly or indirectly minister to corrupt nature and the powers of darkness.

The art of painting, however, is peculiar: music and architecture are more ideal, and their respective archetypes, even if not supernatural, at least are abstract and unearthly; and yet what I have been observing about painting holds, I suppose, analogously, in the marvellous development which musical science has undergone in the last century. Doubtless here too the highest genius may be made subservient to religion; here too, still more simply than in the case of painting, the science has a field of its own, perfectly innocent, into which religion does not and need not enter; on the other hand here also, in the case of music as of painting, it is certain that religion must be alive and on the defensive, for, if its servants sleep, a potent enchantment will steal over it. Music, I suppose, though this is not the place to enlarge upon it, has an object of its own; as mathematical science also, it is the expression of ideas greater and more profound than any in the visible world, ideas which centre indeed in Him whom Catholicism manifests, who is the seat of all beauty, order, and perfection whatever, still ideas after all which are not those on which revelation directly and principally fixes our gaze. If then a great master in this mysterious science (if I may speak of matters which seem to lie out of my own province) throws himself on his own gift, trusts its inspirations, and absorbs himself in those thoughts which, though they come to him in the way of nature, belong to things above nature, it is obvious he will neglect everything else. Rising in his strength, he will break through the trammels of words, he will scatter human voices, even the sweetest, to the winds; he will be borne upon nothing less than the fullest flood of sounds which art has enabled him to draw from mechanical contrivances; he will go forth as a giant, as far as ever his instruments can reach, starting from their secret depths fresh and fresh elements of beauty and grandeur as he goes, and pouring them together into still more marvellous and rapturous combinations—and well indeed and lawfully, while he keeps to that line which is his own; but, should he happen to be attracted, as he well may, by the sublimity, so congenial to him, of the Catholic doctrine and ritual, should he engage in sacred themes, should he resolve to do honour to the mass, or the divine office—(he cannot have a more pious, a better purpose, and religion will gracefully accept what he gracefully offers; but)—is it not certain, from the circumstances of the case, that he will rather use religion than minister to it, unless religion is strong on its own ground, and reminds him that, if he would do honour to the highest of subjects, he must make himself its scholar, must humbly follow the thoughts given him, and must aim at the glory, not of his own gift, but of the Great Giver?

As to architecture, it is a remark, if I recollect aright, both of Fénélon and Berkeley, men so different that it carries more with it even than the names of those celebrated men, that the Gothic style is not as *simple* as ecclesiastical structures demand. I understand this to be a similar judgment to that which I have been passing on the cultivation of painting and music. For myself, certainly I think that that style which, whatever be its origin, is called Gothic, is endowed with a profound and a commanding beauty, such as no other style possesses with which we are acquainted, and which probably the Church will not see surpassed till it attain to the Celestial City. No other architecture now used for sacred purposes seems to have an idea in it, whereas the Gothic style is as harmonious and as intellectual as it is graceful. But this feeling should not blind us, rather it should awaken us, to the danger lest what is really a divine gift be incautiously used as an end rather than as a means. It is surely quite within the bounds of possibility that, as the Renaissance three centuries ago carried away its own day, in spite of the Church, into excesses in literature and art, so that revival of an almost forgotten architecture, which is at present taking place in our own countries, in France, and in Germany, may in some way or other run away with us into this or that error, unless we keep a watch over its course. I am not speaking of Ireland; but to English Catholics at least it would be a serious evil, if it came as the emblem and advocate of a past ceremonial or an extinct nationalism. We are not living in an age of wealth and loyalty, of pomp and stateliness, of time-honoured establishments, of pilgrimage and penance, of hermitages and convents in the wild, and of fervent populations supplying the want of education by love, and apprehending in form and symbol what they cannot read in books. Our rules and our rubrics have been altered now to meet the times, and hence an obsolete discipline may be a present heresy.

I have been pointing out to you, gentlemen, how the fine arts may prejudice religion, by laying down the law in cases where they should be subservient. The illustration is analogous rather than strictly proper to my subject, yet I think it is to the point. If then the most loyal and dutiful children of the Church must deny themselves, and do deny themselves, when they would sanctify to a heavenly purpose sciences as sublime and as divine as any which are cultivated by fallen man, it is not wonderful, when we turn to sciences of a different character, of which the object is tangible and material, and the principles belong to the reason, not the imagination, that we should find their disciples, if disinclined to the Catholic faith, acting the part of opponents to it, and that, as may often happen, even against their will and intention. Many men there are who, devoted to one particular subject of thought, and making its principles the measure of all things, become enemies to revealed religion before they know it, and only as time proceeds are aware of their state of mind. These, if they are writers or lecturers, while in this state of unconscious or semi-conscious unbelief, scatter infidel principles under the garb and colour of Christianity; and this simply because they have made their own science, whatever it is, political economy, or geology, or astronomy, not theology, the centre of all truth, and view every part or the chief parts of knowledge as if developed from it, and to be tested and determined by its principles. Others, though conscious to themselves of their antichristian opinions, have too much good feeling and good taste to wish to obtrude them upon the world. They neither wish to shock people nor to earn for themselves a confessorship which brings with it no gain. They know the strength of prejudice, and the penalty of innovation; they wish to go through life quietly; they scorn polemics; they shrink, as from a real humiliation, from being mixed up in religious controversy; they are ashamed of the very name. However, they have had occasion at some time to publish on some literary or scientific subject; they have wished to give no offence; but after all, to their great annoyance, they find when they least expect it, or when they have taken considerable pains to avoid it, that they have roused by their publication what they would style the bigoted and bitter hostility of a party. This misfortune is easily conceivable, and has befallen many a man. Before he knows where he is a cry is raised on all sides of him; and so little does he know what we may call the *lie* of the land that his attempts at apology perhaps only make matters worse. In other words, an exclusive line of study has led him, whether he will or no, to run counter to the principles of religion; which principles he has never made his landmarks, and which, whatever might be their effect upon himself, at least would have warned him against practising upon the faith of others, had they been authoritatively held up before him.

Instances of this kind are far from uncommon. Men who are old enough will remember the trouble which came upon a person, eminent as a professional man in London even at that distant day, and still more eminent since, in consequence of his publishing a book in which he so treated the subject of comparative anatomy as to seem to deny the immateriality of the soul. I speak here neither as excusing nor reprobating sentiments about which I have not the means of forming a judgment; all indeed I have heard of him makes me mention him with interest and respect; anyhow of this I am sure, that if there be a calling which feels its position and its dignity to lie in abstaining from controversy and cultivating kindly feelings with men of all opinions, it is the medical profession, and I cannot believe that the person in question would purposely have raised the indignation and incurred the censure of the religious public. What then must have been his fault or mistake, but that he unsuspiciously threw himself upon his own particular science, which is of a material character, and allowed it to carry him forward into a subject-matter where it had no right to give the law, viz. that of spiritual beings, which directly belongs to the science of theology?

Another instance occurred at a later date. A living dignitary of the Established Church wrote a History of the Jews in which, with what I consider at least bad judgment, he took an external view of it, and hence was led to assimilate it as nearly as possible to secular history. A great sensation was the consequence among the members of his own communion, from which he still suffers. Arguing from the dislike and contempt of polemical demonstrations which that accomplished writer has ever shown, I must conclude that he was simply betrayed into a false step by the treacherous fascination of what is called the philosophy of history, which is good in its place, but can scarcely be applied in cases where the Almighty has superseded the natural laws of society and history. From this he would have been saved had he been a Catholic; but in the Establishment he knew of no teaching to which he was bound to defer, which ruled that to be false which attracted him by its speciousness.

I will now take an instance from another science. Political economy is the science, I suppose, of wealth—a science simply lawful and useful, for it is no sin to make money, any more than it is a sin to seek honour; a science at the same time dangerous and leading to occasions of sin, as is the pursuit of honour too; and in consequence, if studied by itself, and apart from the control of revealed truth, sure to conduct a speculator to unchristian conclusions. Holy Scripture tells us distinctly that 'covetousness,' or more literally the love of money, 'is the root of all evils'; and that 'thye that would become rich fall into temptation'; and that 'hardly shall they that have riches enter into the kingdom of God'; and after drawing the picture of a wealthy and flourishing people, it adds: 'That have called the people happy that hath these things; but happy is that people whose God is the Lord'—while on the other hand it says with equal distinctness: 'If any will not work, neither let him eat'; and: 'If any man have not care of his own, and especially of those of his house, he hath denied the faith, and is worse than an infidel.' These opposite injunctions are summed up in the wise man's prayer, who says: 'Give me neither beggary nor riches, give me only the necessaries of life.' With this most precise view of a Christian's duty, viz. to labour indeed, but to labour for a competency for

himself and his, and to be jealous of wealth, whether personal
or national, the holy fathers are, as might be expected, in
simple accordance. 'Judas,' says St Chrysostom, 'was
with Him who knew not where to lay His head, yet could
not restrain himself; and how canst thou hope to escape
the contagion without anxious effort?' 'It is ridiculous,'
says St Jerome, 'to call it idolatry to offer to the creature
the grains of incense that are due to God, and not to call it
so, to offer the whole service of one's life to the creature.'
'There is not a trace of justice in that heart,' says St Leo,
'in which the love of gain has made itself a dwelling.' The
same thing is emphatically taught us by the counsels of
perfection, and by every holy monk and nun anywhere, who
has ever embraced them; but it is needless to collect when
Scripture is so clear.

Now observe, gentlemen, my drift in setting Scripture
and the fathers over against political economy. Of
course if there is a science of wealth, it must give rules for
gaining wealth and disposing of wealth, and can do nothing
more; it cannot itself declare that it is a subordinate science,
that its end is not the ultimate end of all things, and that its
conclusions are only hypothetical, depending on its premises
and liable to be overruled by a higher teaching. I do not
then blame the political economist for anything which
follows from the very idea of his science, from the very
moment that it is recognized as a science. He must of
course direct his inquiries towards his end; but then at the
same time it must be recollected that so far he is not
practical, but only pursues an abstract study, and is busy
himself in establishing logical conclusions from indisputable
premises. Given that wealth is to be sought, this and that
is the method of gaining it. This is the extent to which a
political economist has a right to go; he has no right to
determine that wealth is at any rate to be sought, or that
it is the way to be virtuous and the price of happiness; I

say this is to pass the bounds of his science, independent of the question whether he be right or wrong in so determining, for he is only concerned with an hypothesis.

To take a parallel case. A physician may tell you that if you are to preserve your health you must give up your employment and retire to the country. He distinctly says 'if'; that is all in which he is concerned, he is no judge whether there are objects dearer to you, more urgent upon you, than the preservation of your health; he does not enter into your circumstances, your duties, your liabilities, the persons dependent on you; he knows nothing about what is advisable or what is not; he only says: 'I speak *as* a physician; if you would be well, give up your profession, your trade, your office, whatever it is.' However he may wish it, it would be impertinent to him to say more, unless indeed he spoke not as a physician but as a friend; and it would be extravagant if he asserted that bodily health was the *summum bonum*, and that no one could be virtuous whose animal system was not in good order.

But now let us turn to the teaching of the political economist, a fashionable philosopher just now. I will take a very favourable instance of him; he shall be represented by a gentleman of high character whose religious views are sufficiently guaranteed to us by his being the special choice, in this department of science, of a university removed more than any other Protestant body of the day from sordid or unchristian principles on the subject of money-making. I say, if there be a place where political economy would be kept in order, and would not be suffered to leave the high road and ride across the pastures and the gardens dedicated to other studies, it is the university of Oxford. And if a man could anywhere be found who would have too much good taste to offend the religious feeling of the place, or to say anything which he would himself allow to be inconsistent with revelation, I conceive it is the person whose temperate and well-considered composition, as it would be generally accounted, I am going to offer to your notice. Nor did it occasion any excitement whatever on the part of the academical or the religious public, as did the instances which I have hitherto been adducing. I am representing then the science of political economy, in its independent or unbridled action, to great advantage when I select, as its specimen, the inaugural lecture upon it, delivered in the university in question, by its first professor. Yet with all these circumstances in its favour, you will soon see, gentlemen, into what extravagance, for so I must call it, a grave lawyer is led in praise of his chosen science, merely from the circumstance that he has fixed his mind upon it, till he has forgotten there are subjects of thought higher and more heavenly than it. You will find beyond mistake that it is his object to recommend the science of wealth by claiming for it an *ethical* quality, viz. by extolling it as the road to virtue and happiness, whatever Scripture and holy men may say to the contrary.

He begins by predicting of political economy that in the course of a very few years, 'it will rank in public estimation among the first of *moral* sciences in interest and in utility.' Then he explains most lucidly its objects and duties, considered as 'the science which teaches in what wealth consists, by what agents it is produced, and according to what laws it is distributed, and what are the institutions and customs by which production may be facilitated and distribution regulated, so as to give the largest possible amount of wealth to each individual.' And he dwells upon the interest which attaches to the inquiry 'whether England has run her full career of wealth and improvement, but stands safe where she is, or whether to remain stationary is impossible.' After this he notices a certain objection, which I shall set before you in his own words, as they will furnish me with the illustration I propose.

This objection, he says, is that 'as the pursuit of wealth is one of the humblest of human occupations, far inferior to the pursuit of virtue, or of knowledge, or even of reputation, and as the possession of wealth is not necessarily joined—perhaps it will be said, is not conducive—to happiness, a science of which the only subject is wealth cannot claim to rank as the first, or nearly the first, of moral sciences.' [1] Certainly, to an enthusiast in behalf of any science whatever, the temptation is great to meet an objection urged against its dignity and worth; however, from the very form of it, such an objection cannot receive a satisfactory answer by means of the science itself. It is an objection external to the science, and reminds us of the truth of Lord Bacon's remark: 'No perfect discovery can be made upon a flat or a level; neither is it possible to discover the more remote and deeper parts of any science, if you stand upon the level of the science, and ascend not to a higher science.' [2] The objection that political economy is inferior to the science of virtue, or does not conduce to happiness, is an ethical or theological objection; the question of its 'rank' belongs to that architectonic science or philosophy, whatever it be, which is itself the arbiter of all truth, and which disposes of the claims and arranges the places of all the departments of knowledge which man is able to master. I say, when an opponent of a particular science asserts that it does not conduce to happiness, and much more when its champion contends in reply that it certainly does conduce to virtue, as this author proceeds to contend, the obvious question which occurs to one to ask is, what does religion, what does revelation, say on the point? Political economy must not be allowed to give judgment in its own favour, but must come before a higher tribunal. The objection is an appeal to the theologian;

[1] Introductory Lecture on Political Economy, pp. 11, 12.
[2] *Advancement of Learning*.

however, the professor does not so view the matter; he does not consider it a question for philosophy; nor indeed on the other hand a question for political economy; not a question for science at all, but for private judgment—so he answers it himself, and as follows:

'My answer,' he says, 'is, first, that the pursuit of wealth, that is, the endeavour to accumulate the means of future subsistence and enjoyment, is, to the mass of mankind, the great source of *moral* improvement.' Now observe, gentlemen, how exactly this bears out what I have been saying. It is just so far true as to be able to instil what is false, far as the author was from any such design. I grant then that beggary is not the means of moral improvement; and that the orderly habits which attend upon the hot pursuit of gain, not only may effect an external decency, but may at least shelter the soul from the temptations of vice. Moreover, these habits of good order guarantee regularity in a family or household, and thus are accidentally the means of good; moreover, they lead to the education of its younger branches, and they thus accidentally provide the rising generation with a virtue or a truth which the present has not: but without going into these considerations, further than to allow them generally, and under circumstances, let us rather contemplate what the author's direct assertion is. He says 'the endeavour to *accumulate*,' the words should be weighed, and for what? 'for *enjoyment*' —'to accumulate the means of future subsistence and enjoyment is, to the mass of mankind, *the great* source,' not merely *a* source, but *the great* source, and of what? of social and political progress?—such an answer would have been more within the limits of his art—no, but of something individual and personal, 'of *moral improvement*.' The soul, to speak of the 'mass of mankind,' improves in moral excellence from this more than anything else, viz. from heaping up the means of enjoying this world in time to come! I really should on every account be sorry, gentle-men, to exaggerate, but indeed one is taken by surprise on meeting with so very categorical a contradiction of our Lord, St Paul, St Chrysostom, St Leo, and all saints.

'No institution,' he continues, 'could be more beneficial to the morals of the lower orders, that is, to at least nine-tenths of the whole body of any people, than one which should increase their power and their wish to accumulate; none more mischievous than one which should diminish their motives and means to save.' No institution more beneficial than one which should increase the *wish* to *accumulate*! Then Christianity is not one of such bene-ficial institutions, for it expressly says: '*Lay not up to* yourselves *treasures* on earth . . . for where thy treasure is, there is thy heart also'—no institution more mischievous than one which should diminish the *motives to save*! Then Christianity is one of such mischiefs, for the inspired text proceeds: 'Lay up to yourselves treasures *in heaven, where* neither the rust nor the moth doth consume, and where thieves do not dig through nor steal.'

But it is not enough that morals and happiness are made to depend on gain and accumulation: the practice of religion is ascribed to these causes also, and in the follow-ing way. Wealth depends upon the pursuit of wealth; education depends upon wealth; knowledge depends on education, and religion depends on knowledge; therefore religion depends on the pursuit of wealth. He says, after speaking of a poor and savage people: 'Such a population must be grossly ignorant. The desire of knowledge is one of the last results of refinement; it requires in general to have been implanted in the mind during childhood; and it is absurd to suppose that persons thus situated would have the power or the will to devote much to the education of their children. A further consequence is the *absence of all real religion*; for the religion of the grossly ignorant, if they

have any, scarcely ever amounts to more than a debasing
superstition.'[1]   The pursuit of gain, then, is the basis of
virtue, religion, happiness; though it is all the while, as a
Christian knows, the 'root of all evils,' and the 'poor on the
contrary are blessed, for theirs is the kingdom of God.'

As to the argument contained in the logical sorites which
I have been drawing out, I anticipated just now what I
should say to it in reply. I repeat, doubtless 'beggary,'
as the wise man says, is not desirable; doubtless, if men will
not work, they should not eat; there is doubtless a sense in
which it may be said that mere social or political virtue tends
to moral and religious excellence; but the sense needs to be
defined and the statement to be kept within bounds.   This
is the very point on which I am all along insisting.   I am
not denying, I am granting, I am assuming, that there is
reason and truth in the 'leading ideas,' as they are called,
and 'large views' of scientific men; I only say that, though
they speak truth, they do not speak the whole truth; that
they speak a narrow truth, and think it a broad truth;
that their deductions must be compared with other truths,
which are acknowledged as such in order to verify, complete, and correct them.   They say what is true, *exceptis
excipiendis*; what is true, but requires guarding; true, but
must not be ridden too hard, or made what is called a
hobby; true, but not the measure of all things; true, but if
thus inordinately, extravagantly, ruinously carried out, in
spite of other sciences, in spite of theology, sure to become
but a great bubble, and to burst.

I am getting to the end of this discourse, before I have
noticed one-tenth part of the instances with which I might
illustrate the subject of it.   Else I should have wished
especially to have dwelt upon the not unfrequent perversion which occurs of antiquarian and historical research, to
the prejudice of theology.   It is undeniable that the records

[1] Ibid, p. 16.

of former ages are of primary importance in determining religious truth; it is undeniable also that there is a silence or a contrariety abstractedly conceivable in those records, as to an alleged portion of that truth, sufficient to invalidate its claims; but it is quite as undeniable that the existing documentary evidences of Catholicism and Christianity may be so unduly exalted as to be made the absolute measure of revelation, as if no part of theological teaching were true which cannot bring its express text, as it is called, from Scripture, and authorities from the fathers or profane writers—whereas there are numberless facts in past times which we cannot deny, for they are indisputable, though history is silent about them. I suppose, on this score, we ought to deny that the round towers of this country had any origin, because history does not disclose it; or that any individual came from Adam who cannot produce the table of his ancestry. Yet Gibbon argues against the darkness at the Passion, from the accident that it is not mentioned by pagan historians: as well might he argue against the existence of Christianity itself in the first century, because Seneca, Pliny, Plutarch, the Jewish Mishna, and other authorities are silent about it. In a parallel way Protestants argue against transubstantiation, and Arians against our Lord's divinity, viz. because extant writings of certain fathers do not witness those doctrines to their satisfaction: as well might they say that Christianity was not spread by the Twelve Apostles, because we know so little of their labours. The evidence of history, I say, is invaluable in its place; but, if it assumes to be the sole means of gaining religious truth, it goes beyond its place. We are putting it to a larger office than it can undertake if we countenance the usurpation; and we are turning a true guide and blessing into a source of inexplicable difficulty and interminable doubt.

And so of other sciences: just as comparative anatomy,

political economy, the philosophy of history, and the science of antiquities may be and are turned against religion, by being taken by themselves, as I have been showing, so a like mistake may befall any other. Grammar, for instance, at first sight does not appear to admit of a perversion; yet Horne Tooke made it the vehicle of his peculiar scepticism. Law would seem to have enough to do with its own clients, and their affairs; and yet Mr Bentham made a treatise on judicial proofs a covert attack upon the miracles of revelation. And in like manner physiology may deny moral evil and human responsibility; geology may deny Moses; and logic may deny the Holy Trinity; [1] and other sciences, now rising into notice, are or will be victims of a similar abuse.

And now to sum up what I have been saying in a few words. My object, it is plain, has been—not to show that secular science in its various departments may take up a position hostile to theology—this is rather the basis of the objection with which I opened this discourse—but to point out the cause of an hostility to which all parties will bear witness. I have been insisting then on this, that the hostility in question, when it occurs, is coincident with an evident deflection or exorbitance of science from its proper course; and that this exorbitance is sure to take place almost from the necessity of the case, if theology be not present to defend its own boundaries and to hinder the encroachment. The human mind cannot keep from speculating and systematizing; and if theology is not allowed to occupy its own territory, adjacent sciences, nay, sciences which are quite foreign to theology, will take possession of it. And it is proved to be a usurpation by this circumstance, that those sciences will assume certain principles as true, and act upon them, which they neither have authority to lay down themselves, nor appeal to any

[1] *Vide* Abelard, for instance.

other higher science to lay down for them. For example, it is a mere unwarranted assumption to say with the antiquarian: 'Nothing has ever taken place but is to be found in historical documents'; or with the philosophic historian: 'There is nothing in Judaism different from other political institutions'; or with the anatomist: 'There is no soul beyond the brain'; or with the political economist: 'Easy circumstances make men virtuous.' These are enunciations, not of science, but of private judgment; and it is private judgment that infects every science which it touches with a hostility to theology, a hostility which properly attaches to no science in itself whatever.

If then, gentlemen, I now resist such a course of acting as unphilosophical, what is this but to do as men of science do when the interests of their own respective pursuits are at stake? If they certainly would resist the divine who determined the orbit of Jupiter by the pentateuch, why am I to be accused of cowardice or illiberality, because I will not tolerate their attempt in turn to theologize by means of science? And if experimentalists would be sure to cry out, did I attempt to install the Thomist philosophy in the schools of astronomy and medicine, why may not I, when divine science is ostracized, and La Place, or Buffon, or Humboldt sits down in its chair, why may not I fairly protest against their exclusiveness, and demand the emancipation of theology?

And now I consider I have said enough in proof of the first point which I undertook to maintain, viz. the claim of theology to be represented among the chairs of a university. I have shown, I think, that exclusiveness really attaches, not to those who support that claim, but to those who dispute it. I have argued in its behalf, first, from the consideration that, whereas it is the very profession of a university to teach all sciences, on this account it cannot exclude theology without being untrue to its profession.

Next, I have said that, all sciences being connected together, and having bearings one on another, it is impossible to teach them all thoroughly, unless they all are taken into account, and theology among them. Moreover, I have insisted on the important influence which theology in matter of fact does and must exercise over a great variety of sciences, completing and correcting them; so that, granting it to be a real science occupied upon truth, it cannot be omitted without great prejudice to the teaching of the rest. And lastly, I have urged that, supposing theology be not taught, its province will not simply be neglected, but will be actually usurped by other sciences, which will teach, without warrant, conclusions of their own in a subject-matter which needs its own proper principles for its due formation and disposition.

Abstract statements are always unsatisfactory; these, as I have already observed, could be illustrated at far greater length than the time allotted to me for the purpose has allowed. Let me hope that I have said enough upon the subject to suggest thoughts which those who take an interest in it may pursue for themselves.

DISCOURSE IV

A UNIVERSITY may be considered with reference either to its students or to its studies; and the principle that all knowledge is a whole and the separate sciences parts of one, which I have hitherto been using in behalf of its studies, is equally important when we direct our attention to its students. Now then I turn to the students, and shall consider the education which, by virtue of this principle, a university will give them; and thus I shall be introduced, gentlemen, to the second question which I proposed to discuss, viz. whether and in what sense its teaching, viewed relatively to the taught, carries the attribute of utility along with it.

I have said that all branches of knowledge are connected together, because the subject-matter of knowledge is intimately united in itself, as being the great Creator and His work. Hence it is that the sciences into which our knowledge may be said to be cast have multiplied bearings one on another, and an internal sympathy, and admit, or rather demand, comparison and adjustment. They complete, correct, balance each other. This consideration, if well founded, must be taken into account, not only as regards the attainment of truth, which is their common end, but as regards the influence which they exercise upon those whose education consists in the study of them. I have said already that to give undue prominence to one is to be unjust to another; to neglect or supersede these is to divert those from their proper object. It is to unsettle the boundary lines between science and science, to disturb their action, to destroy the harmony which binds them together. Such a proceeding will have a corresponding effect when introduced into a place of education. There is no science but tells a different tale, when viewed as a portion of a whole, from what it is likely to suggest when taken by itself, without the safeguard, as I may call it, of others.

Let me make use of an illustration. In the combination of colours, very different effects are produced by a difference in their selection and juxtaposition; red, green, and white change their shades, according to the contrast to which they are submitted. And, in like manner, the drift and meaning of a branch of knowledge varies with the company in which it is introduced to the student. If this reading is confined simply to one subject, however such division of labour may favour the advancement of a particular pursuit, a point into which I do not here enter, certainly it has a tendency to contract his mind. If it is incorporated with others, it depends on those others as to the kind of influence which it exerts upon him. Thus the classics, which in England are the means of refining the taste, have in France subserved the spread of revolutionary and deistical doctrines. In metaphysics, again, Butler's *Analogy of Religion*, which has had so much to do with the conversion of members of the university of Oxford, appeared to Pitt and others, who had received a different training, to operate only in the direction of infidelity. And so again Watson, Bishop of Llandaff, as I think he tells us in the narrative of his life, felt the science of mathematics to indispose the mind to religious belief, while others see in its investigations the best defence of the Christian mysteries. In like manner, I suppose, Arcesilas would not have handled logic as Aristotle, nor Aristotle have criticized poets as Plato; yet reasoning and poetry are subject to scientific rules.

It is a great point then to enlarge the range of studies which a university professes, even for the sake of the students; and, though they cannot pursue every subject which is open to them, they will be the gainers by living among those and under those who represent the whole circle. This I conceive to be the advantage of a seat of universal learning, considered as a place of education. An assemblage of learned men, zealous for their own sciences, and rivals of each other, are brought, by familiar intercourse and for the sake of intellectual peace, to adjust together the claims and relations of their respective subjects of investigation. They learn to respect, to consult, to aid each other. Thus is created a pure and clear atmosphere of thought, which the student also breathes, though in his own case he only pursues a few sciences out of the multitude. He profits by an intellectual tradition which is independent of particular teachers, which guides him in his choice of subjects, and duly interprets for him those which he chooses. He apprehends the great outlines of knowledge, the principles on which it rests, the scale of its parts, its lights and its shades, its great points and its little, as he otherwise cannot apprehend them. Hence it is that his education is called liberal. A habit of mind is formed which lasts through life, of which the attributes are freedom, equitableness, calmness, moderation, and wisdom; or what in a former discourse I have ventured to call a philosophical habit. This then I would assign as the special fruit of the education furnished at a university, as contrasted with other places of teaching or modes of teaching. This is the main purpose of a university in its treatment of its students.

And now the question is asked me: What is the *use* of it? and my answer will constitute the main subject of the discourses which are to follow.

Cautious and practical thinkers, I say, will ask of me

what, after all, is the gain of this philosophy, of which I
make such account, and from which I promise so much.
Even supposing it to enable us to give the degree of confidence exactly due to every science respectively, and to
estimate precisely the value of every truth which is anywhere to be found, how are we better for this master view
of things which I have been extolling? Does it not reverse
the principle of the division of labour? Will practical
objects be obtained better or worse by its cultivation? To
what then does it lead? Where does it end? What does
it do? How does it profit? What does it promise?
Particular sciences are respectively the basis of definite arts,
which carry on to results tangible and beneficial the truths
which are the subjects of the knowledge attained. What
is the art of this science of sciences? What is the fruit of
such a philosophy? What are we proposing to effect,
what inducements do we hold out to the Catholic community, when we set about the enterprise of founding a
university?

I am asked what is the end of university education, and
of the liberal or philosophical knowledge which I conceive
it to impart: I answer, that what I have already said has
been sufficient to show that it has a very tangible, real, and
sufficient end, though the end cannot be divided from that
knowledge itself. Knowledge is capable of being its own
end. Such is the constitution of the human mind that any
kind of knowledge, if it be really such, is its own reward.
And if this is true of all knowledge, it is true also of that
special philosophy, which I have made to consist in a
comprehensive view of truth in all its branches, of the
relations of science to science, of their mutual bearings,
and their respective values. What the worth of such an
acquirement is, compared with other objects which we
seek—wealth or power or honour or the conveniences and
comforts of life—I do not profess here to discuss; but I

would maintain, and mean to show, that it is an object in its own nature so really and undeniably good, as to be the compensation of a great deal of thought in the compassing, and a great deal of trouble in the attaining.

Now, when I say that knowledge is, not merely a means to something beyond it, or the preliminary of certain arts into which it naturally resolves, but an end sufficient to rest in and to pursue for its own sake, surely I am uttering no paradox, for I am stating what is both intelligible in itself, and has ever been the common judgment of philosophers and the ordinary feeling of mankind. I am saying what at least the public opinion of this day ought to be slow to deny, considering how much we have heard of late years, in opposition to religion, of entertaining, curious, and various knowledge. I am but saying what whole volumes have been written to illustrate, by a 'selection from the records of philosophy, literature, and art, in all ages and countries, of a body of examples, to show how the most unpropitious circumstances have been unable to conquer an ardent desire for the acquisition of knowledge.' [1] That further advantages accrue to us and redound to others by its possession, over and above what it is in itself, I am very far indeed from denying; but, independent of these, we are satisfying a direct need of our nature in its very acquisition; and, whereas our nature, unlike that of the inferior creation, does not at once reach its perfection, but depends, in order to it, on a number of external aids and appliances, knowledge, as one of the principal gifts or accessories by which it is completed, is valuable for what its very presence in us does for us by a sort of *opus operatum*, even though it be turned to no further account, nor subserve any direct end.

Hence it is that Cicero, in enumerating the various heads of mental excellence, lays down the pursuit of knowledge

Pursuit of Knowledge under Difficulties. Introduction.

for its own sake as the first of them. 'This pertains most of all to human nature,' he says, 'for we are all of us drawn to the pursuit of knowledge; in which to excel we consider excellent, whereas to mistake, to err, to be ignorant, to be deceived, is both an evil and a disgrace.'[1] And he considers knowledge the very first object to which we are attracted, after the supply of our physical wants. After the calls and duties of our animal existence, as they may be termed, as regards ourselves, our family, and our neighbours, follows, he tells us, 'the search after truth. Accordingly, as soon as we escape from the pressure of necessary cares, forthwith we desire to see, to hear, to learn; and consider the knowledge of what is hidden or is wonderful a condition of our happiness.'

This passage, though it is but one of many similar passages in a multitude of authors, I take for the very reason that it is so familiarly known to us; and I wish you to observe, gentlemen, how distinctly it separates the pursuit of knowledge from those ulterior objects to which certainly it can be made to conduce, and which are, I suppose, solely contemplated by the persons who would ask of me the use of a university of liberal education. So far from dreaming of the cultivation of knowledge directly and mainly in order to our physical comfort and enjoyment, for the sake of life and person, of health, of the conjugal and family union, of the social tie and civil security, the great orator implies that it is only after our physical and political needs are supplied, and when we are 'free from necessary duties and cares,' that we are in a condition for 'desiring to see, to hear, and to learn.' Nor does he contemplate in the least degree the reflex or subsequent action of knowledge, when acquired, upon those material goods which we set out by securing before we seek it; on the contrary, he expressly denies its bearing upon social life

[1] Cicero, *Offic. init.*

altogether, strange as such a procedure is to those who
live after the rise of the Baconian philosophy, and he
cautions us against such a cultivation of it as will interfere
with our duties to our fellow creatures. 'All these methods,'
he says, 'are engaged in the investigation of truth; by the
pursuit of which to be carried off from public occupations
is a transgression of duty. For the praise of virtue lies
altogether in action; yet intermissions often occur, and
then we recur to such pursuits; not to say that the incessant
activity of the mind is vigorous enough to carry us on in the
pursuit of knowledge, even without any exertion of our
own.' The idea of benefiting society by means of 'the
pursuit of science and knowledge' did not enter at all into
the motives which he would assign for their cultivation.

This was the ground of the opposition which the elder
Cato made to the introduction of Greek philosophy among
his countrymen, when Carneades and his companions, on
occasion of their embassy, were charming the Roman
youth with their eloquent expositions of it. The fit representative of a practical people, Cato estimated everything
by what it produced; whereas the pursuit of knowledge
promised nothing beyond knowledge itself. He despised
that refinement or enlargement of mind of which he had no
experience.

Things which can bear to be cut off from everything else
and yet persist in living must have life in themselves;
pursuits which issue in nothing, and still maintain their
ground for ages, which are regarded as admirable, though
they have not as yet proved themselves to be useful, must
have their sufficient end in themselves, whatever it turn out
to be. And we are brought to the same conclusion by
considering the force of the epithet by which the knowledge
under consideration is popularly designated. It is common to
speak of '*liberal* knowledge,' of the '*liberal* arts and studies,'
and of a '*liberal* education,' as the especial characteristic

or property of a university and of a gentleman; what
is really meant by the word? Now, first, in its gram-
matical sense it is opposed to *servile*; and by 'servile work'
is understood, as our catechisms inform us, bodily labour,
mechanical employment, and the like, in which the mind
has little or no part. Parallel to such works are those arts,
if they deserve the name, of which the poet speaks,[1] which
owe their origin and their method to hazard, not to skill;
as for instance the practice and operations of an empiric.
As far as this contrast may be considered as a guide into the
meaning of the word, liberal knowledge and liberal pursuits
are such as belong to the mind, not to the body.

But we want something more for its explanation, for there
are bodily exercises which are liberal, and mental exercises
which are not so. For instance, in ancient times the
practitioners in medicine were commonly slaves; yet it was
an art as intellectual in its nature, in spite of the pretence,
fraud, and quackery with which it might then, as now, be
debased, as it was heavenly in its aim. And so in like
manner we contrast a liberal education with a commercial
education or a professional; yet no one can deny that commerce and the professions afford scope for the highest and
most diversified powers of mind. There is then a great
variety of intellectual exercises which are not technically
called liberal; on the other hand, I say, there are exercises
of the body which do receive that appellation. Such, for
instance, was the palaestra in ancient times; such the
Olympic Games, in which strength and dexterity of body as
well as of mind gained the prize. In Xenophon we read of
the young Persian nobility being taught to ride on horse-
back and to speak the truth; both being among the accomplishments of a gentleman. War, too, however rough a
profession, has ever been accounted liberal, unless in cases

---

[1] Τέχνη τύχην ἔστερξε καὶ τύχη τέχνην.
              Vide Aristotle, *Nic. Ethic.*, vi.

when it becomes heroic, which would introduce us to another subject.

Now comparing these instances together, we shall have no difficulty in determining the principle of this apparent variation in the application of the term which I am examining. Manly games, or games of skill, or military prowess, though bodily, are, it seems, accounted liberal; on the other hand, what is merely professional, though highly intellectual, nay, though liberal in comparison of trade and manual labour, is not simply called liberal, and mercantile occupations are not liberal at all. Why this distinction? Because that alone is liberal knowledge which stands on its own pretensions, which is independent of sequel, expects no complement, refuses to be *informed* (as it is called) by any end, or absorbed into any art, in order duly to present itself to our contemplation. The most ordinary pursuits have this specific character, if they are self-sufficient and complete; the highest lose it, when they minister to something beyond them. It is absurd to balance, in point of worth and importance, a treatise on reducing fractures with a game of cricket or a fox-chase; yet of the two the bodily exercise has that quality which we call liberal, and the intellectual has it not. And so of the learned professions altogether, considered merely as professions; although one of them be the most popularly beneficial, and another the most politically important, and the third the most intimately divine of all human pursuits, yet the very greatness of their end, the health of the body, or of the commonwealth, or of the soul, diminishes, not increases, their claim to the appellation in question, and that still more if they are cut down to the strict exigencies of that end. If, for instance, theology, instead of being cultivated as a contemplation, be limited to the purposes of the pulpit or be represented by the catechism, it loses—not its usefulness, not its divine character, not its meritoriousness (rather it

increases these qualities by such charitable condescension)
—but it does lose the particular attribute which I am
illustrating; just as a face worn by tears and fasting loses
its beauty, or a labourer's hand loses its delicateness; for
theology thus exercised is not simple knowledge, but
rather is an art or a business making use of theology. And
thus it appears that even what is supernatural need not be
liberal, nor need a hero be a gentleman, for the plain
reason that one idea is not another idea. And in like
manner the Baconian philosophy, by using its physical
sciences for the purpose of fruit, does thereby transfer them
from the order of liberal pursuits to, I do not say the inferior, but the distinct class of the useful. And, to take a
different instance, hence again, as is evident, whenever
personal gain is the motive, still more distinctive an effect
has it upon the character of a given pursuit; thus racing,
which was a liberal exercise in Greece, forfeits its rank
in times like these, so far as it is made the occasion of
gambling.

All that I have been now saying is summed up in a few
characteristic words of the great philosopher. 'Of possessions,' he says, 'those rather are useful which bear
fruit; those *liberal which tend to enjoyment*. By fruitful I
mean, which yield revenue; by enjoyable, where *nothing
accrues of consequence beyond the use*.' [1]

Do not suppose, gentlemen, that in thus appealing to
the ancients I am throwing back the world two thousand
years, and fettering philosophy with the reasonings of
paganism. While the world lasts will Aristotle's doctrine
on these matters last, for he is the oracle of nature and of
truth. While we are men we cannot help, to a great
extent, being Aristotelians, for the great master does but
analyse the thoughts, feelings, views, and opinions of human
kind. He has told us the meaning of our own words and

[1] Aristotle, *Rhet.*, i. 5.

ideas, before we were born. In many subject-matters, to think correctly is to think like Aristotle; and we are his disciples whether we will or no, though we may not know it. Now, as to the particular instance before us, the word liberal as applied to knowledge and education expresses a specific idea, which ever has been, and ever will be, while the nature of man is the same, just as the idea of the beautiful is specific, or of the sublime, or of the ridiculous, or of the sordid. It is in the world now, it was in the world then; and, as in the case of the dogmas of faith, it is illustrated by a continuous historical tradition, and never was out of the world, from the time it came into it. There have indeed been differences of opinion from time to time as to what pursuits and what arts came under that idea, but such differences are but an additional evidence of its reality. That idea must have a substance in it which has maintained its ground amid these conflicts and changes, which has ever served as a standard to measure things withal, which has passed from mind to mind unchanged, when there was so much to colour, so much to influence any notion or thought whatever, which was not founded in our very nature. Were it a mere generalization, it would have varied with the subjects from which it was generalized; but though its subjects vary with the age, it varies not itself. The palaestra may seem a liberal exercise to Lycurgus, and illiberal to Seneca; coach-driving and prize-fighting may be recognized in Elis, and be condemned in England; music may be despicable in the eyes of certain moderns, and be in the highest place with Aristotle and Plato—(and the case is the same in the particular application of the idea of beauty, or of goodness, or of moral virtue, there is a difference of tastes, a difference of judgments)—still these variations imply, instead of discrediting, the archetypal idea, which is but a previous hypothesis or condition, by means of which issue is joined between contending opinions, and without which there would be nothing to dispute about.

I consider then that I am chargeable with no paradox when I speak of a knowledge which is its own end, when I call it liberal knowledge, or a gentleman's knowledge, when I educate for it, and make it the scope of a university. And still less am I incurring such a charge when I make this acquisition consist, not in knowledge in a vague and ordinary sense, but in that knowledge which I have especially called philosophy or, in an extended sense of the word, science; for whatever claims knowledge has to be considered as a good, these it has in a higher degree when it is viewed not vaguely, not popularly, but precisely and transcendently as philosophy. Knowledge, I say, is then especially liberal, or sufficient for itself, apart from every external and ulterior object, when and so far as it is philosophical, and this I proceed to show.

Now bear with me, gentlemen, if what I am about to say has at first sight a fanciful appearance. Philosophy, then, or science, is related to knowledge in this way: knowledge is called by the name of science or philosophy when it is acted upon, informed, or if I may use a strong figure, impregnated by reason. Reason is the principle of that intrinsic fecundity of knowledge which, to those who possess it, is its special value, and which dispenses with the necessity of their looking abroad for any end to rest upon external to itself. Knowledge, indeed, when thus exalted into a scientific form, is also power; not only is it excellent in itself, but whatever such excellence may be it is something more, it has a result beyond itself. Doubtless; but that is a further consideration, with which I am not concerned. I only say that, prior to its being a power, it is a good; that it is, not only an instrument, but an end. I know well it may resolve itself into an art, and terminate in a mechanical process, and in tangible fruit; but it also may fall back upon reason, and resolve itself into philosophy. In one case it is called useful knowledge, in the other liberal. The same person may cultivate it in both ways at once; but this again is a matter foreign to my subject; here I do but say that there are two ways of using knowledge, and in matter of fact those who use it in one way are not likely to use it in the other, or at least in a very limited measure. You see, then, gentlemen, here are two methods of education; the one aspires to be philosophical, the other to be mechanical; the one rises towards ideas, the other is exhausted upon what is particular and external. Let me not be thought to deny the necessity, or to decry the benefit, of such attention to what is particular and practical, the useful or mechanical arts; life could not go on without them; we owe our daily welfare to them; their exercise is the duty of the many, and we owe to the many a debt of gratitude for fulfilling it. I only say that knowledge, in proportion as it tends more and more to be particular, ceases to be knowledge. It is a question whether knowledge can in any proper sense be predicated of the brute creation; without pretending to metaphysical exactness of phraseology, which would be unsuitable to an occasion like this, I say, it seems to me improper to call that passive sensation or perception of things which brutes seem to possess by the name of knowledge. When I speak of knowledge, I mean something intellectual, something which grasps what it perceives through the senses; something which takes a view of things; which sees more than the senses convey; which reasons upon what it sees, and while it sees; which invests it with an idea. It expresses itself, not in a mere enunciation, but by an enthymeme: it is of the nature of science from the first, and in this consists its dignity. The principle of real dignity in knowledge, its worth, its desirableness, considered irrespectively of its results, is this germ within it of a scientific or a philosophical process. This is how it comes to be an end in itself; this is why it admits of being called liberal. Not to know the relative disposition of things is the state of slaves or children; to have mapped out the universe is the boast of philosophy.

Moreover, such knowledge is not a mere extrinsic or accidental advantage, which is ours to-day and another's to-morrow, which may be got up from a book, and easily forgotten again, which we can command or communicate at our pleasure, which we can borrow for the occasion, carry about in our hand, and take into the market; it is an acquired illumination, it is a habit, a personal possession, and an inward endowment. And this is the reason why it is more correct, as well as more usual, to speak of a university as a place of education than of instruction, though, when knowledge is concerned, instruction would at first sight have seemed the more appropriate word. We are instructed, for instance, in manual exercises, in the fine and useful arts, in trades, and in ways of business; for these are methods which have little or no effect upon the mind itself, are contained in rules committed to memory, to tradition, or to use, and bear upon an end external to themselves. But education is a higher word; it implies an action upon our mental nature, and the formation of a character; it is something individual and permanent, and is commonly spoken of in connection with religion and virtue. When, then, we speak of the communication of knowledge as being education, we thereby really imply that that knowledge is a state or condition of mind; and since cultivation of mind is surely worth seeking for its own sake, we are thus brought once more to the conclusion, which the word liberal and the word philosophy have already suggested, that there is a knowledge which is desirable though nothing come of it, as being of itself a treasure, and a sufficient remuneration of years of labour.

This, then, is the answer which I am prepared to give to the question with which I opened this discourse. Before going on to speak of the object of the Church in taking up philosophy, and the uses to which she puts it, I am prepared to maintain that philosophy is its own end, and, as I conceive, I have now begun proving it. I am prepared to maintain that there is a knowledge worth possessing for what it is, and not merely for what it does; and what minutes remain to me to-day I shall devote to the removal of some portion of the indistinctness and confusion with which the subject may in some minds be surrounded.

It may be objected then that, when we profess to seek knowledge for some end or other beyond itself, whatever it be, we speak intelligibly; but that, whatever men may have said, however obstinately the idea may have kept its ground from age to age, still it is simply unmeaning to say that we seek knowledge for its own sake, and for nothing else; for that it ever leads to something beyond itself, which therefore is its end, and the cause why it is desirable; moreover, that this end is twofold, either of this world or of the next; that all knowledge is cultivated either for secular objects or for eternal; that if it is directed to secular objects it is called useful knowledge, if to eternal, religious or Christian knowledge; in consequence, that if, as I have allowed, this liberal knowledge does not benefit the body or estate, it ought to benefit the soul; but if the fact be really so, that it is neither a physical nor a secular good on the one hand, nor a moral good on the other, it cannot be a good at all, and is not worth the trouble which is necessary for its acquisition.

And then I may be reminded that the professors of this liberal or philosophical knowledge have themselves, in every age, recognized this exposition of the matter, and have submitted to the issue in which it terminates; for they have ever been attempting to make men virtuous; or, if not, at least have assumed that refinement of mind was virtue, and that they themselves were the virtuous portion of mankind. This they have professed on the one hand; and on the other, they have utterly failed in their professions, so as ever to make themselves a proverb among men, and a laughing-stock both to the grave and the dissipated portion of mankind, in consequence of them. Thus they have furnished against themselves both the ground and the means of their own exposure, without any trouble at all to anyone else. In a word, from the time that Athens was the university of the world, what has philosophy taught men, but to promise without practising, and to aspire without attaining? What has the deep and lofty thought of its disciples ended in but eloquent words? Nay, what has its teaching ever meditated, when it was boldest in its remedies for human ill, beyond charming us to sleep by its lessons, that we might feel nothing at all? Like some melodious air, or rather like those strong and transporting perfumes which at first spread their sweetness over everything they touch, but in a little while do but offend in proportion as they once pleased us. Did philosophy support Cicero under the disfavour of the fickle populace, or nerve Seneca to oppose an imperial tyrant? It abandoned Brutus, as he sorrowfully confessed, in his greatest need, and it forced Cato, as his panegyrist strangely boasts, into the false position of defying heaven. How few can be counted among its professors who, like Polemo, were thereby converted from a profligate course, or like Anaxagoras thought the world well lost in exchange for its possession. The philosopher in Rasselas taught a super-human doctrine, and then succumbed without an effort to a trial of human affection.

'He discoursed,' we are told, 'with great energy on the government of the passions. His look was venerable, his action graceful, his pronunciation clear, and his diction

elegant.   He showed, with great strength of sentiment and
variety of illustration, that human nature is degraded and
debased, when the lower faculties predominate over the
higher.   He communicated the various precepts given,
from time to time, for the conquest of passion, and displayed the happiness of those who had obtained the important victory, after which man is no longer the slave of
fear, nor the fool of hope. . . .   He enumerated many
examples of heroes immovable by pain or pleasure, who
looked with indifference on those modes or accidents to
which the vulgar give the names of good and evil.'

Rasselas in a few days found the philosopher in a room
half darkened, with his eyes misty, and his face pale.   'Sir,'
said he, 'you have come at a time when all human friendship is useless; what I suffer cannot be remedied, what I
have lost cannot be supplied.   My daughter, my only
daughter, from whose tenderness I expected all the comforts of my age, died last night of a fever.'   'Sir,' said the
prince, 'mortality is an event by which a wise man can
never be surprised; we know that death is always near, and
it should therefore always be expected.'   'Young man,'
answered the philosopher, 'you speak like one who has
never felt the pangs of separation.'   'Have you, then,
forgot the precept,' said Rasselas, 'which you so power-
fully enforced? . . . consider that external things are
naturally variable, but truth and reason are always the
same.'   'What comfort,' said the mourner, 'can truth and
reason afford me?   Of what effect are they now, but to
tell me that my daughter will not be restored?'

Better, far better, to make no professions, you will say,
than to cheat others with what we are not, and to scan-
dalize them with what we are.   The sensualist or the man
of the world at any rate is not the victim of fine words, but
pursues a reality and gains it.   The philosophy of utility,
you will say, gentlemen, has at least done its work; it

aimed low, but it has fulfilled its aim. If that man of great
intellect who has been its prophet in the conduct of life
played false to his own professions, he was not bound by
his philosophy to be true to his friend or faithful in his
trust. Moral virtue was not the line in which he undertook to instruct men; and though, as the poet calls him, he
were the 'meanest' of mankind, he was so in what may be
called his private capacity, and without any prejudice to
the theory of induction. He had a right to be so, if he
chose, for anything that the idols of the den or the theatre
had to say to the contrary. His mission was the increase
of physical enjoyment and social comfort; [1] and most
wonderfully, most awfully has he fulfilled his conception
and his design. Almost day by day have we fresh and fresh
shoots, and buds, and blossoms, which are to ripen into
fruit, on that magical tree of knowledge which he planted,
and to which none of us perhaps, except the very poor, but
owes, if not his present life, at least his daily food, his
health, and general well-being. He was the divinely provided minister of temporal benefits to all of us so great that,
whatever I am forced to think of him as a man, I have not
the heart, from mere gratitude, to speak of him severely.
And, in spite of the tendencies of his philosophy, which are,
as we see at this day, to depreciate or to trample on theology,
he has himself, in his writings, gone out of his way, as if
with a prophetic misgiving of those tendencies, to insist
on it as the instrument of that beneficent Father [2] who,
when He came on earth in visible form, took on Him first
and most prominently the office of assuaging the bodily

[1] It will be seen that on the whole I agree with Lord Macaulay in his
essay on Bacon's philosophy. I do not know whether he would agree
with me.

[2] *De Augment.*, iv. 2, *vide* Macaulay's essay; *vide* also 'In principio
operrs ad Deum Patrem, Deum Verbum, Deum Spiritum, preces
fundimus humillimas et ardentissimas, ut humani generis aerumnarum
memores, et peregrinationis istius vitae, in qua dies paucos et malos
terimus, *novis suis eleemosynis, per manus nostras,* familiam humanam

wounds of human nature.   And truly, like the old mediciner in the tale, 'he sat diligently at his work, and hummed, with cheerful countenance, a pious song'; and then in turn 'went out singing into the meadows so gaily, that those who had seen him from afar might well have thought it was a youth gathering flowers for his beloved, instead of an old physician gathering healing herbs in the morning dew.' [1]

Alas, that men, in the action of life or in their heart of hearts, are not what they seem to be in their moments of excitement, or in their trances or intoxications of genius— so good, so noble, so serene!   Alas, that Bacon too [2] in his own way should after all be but the fellow of those heathen philosophers who in their disadvantages had some excuse for their inconsistency, and who surprise us rather in what they did say than in what they did not do!   Alas, that he too, like Socrates or Seneca, must be stripped of his holy-day coat, which looks so fair, and should be but a mockery amid his most majestic gravity of phrase; and, for all his vast abilities, should, in the littleness of his own moral being, but typify the intellectual narrowness of his school!   However, granting all this, heroism after all was not his philosophy: I cannot deny he has abundantly achieved what he proposed.   His is simply a method whereby bodily discomforts and temporal wants are to be most effectually removed from the greatest number; and already, before it has shown any signs of exhaustion, the gifts of nature, in their most artificial shapes and luxurious profusion and diversity, from all quarters of the earth, are, it is undeniable, by its means brought even to our doors, and we rejoice in them.

---

dotare dignentur.   Atque illud insuper supplices rogamus, ne *humana divinis officiant*; neve *ex reseratione viarum sensûs*, et accensione majore luminis naturalis, *aliquid incredulitatis* et noctis, animis nostris erga divina mysteria oriatur,' etc.   *Praef.* Instaur. Magn.

[1] Fouqué's *Unknown Patient*.

[2] Te maris et terrae, etc.   Horace, *Od.*, i. 28.

Useful knowledge then certainly has done its work; and liberal knowledge as certainly has not done its work—supposing, that is, as the objectors assume, its direct end, like religious knowledge, is to make men better; but this I will not for an instant allow. For all its friends, or its enemies, may say, I insist upon it, that it is as real a mistake to burden it with virtue or religion as with the mechanical arts. Its direct business is not to steel the soul against temptation, or to console it in affliction, any more than to set the loom in motion, or to direct the steam carriage; be it ever so much the means or the condition of both material and moral advancement; still, taken by and in itself, it as little mends our hearts as it improves our temporal circumstances. And if its eulogists claim for it such a power, they commit the very same kind of encroachment on a province not their own as the political economist who should maintain that his science educated him for casuistry or diplomacy. Knowledge is one thing, virtue is another; good sense is not conscience, refinement is not humility, nor is largeness and justness of view faith. Philosophy, however enlightened, however profound, gives no command over the passions, no influential motives, no vivifying principles. Liberal education makes not the Christian, not the Catholic, but the gentleman. It is well to be a gentleman, it is well to have a cultivated intellect, a delicate taste, a candid, equitable, dispassionate mind, a noble and courteous bearing in the conduct of life—these are the connatural qualities of a large knowledge; they are the objects of a university; I am advocating, I shall illustrate and insist upon them; but still, I repeat, they are no guarantee for sanctity or even for conscientiousness, they may attach to the man of the world, to the profligate, to the heartless—pleasant, alas, and attractive as he shows when decked out in them. Taken by themselves, they do but seem to be what they are not; they look like virtue at a distance, but they are detected by close observers, and on the long run; and hence it is that they are popularly accused of pretence and hypocrisy, not, I repeat, from their own fault, but because their professors and their admirers persist in taking them for what they are not, and are officious in arrogating for them a praise to which they have no claim. Quarry the granite rock with razors, or moor the vessel with a thread of silk; then may you hope with such keen and delicate instruments as human knowledge and human reason to contend against these giants, the passion and the pride of man.

Surely we are not driven to theories of this kind in order to vindicate the value and dignity of liberal knowledge. Surely the real grounds on which its pretensions rest are not so very subtle or abstruse, so very strange or improbable. Surely it is very intelligible to say, and that is what I say here, that liberal education, viewed in itself, is simply the cultivation of the intellect as such, and its object is nothing more or less than intellectual excellence. Everything has its own perfection, be it higher or lower in the scale of things; and the perfection of one is not the perfection of another. Things animate, inanimate, visible, invisible, all are good in their kind, and have a *best* of themselves, which is an object of pursuit. Why do you take such pains with your garden or your park? You see to your walks and turf and shrubberies, to your trees and drives; not as if you meant to make an orchard of the one, or corn or pasture land of the other, but because there is a special beauty in all that is goodly in wood, water, plain, and slope, brought all together by art into one shape, and grouped into one whole. Your cities are beautiful, your palaces, your public buildings, your territorial mansions, your churches; and their beauty leads to nothing beyond itself. There is a physical beauty and a moral: there is a beauty of person, there is a beauty of our moral being, which is natural virtue; and in like manner there is a beauty, there is a perfection, of the intellect. There is an ideal perfection in these various subject-matters, towards which individual instances are seen to rise, and which are the standards for all instances whatever. The Greek divinities and demigods, as the statuary has moulded them, with their symmetry of figure, and their high forehead and their regular features, are the perfection of physical beauty. The heroes of whom history tells, Alexander, or Caesar, or Scipio, or Saladin, are the representatives of that magnanimity or self-mastery which is the greatness of human nature. Christianity too has its heroes, and in the supernatural order, and we call them saints. The artist puts before him beauty of feature and form; the poet, beauty of mind; the preacher, the beauty of grace: then intellect too, I repeat, has its beauty, and it has those who aim at it. To open the mind, to correct it, to refine it, to enable it to know, and to digest, master, rule, and use its knowledge, to give it power over its own faculties, application, flexibility, method, critical exactness, sagacity, resource, address, eloquent expression, is an object as intelligible (for here we are inquiring, not what the object of a liberal education is worth, nor what use the Church makes of it, but what it is in itself), I say, an object as intelligible as the cultivation of virtue, while, at the same time, it is absolutely distinct from it.

This indeed is but a temporal object, and a transitory possession: but so are other things in themselves which we make much of and pursue. The moralist will tell us that man, in all his functions, is but a flower which blossoms and fades, except so far as a higher principle breathes upon him, and makes him and what he is immortal. Body and mind are carried on into an eternal state of being by the gifts of divine munificence; but at first they do but fail in a failing world; and if the powers of intellect decay, the powers of the body have decayed before them, and, as an hospital or an alms-house, though its end be ephemeral, may be sanctified to the service of religion, so surely may a university, even were it nothing more than I have as yet described it. We attain to heaven by using this world well, though it is to pass away; we perfect our nature, not by undoing it, but by adding to it what is more than nature, and directing it towards aims higher than its own.

DISCOURSE V

LIBERAL KNOWLEDGE VIEWED IN RELATION TO LEARNING

IT were well if the English, like the Greek language, possessed some definite word to express, simply and generally, intellectual proficiency or perfection, such as health, as used with reference to the animal frame, and virtue, with reference to our moral nature. I am not able to find such a term: talent, ability, genius belong distinctly to the raw material, which is the subject-matter, not to that excellence which is the result of exercise and training. When we turn, indeed, to the particular kinds of intellectual perfection, words are forthcoming for our purpose, as for instance judgment, taste, and skill; yet even these belong, for the most part, to powers or habits bearing upon practice or upon art, and not to any perfect condition of the intellect, considered in itself. Wisdom, again, which is a more comprehensive word than any other, certainly has a direct relation to conduct and to human life. Knowledge, indeed, and science express purely intellectual ideas, but still not a state or habit of the intellect; for knowledge, in its ordinary sense, is but one of its circumstances, denoting a possession or a faculty; and science has been appropriated to the subject-matter of the intellect, instead of belonging at present, as it ought to do, to the intellect itself. The consequence is that, on an occasion like this, many words are necessary, in order, first, to bring out and convey what surely is no difficult idea in itself—that of the cultivation of the intellect as an end; next, in order to recommend what surely is no unreasonable object; and lastly, to describe and make the mind realize the particular perfection in which that object consists. Everyone knows practically what are the constituents of health or of virtue; and everyone recognizes health and virtue as ends to be pursued; it is otherwise with intellectual excellence, and this must be my excuse, if I seem to anyone to be bestowing a good deal of labour on a preliminary matter.

In default of a recognized term, I have called the perfection or virtue of the intellect by the name of philosophy, philosophical knowledge, enlargement of mind, or illumination; terms which are not uncommonly given to it by writers of this day: but, whatever name we bestow on it, it is, I believe, as a matter of history, the business of a university to make this intellectual culture its direct scope, or to employ itself in the education of the intellect—just as the work of a hospital lies in healing the sick or wounded; of a riding or fencing school, or of a gymnasium, in exercising the limbs; of an alms-house in aiding and solacing the old; of an orphanage in protecting innocence; of a penitentiary in restoring the guilty. I say a university, taken in its bare idea, and before we view it as an instrument of the Church, has this object and this mission; it contemplates neither moral impression nor mechanical production; it professes to exercise the mind neither in art nor in duty; its function is intellectual culture: here it may leave its scholars, and it has done its work when it has done as much as this. It educates the intellect to reason well in all matters, to reach out towards truth, and to grasp it.

This, I said in my foregoing discourse, was the object of a university, viewed in itself, and apart from the Catholic Church, or from the State, or from any other power which may use it; and I illustrated this in various ways. I said that the intellect must have an excellence of its own, for there was nothing which had not its specific good; that the word educate would not be used of intellectual culture, as it is used, had not the intellect had an end of its own; that, had it not such an end, there would be no meaning in calling certain intellectual exercises liberal, in contrast with useful, as is commonly done; that the very notion of a philosophical temper implied it, for it threw us back upon research and system as ends in themselves, distinct from effects and works of any kind; that a philosophical scheme of knowledge, or system of sciences, could not, from the nature of the case, issue in any one definite art or pursuit, as its end; and that, on the other hand, the discovery and contemplation of truth, to which research and systematizing led, were surely sufficient ends, though nothing beyond them were added, and that they had ever been accounted sufficient by mankind.

Here then I take up the subject; and having determined that the cultivation of the intellect is an end distinct and sufficient in itself, and that, so far as words go, it is an enlargement or illumination, I proceed to inquire what this mental breadth, or power, or light, or philosophy consists in. A hospital heals a broken limb or cures a fever; what does an institution effect, which professes the health, not of the body, not of the soul, but of the intellect? What is this good, which in former times, as well as our own, has been found worth the notice, the appropriation, of the Catholic Church?

I have then to investigate, in the discourses which follow, those qualities and characteristics of the intellect in which its cultivation issues or rather consists; and, with a view of assisting myself in this undertaking, I shall recur to certain questions which have already been touched upon. These questions are three: viz. the relation of intellectual culture, first, to *mere* knowledge; secondly, to *professional* knowledge; and thirdly, to *religious* knowledge. In other words, are *acquirements* and *attainments* the scope of a university education? or *expertness in particular arts and pursuits*? or *moral and religious proficiency*? or something besides these three? These questions I shall examine in succession, with the purpose I have mentioned; and I hope to be excused if, in this anxious undertaking, I am led to repeat what, either in these discourses or elsewhere,[1] I have already put upon paper. And first, of *mere knowledge*, or learning, and its connection with intellectual illumination or philosophy.

I suppose the *prima facie* view which the public at large would take of a university, considered as a place of education, is nothing more or less than a place for acquiring a great deal of knowledge on a great many subjects. Memory is one of the first developed of the mental faculties; a boy's business when he goes to school is to learn, that is, to store up things in his memory. For some years his intellect is little more than an instrument for taking in facts, or a receptacle for storing them; he welcomes them as fast as they come to him; he lives on what is without; he has his eyes ever about him; he has a lively susceptibility of impressions; he imbibes information of every kind; and little does he make his own in a true sense of the word, living rather upon his neighbours all around him. He has opinions, religious, political, and literary, and, for a boy, is very positive in them and sure about them; but he gets them from his schoolfellows, or his masters, or his parents, as the case may be. Such as he is in his other relations, such also is he in his school exercises; his mind is observant, sharp, ready, retentive; he is almost passive in the acquisition of knowledge. I say this in no disparagement of the idea of a clever boy. Geography, chronology, history, language, natural history, he heaps up the matter of these studies as treasures for a future day. It is the seven years of plenty with him: he gathers in by handfuls, like the Egyptians, without counting; and though, as time goes on, there

[1] *Vide* the author's University (Oxford) Sermons.

is exercise for his argumentative powers in the elements of mathematics, and for his taste in the poets and orators, still, while at school, or at least till quite the last years of his time, he acquires and little more; and when he is leaving for the university, he is mainly the creature of foreign influences and circumstances, and made up of accidents, homogeneous or not, as the case may be. Moreover, the moral habits which are a boy's praise encourage and assist this result; that is, diligence, assiduity, regularity, dispatch, persevering application; for these are the direct conditions of acquisition, and naturally lead to it. Acquirements, again, are emphatically producible, and at a moment; they are a something to show, both for master and scholar; an audience, even though ignorant themselves of the subjects of an examination, can comprehend when questions are answered and when they are not. Here again is a reason why mental culture should in the minds of men be identified with the acquisition of knowledge.

The same notion possesses the public mind when it passes on from the thought of a school to that of a university: and with the best of reasons so far as this, that there is no true culture without acquirements, and that philosophy presupposes knowledge. It requires a great deal of reading, or a wide range of information, to warrant us in putting forth our opinions on any serious subject; and without such learning the most original mind may be able indeed to dazzle, to amuse, to refute, to perplex, but not to come to any useful result or any trustworthy conclusion. There are indeed persons who profess a different view of the matter, and even act upon it. Every now and then you will find a person of vigorous or fertile mind who relies upon his own resources, despises all former authors, and gives the world, with the utmost fearlessness, his views upon religion, or history, or any other popular subject. And his works may sell for a while; he may get a name in his day; but this will be all. His readers are sure to find in the long run that his doctrines are mere theories, and not the expression of facts, that they are chaff instead of bread, and then his popularity drops as suddenly as it rose.

Knowledge, then, is the indispensable condition of expansion of mind, and the instrument of attaining to it; this cannot be denied, it is ever to be insisted on; I begin with it as a first principle; however, the very truth of it carries men too far, and confirms to them the notion that it is the whole of it. A narrow mind is thought to be that which contains little knowledge; and an enlarged mind that which holds a deal; and what seems to put the matter beyond dispute is the fact of the number of studies which are pursued in a university, by its very profession. Lectures are given on every kind of subject; examinations are held; prizes awarded. There are moral, metaphysical, physical professors; professors of languages, of history, of mathematics, of experimental science. Lists of questions are published, wonderful for their range and depth, variety, and difficulty; treatises are written, which carry upon their very face the evidence of extensive reading or multifarious information; what then is wanted for mental culture to a person of large reading and scientific attainments? What is grasp of mind but acquirement? Where shall philosophical repose be found, but in the consciousness and enjoyment of large intellectual possessions?

And yet this notion is, I conceive, a mistake, and my present business is to show that it is one, and that the end of a liberal education is not mere knowledge, or knowledge considered in its *matter*; and I shall best attain my object by actually setting down some cases which will be generally granted to be instances of the process of enlightenment or enlargement of mind, and others which are not, and thus, by the comparison, you will be able to judge for yourselves, gentlemen, whether knowledge, that is, acquirement, is after all the real principle of the enlargement, or whether that principle is not rather something beyond it.

For instance, let a person whose experience has hitherto been confined to the more calm and unpretending scenery of these islands, whether here or in England, go for the first time into parts where physical nature puts on her wilder and more awful forms, whether at home or abroad, as into mountainous districts; or let one who has ever lived in a quiet village go for the first time to a great metropolis— then I suppose he will have a sensation which perhaps he never had before. He has a feeling not in addition or increase of former feelings, but of something different in its nature. He will perhaps be borne forward, and find for a time that he has lost his bearings. He has made a certain progress, and he has a consciousness of mental enlargement; he does not stand where he did, he has a new centre, and a range of thoughts to which he was before a stranger.

Again, the view of the heavens which the telescope opens upon us, if allowed to fill and possess the mind, may almost whirl it round and make it dizzy. It brings in a flood of ideas, and is rightly called an intellectual enlargement, whatever is meant by the term.

And so again, the sight of beasts of prey and other foreign animals, their strangeness, the originality (if I may use the term) of their forms and gestures and habits, and their variety and independence of each other, throw us out of ourselves into another creation, and as if under another Creator, if I may so express the temptation which may come on the mind. We seem to have new faculties, or a new exercise for our faculties, by this addition to our knowledge; like a prisoner who, having been accustomed to wear manacles or fetters, suddenly finds his arms and legs free.

Hence physical science generally, in all its departments, as bringing before us the exuberant riches and resources, yet the orderly course, of the universe, elevates and excites the student, and at first, I may say, almost takes away his breath, while in time it exercises a tranquillizing influence upon him.

Again, the study of history is said to enlarge and enlighten the mind, and why? Because, as I conceive, it gives it a power of judging of passing events, and of all events; and a conscious superiority over them, which before it did not possess.

And in like manner, what is called seeing the world, entering into active life, going into society, travelling, gaining acquaintance with the various classes of the community, coming into contact with the principles and modes of thought of various parties, interests, and races, their views, aims, habits, and manners, their religious creeds and forms of worship—gaining experience how various yet how alike men are, how low-minded, how bad, how opposed, yet how confident in their opinions; all this exerts a perceptible influence upon the mind, which it is impossible to mistake, be it good or be it bad, and is popularly called its enlargement.

And then again, the first time the mind comes across the arguments and speculations of unbelievers, and feels what a novel light they cast upon what he has hitherto accounted sacred; and still more, if it gives in to them and embraces them, and throws off as so much prejudice what it has hitherto held, and, as if waking from a dream, begins to realize to its imagination that there is now no such thing as law and the transgression of law, that sin is a phantom, and punishment a bugbear, that it is free to sin, free to enjoy the world and the flesh; and still further, when it does enjoy them, and reflects that it may think and hold just what it will, that 'the world is all before it where to choose,' and what system to build up as its own private persuasion; when this torrent of bad thoughts rushes over and inundates

it, who will deny that the fruit of the tree of knowledge, or what the mind takes for knowledge, has made it
one of the gods, with a sense of expansion and elevation—
an intoxication in reality, still, so far as the subjective state
of the mind goes, an illumination? Hence the fanaticism
of individuals or nations who suddenly cast off their
Maker. Their eyes are opened, and, like the judgment-
stricken king in the tragedy, they see two suns, and a magic
universe, out of which they look back upon their former
state of faith and innocence with a sort of contempt and
indignation, as if they were then but fools, and the dupes of
imposture.

On the other hand, religion has its own enlargement, and
an enlargement, not of tumult, but of peace. It is often
remarked of uneducated persons, who have hitherto
thought little of the unseen world, that, on their turning
to God, looking into themselves, regulating their hearts,
reforming their conduct, and meditating on death and
judgment, heaven and hell, they seem to become, in point
of intellect, different beings from what they were. Before,
they took things as they came, and thought no more of one
thing than another. But now every event has a meaning;
they have their own estimate of whatever happens to them;
they are mindful of times and seasons, and compare the
present with the past; and the world, no longer dull,
monotonous, unprofitable, and hopeless, is a various and
complicated drama, with parts and an object, and an awful
moral.

Now from these instances, to which many more might be
added, it is plain, first, that the communication of knowledge certainly is either a condition or the means of that
sense of enlargement or enlightenment, of which at this day
we hear so much in certain quarters: this cannot be denied;
but next, it is equally plain that such communication is not
the whole of the process. The enlargement consists, not

merely in the passive reception into the mind of a number of ideas hitherto unknown to it, but in the mind's energetic and simultaneous action upon and towards and among those new ideas which are rushing in upon it. It is the action of a formative power, reducing to order and meaning the matter of our acquirements; it is making the objects of our knowledge subjectively our own, or, to use a familiar word, it is a digestion of what we receive into the substance of our previous state of thought; and without this no enlargement is said to follow. There is no enlargement unless there be a comparison of ideas one with another, as they come before the mind, and a systematizing of them. We feel our minds to be growing and expanding *then*, when we not only learn, but refer what we learn to what we know already. It is not a mere addition to our knowledge which is the illumination; but the locomotion, the movement onwards, of that mental centre to which both what we know and what we are learning, the accumulating mass of our requirements, gravitates. And therefore a truly great intellect, and recognized to be such by the common opinion of mankind, such as the intellect of Aristotle, or of St Thomas, or of Newton, or of Goethe (I purposely take instances within and without the Catholic pale, when I would speak of the intellect as such), is one which takes a connected view of old and new, past and present, far and near, and which has an insight into the influence of all these one on another; without which there is no whole, and no centre. It possesses the knowledge, not only of things, but also of their mutual and true relations; knowledge not merely considered as acquirement, but as philosophy.

Accordingly, when this analytical, distributive, harmonizing process is away, the mind experiences no enlargement, and is not reckoned as enlightened or comprehensive, whatever it may add to its knowledge. For instance, a great memory, as I have already said, does not make a philosopher, any more than a dictionary can be called a grammar. There are men who embrace in their minds a vast multitude of ideas, but with little sensibility about their real relations towards each other. These may be anti-quarians, annalists, naturalists; they may be learned in the law; they may be versed in statistics; they are most useful in their own place; I should shrink from speaking dis-respectfully of them; still, there is nothing in such attain-ments to guarantee the absence of narrowness of mind. If they are nothing more than well-read men, or men of information, they have not what specially deserves the name of culture of mind, or fulfils the type of liberal education.

In like manner we sometimes fall in with persons who have seen much of the world, and of the men who, in their day, have played a conspicuous part in it, but who gener-alize nothing, and have no observation, in the true sense of the word. They abound in information in detail, curious and entertaining, about men and things; and, having lived under the influence of no very clear or settled principles, religious or political, they speak of everyone and every-thing only as so many phenomena which are complete in themselves, and lead to nothing, not discussing them, or teaching any truth, or instructing the hearer, but simply talking. No one would say that these persons, well informed as they are, had attained to any great culture of intellect or to philosophy.

The case is the same still more strikingly where the persons in question are beyond dispute men of inferior powers and deficient education. Perhaps they have been much in foreign countries, and they receive, in a passive, otiose, unfruitful way, the various facts which are forced upon them there. Seafaring men, for example, range from one end of the earth to the other; but the multiplicity of external objects which they have encountered forms no symmetrical and consistent picture upon their imagination; they see the tapestry of human life as it were on the wrong side, and it tells no story. They sleep, and they rise up, and they find themselves now in Europe, now in Asia; they see visions of great cities and wild regions; they are in the marts of commerce or amid the islands of the South; they gaze on Pompey's Pillar or on the Andes; and nothing which meets them carries them forward or backward to any idea beyond itself. Nothing has a drift or relation; nothing has a history or a promise. Everything stands by itself, and comes and goes in its turn, like the shifting scenes of a show, which leave the spectator where he was. Perhaps you are near such a man on a particular occasion, and expect him to be shocked or perplexed at something which occurs; but one thing is much the same to him as another, or, if he is perplexed, it is as not knowing what to say, whether it is right to admire, or to ridicule, or to disapprove, while conscious that some expression of opinion is expected from him; for in fact he has no standard of judgment at all, and no landmarks to guide him to a conclusion. Such is mere acquisition, and, I repeat, no one would dream of calling it philosophy.

Instances such as these confirm, by the contrast, the conclusion I have already drawn from those which preceded them. That only is true enlargement of mind which is the power of viewing many things at once as one whole, of referring them severally to their true place in the universal system, of understanding their respective values, and determining their mutual dependence. Thus is that form of universal knowledge, of which I have on a former occasion spoken, set up in the individual intellect, and constitutes its perfection. Possessed of this real illumination, the mind never views any part of the extended subject-matter of knowledge without recollecting that it is but a part, or without the associations which spring from this recollection. It makes everything in some sort lead to everything else; it would communicate the image of the whole to every separate portion, till that whole becomes in imagination like a spirit, everywhere pervading and penetrating its component parts, and giving them one definite meaning. Just as our bodily organs, when mentioned, recall their function in the body, as the word creation suggests the Creator, and subjects a sovereign, so, in the mind of the philosopher, as we are abstractedly conceiving of him, the elements of the physical and moral world, sciences, arts, pursuits, ranks, offices, events, opinions, individualities, are all viewed as one, with correlative functions, and as gradually by successive combinations converging, one and all, to the true centre.

To have even a portion of this illuminative reason and true philosophy is the highest state to which nature can aspire in the way of intellect; it puts the mind above the influences of chance and necessity, above anxiety, suspense, tumult, and superstition, which are the portion of the many. Men whose minds are possessed with some one object take exaggerated views of its importance, are feverish in the pursuit of it, make it the measure of things which are utterly foreign to it, and are startled and despond if it happens to fail them. They are ever in alarm or in transport. Those on the other hand who have no object or principle whatever to hold by lose their way, every step they take. They are thrown out, and do not know what to think or say, at every fresh juncture; they have no view of persons, or occurrences, or facts, which come suddenly upon them, and they hang upon the opinion of others, for want of internal resources. But the intellect which has been disciplined to the perfection of its powers, which knows, and thinks while it knows, which has learned to leaven the dense mass of facts and events with the elastic force of reason, such an intellect cannot be partial, cannot be exclusive, cannot be impetuous, cannot be at a loss, cannot but be patient, collected, and majestically calm, because it discerns the end in every beginning, the origin in every end, the law in every interruption, the limit in each delay; because it ever knows where it stands, and how its path lies from one point to another. It is the τετράγωνος of the Peripatetic, and has the 'nil admirari' of the Stoic:

> Felix qui potuit rerum cognoscere causas,
> Atque metus omnes, et inexorabile fatum
> Subjecit pedibus, strepitumque Acherontis avari.

There are men who, when in difficulties, originate at the moment vast ideas or dazzling projects; who, under the influence of excitement, are able to cast a light, almost as if from inspiration, on a subject or course of action which comes before them; who have a sudden presence of mind equal to any emergency, rising with the occasion, and an undaunted magnanimous bearing, and an energy and keenness which is but made intense by opposition. This is genius, this is heroism; it is the exhibition of a natural gift, which no culture can teach at which no institution can aim; here, on the contrary, we are concerned, not with mere nature, but with training and teaching. That perfection of the intellect which is the result of education, and its beau ideal, to be imparted to individuals in their respective measures, is the clear, calm, accurate vision and comprehension of all things, as far as the finite mind can embrace them, each in its place, and with its own characteristics upon it. It is almost prophetic from its knowledge of history; it is almost heart-searching from its knowledge of human nature; it has almost supernatural charity from its freedom from littleness and prejudice; it has almost the repose of faith, because nothing can startle it; it has almost the beauty and harmony of heavenly contemplation, so intimate is it with the eternal order of things and the music of the spheres.

And now, if I may take for granted that the true and adequate end of intellectual training and of a university is not learning or acquirement, but rather is thought or reason exercised upon knowledge, or what may be called philosophy, I shall be in a position to explain the various mistakes which at the present day beset the subject of university education.

I say then, if we would improve the intellect, first of all we must ascend: we cannot gain real knowledge on a level; we must generalize, we must reduce to method, we must have a grasp of principles, and group and shape our acquisitions by them. It matters not whether our field of operation be wide or limited; in every case, to command it is to mount above it. Who has not felt the irritation of mind and impatience created by a deep, rich country, visited for the first time, with winding lanes, and high hedges, and green steeps, and tangled woods, and everything smiling indeed, but in a maze? The same feeling comes upon us in a strange city, when we have no map of its streets. Hence you hear of practised travellers, when they first come into a place, mounting some high hill or church tower, by way of reconnoitring its neighbourhood. In like manner you must be above your knowledge, gentlemen, not under it, or it will oppress you; and the more you have of it the greater will be the load. The learning of a Salmasius or a Burman, unless you are its master, will be your tyrant. 'Imperat aut servit'; if you can wield it with a strong arm, it is a great weapon; otherwise:

> Vis consili expers
> Mole ruit suâ,

You will be overwhelmed, like Tarpeia, by the heavy wealth which you have exacted from tributary generations.

Instances abound; there are authors who are as pointless as they are inexhaustible in their literary resources. They measure knowledge by bulk, as it lies in the rude block, without symmetry, without design. How many commentators are there on the classics, how many on Holy Scripture, from whom we rise up, wondering at the learning which has passed before us, and wondering why it passed! How many writers are there of ecclesiastical history, such as Mosheim or Du Pin, who, breaking up their subject into details, destroy its life, and defraud us of the whole by their anxiety about the parts! The sermons, again, of the English divines in the seventeenth century, how often are they mere repertories of miscellaneous and officious learning! Of course Catholics also may read without thinking; and in their case, equally as with Protestants, it holds good that that knowledge of theirs is unworthy of the name, knowledge which they have not thought through, and thought out. Such readers are only possessed by their knowledge, not possessed of it; nay, in matter of fact they are often even carried away by it, without any volition of their own. Recollect, the memory can tyrannize as well as the imagination. Derangement, I believe, has been considered as a loss of control over the sequence of ideas. The mind, once set in motion, is henceforth deprived of the power of initiation, and becomes the victim of a train of associations, one thought suggesting another in the way of cause and effect, as if by a mechanical process, or some physical necessity. No one who has had experience of men of studious habits but must recognize the existence of a parallel phenomenon in the case of those who have over-stimulated the memory. In such persons reason acts almost as feebly and as impotently as in the madman; once fairly started on any subject whatever, they have no power of self-control; they passively endure the succession of impulses which are evolved out of the original exciting cause; they are passed on from one idea to another and go steadily forward, plodding along one line of thought in spite of the amplest concessions of the hearer, or wandering from it in endless digression in spite of his remonstrances. Now if, as is very certain, no one would envy the madman the glow and originality of his conceptions, why must we extol the cultivation of that intellect which is the prey, not indeed of barren fancies but of barren facts, of random intrusions from without, though not of morbid imaginations from within? And in thus speaking I am not denying that a strong and ready memory is in itself a real treasure; I am not disparaging a well-stored mind, though it be nothing besides, provided it be sober, any more than I would despise a bookseller's shop: it is of great value to others, even when not so to the owner. Nor am I banishing, far from it, the possessors of deep and multifarious learning from my ideal university; they adorn it in the eyes of men; I do but say that they constitute no type of the results at which it aims; that it is no great gain to the intellect to have enlarged the memory at the expense of faculties which are indisputably higher.

Nor indeed am I supposing that there is any great danger, at least in this day, of over-education; the danger is on the other side. I will tell you, gentlemen, what has been the practical error of the last twenty years—not to load the memory of the student with a mass of undigested knowledge, but to attempt so much that nothing has been really effected, to teach so many things that nothing has properly been learned at all. It has been the error of distracting and enfeebling the mind by an unmeaning profusion of subjects; of implying that a smattering in a dozen branches of study was not shallowness, which it really is, but enlargement; of considering an acquaintance with the learned names of things and persons, and the possession of clever duodecimos, and attendance on eloquent lecturers, and membership with scientific institutions, and the sight of the experiments of a platform and the specimens of a museum, that all this was not dissipation of mind, but progress. All things now are to be learned at once, not first one thing, then another, not one well but many badly. Learning is to be without exertion, without attention, without toil; without grounding, without advance, without finishing. There is to be nothing individual in it; and this, forsooth, is the wonder of the age. What the steam-engine does with matter, the printing press is to do with mind; it is to act mechanically, and the population is to be passively, almost unconsciously, enlightened, by the mere multiplication and dissemination of volumes. Whether it be the schoolboy, or the schoolgirl, or the youth at college, or the mechanic in the town, or the politician in the senate, all have been the victims in one way or other of this most preposterous and pernicious of delusions. Wise men have lifted up their voices in vain; and at length, lest their own institutions should be outshone and should disappear in the folly of the hour, they have been obliged, as far as was conscientiously possible, to humour a spirit which they could not withstand, and make temporizing concessions at which they could not but inwardly smile.

Now I must guard, gentlemen, against any possible misconception of my meaning. Let me frankly declare then that I have no fear at all of the education of the people: the more education they have the better, so that it is really education. Next, as to the cheap publication of scientific and literary works which is now in vogue, I consider it a great advantage, convenience, and gain; that is, to those to whom education has given a capacity for using them. Further, I consider such innocent recreations as science and literature are able to furnish will be a very fit occupation of the thoughts and the leisure of young persons, and may be made the means of keeping them from bad employments and bad companions. Moreover, as to that superficial acquaintance with chemistry, and geology, and astronomy, and political economy, and modern history, and biography, and other branches of knowledge, which periodical literature and occasional lectures and scientific institutions diffuse through the community, I think it a graceful accomplishment, and a suitable, nay, in this day a necessary accomplishment, in the case of educated men. Nor, lastly, am I disparaging or discouraging the thorough acquisition of any one of these studies, or denying that, as far as it goes, such thorough acquisition is a real education of the mind. All I say is, call things by their right names, and do not confuse together ideas which are essentially different. A thorough knowledge of one science and a superficial acquaintance with many are not the same thing; a smattering of a hundred things or a memory for detail is not a philosophical or comprehensive view. Recreations are not education; accomplishments are not education. Do not say the people must be educated, when after all you only mean amused, refreshed, soothed, put into good spirits and good humour, or kept from vicious excesses. I do not say that such amusements, such occupations of mind, are not a great gain; but they are not education. You may as well call drawing and fencing education, as a general knowledge of botany or conchology. Stuffing birds or playing stringed instruments is an elegant pastime, and a resource to the idle, but it is not education; it does not form or cultivate the intellect. Education is a high word; it is the preparation for knowledge, and it is the imparting of knowledge in proportion to that preparation. We require intellectual eyes to know withal, as bodily eyes for sight. We need both objects and organs intellectual; we cannot gain them without setting about it; we cannot gain them in our sleep or by haphazard. The best telescope does not dispense with eyes; the printing press or the lecture room will assist us greatly, but we must be true to ourselves, we must be parties in the work. A university is, according to the usual designation, an Alma Mater, knowing her children one by one, not a foundry, or a mint, or a treadmill.

I protest to you, gentlemen, that if I had to choose between a so-called university which dispensed with residence and tutorial superintendence, and gave its degrees to any person who passed an examination in a wide range of subjects, and a university which had no professors or examinations at all, but merely brought a number of young men together for three or four years, and then sent them away, as the university of Oxford is said to have done some sixty years since, if I were asked which of these two methods was the better discipline of the intellect—mind, I do not say which is *morally* the better, for it is plain that compulsory study must be a good and idleness an intolerable mischief—but if I must determine which of the two courses was the more successful in training, moulding, enlarging the mind, which sent out men the more fitted for their secular duties, which produced better public men, men of the world, men whose names would descend to posterity, I have no hesitation in giving the preference to that university which did nothing, over that which exacted of its members an acquaintance with every science under the sun. And, paradox as this may seem, still if results be the test of systems, the influence of the public schools and colleges of England, in the course of the last century, at least will bear out one side of the contrast as I have drawn it. What would come, on the other hand, of the ideal systems of education which have fascinated the imagination of this age, could they ever take effect, and whether they would not produce a generation frivolous, narrow-minded, and resourceless, intellectually considered, is a fair subject for debate; but so far is certain, that the

universities and scholastic establishments to which I refer,
and which did little more than bring together first boys and
then youths in large numbers, these institutions, with
miserable deformities on the side of morals, with a hollow
profession of Christianity, and a heathen code of ethics—I
say at least they can boast of a succession of heroes and
statesmen, of literary men and philosophers, of men
conspicuous for great natural virtues, for habits of business,
for knowledge of life, for practical judgment, for cultivated
tastes, for accomplishments, who have made England
what it is—able to subdue the earth, able to domineer over
Catholics.

How is this to be explained? I suppose as follows:
When a multitude of young persons, keen, open-hearted,
sympathetic, and observant, as young persons are, come
together and freely mix with each other, they are sure to
learn one from another, even if there be no one to teach
them; the conversation of all is a series of lectures to each,
and they gain for themselves new ideas and views, fresh
matter of thought, and distinct principles for judging and
acting, day by day. An infant has to learn the meaning
of the information which its senses convey to it, and this
seems to be its employment. It fancies all that the eye
presents to it to be close to it, till it actually learns the
contrary, and thus by practice does it ascertain the relations
and uses of those first elements of knowledge which are
necessary for its animal existence. A parallel teaching is
necessary for our social being, and it is secured by a large
school or a college; and this effect may be fairly called in its
own department an enlargement of mind. It is seeing
the world on a small field with little trouble; for the pupils
or students come from very different places, and with
widely different notions, and there is much to generalize,
much to adjust, much to eliminate, there are interrelations
to be defined, and conventional rules to be established, in

the process, by which the whole assemblage is moulded together, and gains one tone and one character. Let it be clearly understood, I repeat it, that I am not taking into account moral or religious considerations; I am but saying that that youthful community will constitute a whole, it will embody a specific idea, it will represent a doctrine, it will administer a code of conduct, and it will furnish principles of thought and action. It will give birth to a living teaching, which in course of time will take the shape of a self-perpetuating tradition, or a *genius loci*, as it is sometimes called; which haunts the home where it has been born, and which imbues and forms, more or less, and one by one, every individual who is successively brought under its shadow. Thus it is that, independent of direct instruction on the part of superiors, there is a sort of self-education in the academic institutions of Protestant England; a characteristic tone of thought, a recognized standard of judgment is found in them which, as developed in the individual who is submitted to it, becomes a two-fold source of strength to him, both from the distinct stamp it impresses on his mind, and from the bond of union which it creates between him and others—effects which are shared by the authorities of the place, for they themselves have been educated in it, and at all times are exposed to the influence of its moral atmosphere. Here then is a real teaching, whatever be its standards and principles, true or false; and it at least tends towards cultivation of the in-tellect; it at least recognizes that knowledge is something more than a sort of passive reception of scraps and details; it is a something, and it does a something, which never will issue from the most strenuous efforts of a set of teachers with no mutual sympathies and no intercommunion, of a set of examiners with no opinions which they dare profess, and with no common principles, who are teaching or questioning a set of youths who do not know them, and do not know each other, on a large number of subjects, different in kind, and connected by no wide philosophy, three times a week, or three times a year, or once in three years, in chill lecture rooms or on a pompous anniversary.

Nay, self-education in any shape, in the most restricted sense, is preferable to a system of teaching which, professing so much, really does so little for the mind. Shut your college gates against the votary of knowledge, throw him back upon the searchings and the efforts of his own mind; he will gain by being spared an entrance into your babel. Few indeed there are who can dispense with the stimulus and support of instructors, or will do anything at all if left to themselves. And fewer still (though such great minds are to be found) who will not, from such unassisted attempts, contract a self-reliance and a self-esteem which are not only moral evils, but serious hindrances to the attainment of truth. And next to none, perhaps, or none, who will not be reminded from time to time of the disadvantage under which they lie by their imperfect grounding, by the breaks, deficiencies, and irregularities of their knowledge, by the eccentricity of opinion and the confusion of principle which they exhibit. They will be too often ignorant of what everyone knows and takes for granted, of that multitude of small truths which fall upon the mind like dust, impalpable and ever accumulating; they may be unable to converse, they may argue perversely, they may pride themselves on their worst paradoxes or their grossest truisms, they may be full of their own mode of viewing things, unwilling to be put out of their way, slow to enter into the minds of others; but, with these and whatever other liabilities upon their heads, they are likely to have more thought, more mind, more philosophy, more true enlargement, than those earnest but ill-used persons who are forced to load their minds with a score of subjects against an examination, who have too much on their hands to indulge themselves in thinking or investigation, who devour premiss and conclusion together with indiscriminate greediness, who hold whole sciences on faith, and commit demonstrations to memory, and who too often, as might be expected, when their period of education is passed, throw up all they have learned in disgust, having gained nothing really by their anxious labours, except perhaps the habit of application.

Yet such is the better specimen of the fruit of that ambitious system which has of late years been making way among us: for its result on ordinary minds, and on the common run of students, is less satisfactory still; they leave their place of education simply dissipated and relaxed by the multiplicity of subjects, which they have never really mastered, and so shallow as not even to know their shallowness. How much better, I say, is it for the active and thoughtful intellect, where such is to be found, to eschew the college and the university altogether, than to submit to a drudgery so ignoble, a mockery so contumelious! How much more profitable for the independent mind, after the mere rudiments of education, to range through a library at random, taking down books as they meet him, and pursuing the trains of thought which his mother wit suggests! How much healthier to wander into the fields, and there with the exiled prince to find 'tongues in the trees, books in the running brooks'! How much more genuine an education is that of the poor boy in the poem [1]—a poem whether in conception or in execution one of the most touching in our language—who, not in the wide world, but ranging day by day around his widowed mother's

---

[1] Crabbe's *Tales of the Hall*. This poem, let me say, I read on its first publication, above thirty years ago, with extreme delight, and have never lost my love of it; and on taking it up lately found I was even more touched by it than heretofore. A work which can please in youth and age seems to fulfil (in logical language) the *accidental definition* of a classic.

home, 'a dexterous gleaner' in a narrow field, and with only such slender outfit

> as the village school and books a few
> Supplied,

contrived from the beach, and the quay, and the fisher's boat, and the inn's fireside, and the tradesman's shop, and the shepherd's walk, and the smuggler's hut, and the mossy moor, and the screaming gulls, and the restless waves, to fashion for himself a philosophy and a poetry of his own!

But in a large subject I am exceeding my necessary limits. Gentlemen, I must conclude abruptly, and postpone any summing up of my argument, should that be necessary, to another day.

DISCOURSE VI

LIBERAL KNOWLEDGE VIEWED IN RELATION TO
PROFESSIONAL

I HAVE been insisting, in my two preceding discourses, first on the cultivation of the intellect, as an end which may reasonably be pursued for its own sake; and next on the nature of that cultivation, or what that cultivation consists in. Truth of whatever kind is the proper object of the intellect; its cultivation then lies in fitting it to apprehend and contemplate truth. Now the intellect in its present state, with exceptions which need not here be specified, does no⁺ discern truth intuitively, or as a whole. We know, not by a direct and simple vision, not at a glance, but as it were by piecemeal and accumulation, by a mental process, by going round an object, by the comparison, the combination, the mutual correction, the continual adaptation of many partial notions, by the joint application and concentration upon it of many faculties and exercises of mind. Such a union and concert of the intellectual powers, such an enlargement and development, such a comprehensiveness, is necessarily a matter of training. And again, such a training is a matter of rule; it is not mere application, however exemplary, which introduces the mind to truth, nor the reading many books, nor the getting up many subjects, nor the witnessing many experiments, nor the attending many lectures. All this is short of enough; a man may have done it all, yet be lingering in the vestibule of knowledge: he may not realize what his mouth utters; he may not see with his mental eye what confronts him; he may have no grasp of things as they are;

128

or at least he may have no power at all of advancing one step forward of himself, in consequence of what he has already acquired, no power of discriminating between truth and falsehood, of sifting out the grains of truth from the mass, of arranging things according to their real value, and, if I may use the phrase, of building up ideas. Such a power is the result of a scientific formation of mind; it is an acquired faculty of judgment, of clear-sightedness, of sagacity, of wisdom, of philosophical reach of mind, and of intellectual self-possession and repose—qualities which do not come of mere acquirement. The bodily eye, the organ for apprehending material objects, is provided by nature; the eye of the mind, of which the object is truth, is the work of discipline and habit.

This process of training, by which the intellect, instead of being formed or sacrificed to some particular or accidental purpose, some specific trade or profession, or study or science, is disciplined for its own sake, for the perception of its own proper object, and for its own highest culture, is called liberal education; and though there is no one in whom it is carried as far as is conceivable, or whose intellect would be a pattern of what intellects should be made, yet there is scarcely anyone but may gain an idea of what real training is, and at least look towards it, and make its true scope and result, not something else, his standard of excellence; and numbers there are who may submit themselves to it, and secure it to themselves in good measure. And to set forth the right standard, and to train according to it, and to help forward all students towards it according to their various capacities, this I conceive to be the business of a university.

Now this is what some great men are very slow to allow; they insist that education should be confined to some particular and narrow end, and should issue in some definite work, which can be weighed and measured. They argue as if everything, as well as every person, had its price; and that where there has been a great outlay they have a right to expect a return in kind. This they call making education and instruction 'useful,' and 'utility' becomes their watchword. With a fundamental principle of this nature, they very naturally go on to ask what there is to show for the expense of a university; what is the real worth in the market of the article called a liberal education, on the supposition that it does not teach us definitely how to advance our manufactures, or to improve our lands, or to better our civil economy; or again, if it does not at once make this man a lawyer, that an engineer, and that a surgeon; or at least if it does not lead to discoveries in chemistry, astronomy, geology, magnetism, and science of every kind.

This question, as might have been expected, has been keenly debated in the present age, and formed one main subject of the controversy to which I referred in the introduction to the present discourses, as having been sustained in the first decade of this century by a celebrated Northern review on the one hand, and defenders of the university of Oxford on the other. Hardly had the authorities of that ancient seat of learning, waking from their long neglect, set on foot a plan for the education of the youth committed to them, than the representatives of science and literature in the city, which has sometimes been called the Northern Athens, remonstrated with their gravest arguments and their most brilliant satire against the direction and shape which the reform was taking. Nothing would content them but that the university should be set to rights on the basis of the philosophy of utility; a philosophy, as they seem to have thought, which needed but to be proclaimed in order to be embraced. In truth, they were little aware of the depth and force of the principles on which the authorities academical were proceeding, and, this being so, it was not to be expected that they would be allowed to walk at leisure over the field of controversy which they had selected. Accordingly they were encountered in behalf of the university by two men of great name and influence in their day, of very different minds, but united, as by collegiate ties, so in the clear-sighted and large view which they took of the whole subject of liberal education; and the defence thus provided for the Oxford studies has kept its ground to this day.

Let me be allowed to devote a few words to the memory of distinguished persons under the shadow of whose name I once lived, and by whose doctrine I am now profiting. In the heart of Oxford there is a small plot of ground, hemmed in by public thoroughfares, which has been the possession and the home of one society for above five hundred years. In the old time of Boniface VIII and John XXII, in the age of Scotus and Occam and Dante, before Wiclif or Huss had kindled those miserable fires which are still raging to the ruin of the highest interests of man, an unfortunate king of England, Edward II, flying from the field of Bannockburn, is said to have made a vow to the Blessed Virgin to found a religious house in her honour if he got back to safety. Prompted and aided by his almoner, he decided on placing this house in the city of Alfred; and the image of our Lady which is opposite its entrance gate is the token of the vow and its fulfilment to this day. King and almoner have long been in the dust, and strangers have entered into their inheritance, and their creed has been forgotten, and their holy rites disowned; but day by day a memento is still made in the holy sacrifice by at least one Catholic priest, once a member of that college, for the souls of those Catholic benefactors who fed him there for so many years. The visitor whose curiosity has been excited by its present fame gazes perhaps with something of disappointment on a collection of buildings which have with them so few of the circumstances of dignity or wealth. Broad quadrangles, high halls and chambers, ornamented cloisters, stately walks, or umbrageous gardens, a throng of students, ample revenues, or a glorious history, none of these things were the portion of that old Catholic foundation; nothing in short which to the common eye sixty years ago would have given tokens of what it was to be. But it had at that time a spirit working within it which enabled its inmates to do, amid its seeming insignificance, what no other body in the place could equal; not a very abstruse gift or extraordinary boast, but a rare one, the honest purpose to administer the trust committed to them in such a way as their conscience pointed out as best. So, whereas the colleges of Oxford are self-electing bodies, the fellows in each perpetually filling up for themselves the vacancies which occur in their number, the members of this foundation determined, at a time when, either from evil custom or from ancient statute, such a thing was not known elsewhere, to throw open their fellowships to the competition of all comers, and in the choice of associates henceforth to cast to the winds every personal motive and feeling, family connection, and friendship, and patronage, and political interest, and local claim, and prejudice, and party jealousy, and to elect solely on public and patriotic grounds. Nay, with a remarkable independence of mind they resolved that even the table of honours awarded to literary merit by the university, in its new system of examination for degrees, should not fetter their judgment as electors; but that at all risks, and whatever criticism it might cause, and whatever odium they might incur, they would select the men, whoever they were, to be children of their founder, whom they thought in their consciences to be most likely from their intellectual and moral qualities to please him if (as they expressed it) he were still upon earth, most likely to do honour to his college, most likely to promote the objects which they believed he had at heart. Such persons did not promise to be the disciples of a low utilitarianism; and consequently, as their collegiate reform synchronized with that reform of the academical body in which they bore a principal part, it was not unnatural that, when the storm broke upon the university from the North, their Alma Mater, whom they loved, should have found her first defenders within the walls of that small college which had first put itself into a condition to be her champion.

These defenders, gentlemen, I have said were two, of whom the more distinguished was the late Dr Copleston, then a fellow of the college, successively its provost, and Protestant Bishop of Llandaff. In that society which owes so much to him his name lives, and ever will live, for the distinction which his talents bestowed on it, for the academical importance to which he raised it, for the generosity of spirit, the liberality of sentiment, and the kindness of heart with which he adorned it, and which even those who had least sympathy with some aspects of his mind and character could not but admire and love. Men come to their meridian at various periods of their lives; the last years of the eminent person I am speaking of were given to duties which, I am told, have been the means of endearing him to numbers, but which afforded no scope for that peculiar vigour and keenness of mind which enabled him, when a young man, single-handed, with easy gallantry, to encounter and overthrow the charge of three giants of the North combined against him. I believe I am right in saying that, in the progress of the controversy, the most scientific, the most critical, and the most witty of that literary company, all of them now, as he himself, removed from this visible scene, Professor Playfair, Lord Jeffrey, and the Reverend Sydney Smith, threw together their several efforts into one article of their review, in order to crush and pound to dust the audacious controvertist who had come out against them in defence of his own institutions.   To have even contended with such men was a sufficient voucher for his ability, even before we open his pamphlets, and have actual evidence of the good sense, the spirit, the scholar-like taste, and the purity of style by which they are distinguished.

He was supported in the controversy, on the same general principles, but with more of method and distinctness, and, I will add, with greater force and beauty and perfection, both of thought and of language, by the other distinguished writer, to whom I have already referred, Mr Davison; who, though not so well known to the world in his day, has left more behind him than the provost of Oriel to make his name remembered by posterity.   This thoughtful man, who was the admired and intimate friend of a very remarkable person, whom, whether he wish it or not, numbers revere and love as the first author of the subsequent movement in the Protestant Church towards Catholicism,[1] this grave and philosophical writer, whose works I can never look into without sighing that such a man was lost to the Catholic Church, as Dr Butler before him, by some early bias or some fault of self-education—he, in a review of a work by Mr Edgeworth on professional education, which attracted a good deal of attention in its day, goes leisurely over the same ground which had already been rapidly traversed by Dr Copleston, and, though professedly employed upon Mr Edgeworth, is really replying to the Northern critic who had brought that writer's work into notice, and to a far greater author than either of them, who in a past age had argued on the same side.

The author to whom I allude is no other than Locke. That celebrated philosopher has preceded the Edinburgh reviewers in condemning the ordinary subjects in which

[1] Mr Keble, vicar of Hursley, late fellow of Oriel, and Professor of Poetry in the university of Oxford.

boys are instructed at school, on the ground that they are not needed by them in after life; and before quoting what his disciples have said in the present century, I will refer to a few passages of the master. ''Tis matter of astonishment,' he says in his work on education, 'that men of quality and parts should suffer themselves to be so far misled by custom and implicit faith. Reason, if consulted with, would advise that their children's time should be spent in acquiring what might be *useful* to them when they come to be men, rather than that their heads should be stuffed with a deal of trash, a great part whereof they usually never do ('tis certain they never need to) think on again as long as they live; and so much of it as does stick by them they are only the worse for.'

And so again, speaking of verse-making, he says: 'I know not what reason a father can have to wish his son a poet, who does not desire him to *bid defiance to all other callings and business*; which is not yet the worst of the case for, if he proves a successful rhymer, and gets once the reputation of a wit, I desire it to be considered what company and places he is likely to spend his time in, nay, and estate too; for it is very seldom seen that anyone discovers *mines of gold or silver in Parnassus*. 'Tis a pleasant air but a barren soil.'

In another passage he distinctly limits utility in education to its bearing on the future profession or trade of the pupil, that is, he scorns the idea of any education of the intellect, simply as such. 'Can there be anything more ridiculous,' he asks, 'than that a father should waste his own money, and his son's time, in setting him to *learn the Roman language*, when at the same time he *designs him for a trade* wherein he, having no use of Latin, fails not to forget that little which he brought from school, and which 'tis ten to one he abhors for the ill-usage it procured him? Could it be believed, unless we have everywhere amongst us examples of it, that a child should be forced to learn the rudiments of a language which *he is never to use in the course of life that he is designed to,* and neglect all the while the writing a good hand, and casting accounts, which are of great advantage in all conditions of life, and to most trades indispensably necessary?' Nothing of course can be more absurd than to neglect in education those matters which are necessary for a boy's future calling; but the tone of Locke's remarks evidently implies more than this, and is condemnatory of any teaching which tends to the general cultivation of the mind.

Now to turn to his modern disciples. The study of the classics has been made the basis of the Oxford education, in the reforms which I have spoken of, and the Edinburgh reviewers protested, after the manner of Locke, that no good could come of a system which was not based upon the principle of utility.

'Classical literature,' they said, 'is the great object at Oxford. Many minds so employed have produced many works and much fame in that department; but if all liberal arts and sciences *useful to human life* had been taught there, if *some* had dedicated themselves to *chemistry,* *some* to *mathematics,* *some* to *experimental philosophy,* and if *every* attainment had been honoured in the mixed ratio of its difficulty and *utility,* the system of such a university would have been much more valuable, but the splendour of its name something less.'

Utility may be made the end of education in two respects: either as regards the individual educated, or the community at large. In which light do these writers regard it? In the latter. So far they differ from Locke, for they consider the advancement of science as the supreme and real end of a university. This is brought into view in the sentences which follow.

'When a university has been doing *useless* things for a

long time, it appears at first degrading to them to be *useful*. A set of lectures on political economy would be discouraged in Oxford, probably despised, probably not permitted. To discuss the inclosure of commons, and to dwell upon imports and exports, to come so near to common life, would seem to be undignified and contemptible. In the same manner, the Parr or the Bentley of the day would be scandalized, in a university, to be put on a level with the discoverer of a neutral salt; and yet *what other measure is there of dignity in intellectual labour but usefulness*? And what ought the term university to mean, but a place where every science is taught which is liberal, and at the same time useful to mankind? Nothing would so much tend to bring classical literature within proper bounds as *a steady and invariable appeal to utility* in our appreciation of all human knowledge. . . . *Looking always to real utility as our guide*, we should see, with equal pleasure, a studious and inquisitive mind arranging the productions of nature, investigating the qualities of bodies, or mastering the difficulties of the learned languages. We should not care whether he was chemist, naturalist, or scholar, because we know it to be as *necessary* that matter should be studied and subdued *to the use of man*, as that taste should be gratified, and imagination inflamed.'

Such then is the enunciation, as far as words go, of the theory of utility in education; and both on its own account, and for the sake of the able men who have advocated it, it has a claim on the attention of those whose principles I am here representing. Certainly it is specious to contend that nothing is worth pursuing but what is useful, and that life is not long enough to expend upon interesting, or curious, or brilliant trifles. Nay, in one sense I will grant it is more than specious, it is true; but if so, how do I propose directly to meet the objection? Why, gentlemen, I have really met it already, viz. in laying down that intellectual culture is its own end; for what has its *end* in itself, has its *use* in itself also. I say, if a liberal education consists in the culture of the intellect, and if that culture be in itself a good, here, without going further, is an answer to Locke's question; for if a healthy body is a good in itself, why is not a healthy intellect? And if a College of Physicians is a useful institution, because it contemplates bodily health, why is not an academical body, though it were simply and solely engaged in imparting vigour and beauty and grasp to the intellectual portion of our nature? And the reviewers I am quoting seem to allow this in their better moments, in a passage which, putting aside the question of its justice in fact, is sound and true in the principles to which it appeals:

'The present state of classical education,' they say, 'cultivates the *imagination* a great deal too much, and other *habits of mind* a great deal too little, and trains up many young men in a style of elegant imbecility, utterly unworthy of the talents with which nature has endowed them. . . . The matter of fact is, that a classical scholar of twenty-three or twenty-four is a man principally conversant with works of imagination. His feelings are quick, his fancy lively, and his taste good. Talents for *speculation* and *original inquiry* he has none, nor has he formed the invaluable *habit of pushing things up to their first principles*, or of collecting dry and unamusing facts as the materials for reasoning. All the solid and masculine parts of his *understanding* are left wholly without *cultivation*; he hates the pain of thinking, and suspects every man whose boldness and originality call upon him to defend his opinions and prove his assertions.'

Now I am not at present concerned with the specific question of classical education; else I might reasonably question the justice of calling an intellectual discipline which embraces the study of Aristotle, Thucydides, and

Tacitus, which involves scholarship and antiquities, *imaginative*; still so far I readily grant, that the cultivation of the 'understanding,' of a 'talent for speculation and original inquiry,' and of 'the habit of pushing things up to their first principles,' is a principal portion of a *good* or *liberal* education. If then the reviewers consider such cultivation the characteristic of a *useful* education, as they seem to do in the foregoing passage, it follows that what they mean by 'useful' is just what I mean by 'good' or 'liberal': and Locke's question becomes a verbal one. Whether youths are to be taught Latin or verse-making will depend on the *fact*, whether these studies tend to mental culture; but, however this is determined, so far is clear, that in that mental culture consists what I have called a liberal or non-professional, and what the reviewers call a useful education.

This is the obvious answer which may be made to those who urge upon us the claims of utility in our plans of education; but I am not going to leave the subject here: I mean to take a wider view of it. Let us take 'useful,' as Locke takes it, in its proper and popular sense, and then we enter upon a large field of thought, to which I cannot do justice in one discourse, though to-day's is all the space that I can give to it. I say, let us take 'useful' to mean, not what is simply good, but what *tends* to good, or is the *instrument* of good; and in this sense also, gentlemen, I will show you how a liberal education is truly and fully a useful, though it be not a professional education. 'Good' indeed means one thing, and 'useful' means another; but I lay it down as a principle which will save us a great deal of anxiety that, though the useful is not always good, the good is always useful. Good is not only good, but reproductive of good; this is one of its attributes; nothing is excellent, beautiful, perfect, desirable for its own sake, but it overflows, and spreads the likeness of itself all around itself. Good is prolific; it is not only good to the eye, but to the taste; it not only attracts us, but it communicates itself; it excites first our admiration and love, then our desire and our gratitude, and that in proportion to its intenseness and fullness in particular instances. A great good will impart great good. If then the intellect is so excellent a portion of us, and its cultivation so excellent, it is not only beautiful, perfect, admirable, and noble in itself, but in a true and high sense it must be useful to the possessor and to all around him; not useful in any low, mechanical, mercantile sense, but as diffusing good, or as a blessing, or a gift, or power, or a treasure, first to the owner, then through him to the world. I say then if a liberal education be good, it must necessarily be useful too.

You will see what I mean by the parallel of bodily health. Health is a good in itself, though nothing came of it, and is especially worth seeking and cherishing; yet after all, the blessings which attend its presence are so great, while they are so close to it and so redound back upon it and encircle it, that we never think of it except as useful as well as good, and praise and prize it for what it does, as well as for what it is, though at the same time we cannot point out any definite and distinct work or production which it can be said to effect. And so as regards intellectual culture, I am far from denying utility in this large sense as the end of education, when I lay it down that the culture of the intellect is a good in itself and its own end; I do not exclude from the idea of intellectual culture what it cannot but be, from the very nature of things; I only deny that we must be able to point out, before we have any right to call it useful, some art, or business, or profession, or trade, or work as resulting from it, and as its real and complete end. The parallel is exact: as the body may be sacrificed to some manual or other toil, whether moderate or oppressive, so may the intellect be devoted to some specific profession; and I do not call *this* the culture of the intellect. Again, as some member or organ of the body may be inordinately used and developed, so may memory, or imagination, or the reasoning faculty; and *this* again is not intellectual culture. On the other hand, as the body may be tended, cherished, and exercised with a simple view to its general health, so may the intellect also be generally exercised in order to its perfect state; and this *is* its cultivation.

Again, as health ought to precede labour of the body, and as a man in health can do what an unhealthy man cannot do, and as of this health the properties are strength, energy, agility, graceful carriage and action, manual dexterity, and endurance of fatigue, so in like manner general culture of mind is the best aid to professional and scientific study, and educated men can do what illiterate cannot; and the man who has learned to think and to reason and to compare and to discriminate and to analyse, who has refined his taste, and formed his judgment, and sharpened his mental vision, will not indeed at once be a lawyer, or a pleader, or an orator, or a statesman, or a physician, or a good landlord, or a man of business, or a soldier, or an engineer, or a chemist, or a geologist, or an antiquarian, but he will be placed in that state of intellect in which he can take up any one of the sciences or callings I have referred to, or any other for which he has a taste or special talent, with an ease, a grace, a versatility, and a success to which another is a stranger. In this sense then, and as yet I have said but a very few words on a large subject, mental culture is emphatically *useful*.

If then I am arguing, and shall argue, against professional or scientific knowledge as the sufficient end of a university education, let me not be supposed, gentlemen, to be disrespectful towards particular studies, or arts, or vocations and those who are engaged in them. In saying that law or medicine is not the end of a university course, I do not mean to imply that the university does not teach law or medicine. What indeed can it teach at all, if it does not teach something particular? It teaches *all* knowledge by teaching all *branches* of knowledge, and in no other way. I do but say that there will be this distinction as regards a professor of law, or of medicine, or of geology, or of political economy, in a university and out of it, that out of a university he is in danger of being absorbed and narrowed by his pursuit, and of giving lectures which are the lectures of nothing more than a lawyer, physician, geologist, or political economist; whereas in a university he will just know where he and his science stand, he has come to it, as it were, from a height, he has taken a survey of all knowledge, he is kept from extravagance by the very rivalry of other studies, he has gained from them a special illumination and largeness of mind and freedom and self-possession, and he treats his own in consequence with a philosophy and a resource which belong not to the study itself, but to his liberal education.

This then is how I should solve the fallacy, for so I must call it, by which Locke and his disciples would frighten us from cultivating the intellect, under the notion that no education is useful which does not teach us some temporal calling, or some mechanical art, or some physical secret. I say that a cultivated intellect, because it is a good in itself, brings with it a power and a grace to every work and occupation which it undertakes, and enables us to be more useful, and to a greater number. There is a duty we owe to human society as such, to the state to which we belong, to the sphere in which we move, to the individuals towards whom we are variously related, and whom we successively encounter in life; and that philosophical or liberal education, as I have called it, which is the proper function of a university, if it refuses the foremost place to professional interests, does but postpone them to the formation of the citizen, and, while it subserves the larger interests of philanthropy, prepares also for the successful prosecution of those merely personal objects which at first sight it seems to disparage.

And now, gentlemen, I wish to be allowed to enforce in detail what I have been saying by some extracts from the writings to which I have already alluded, and to which I am so greatly indebted.

'It is an undisputed maxim in political economy,' says Dr Copleston, 'that the separation of professions and the division of labour tend to the perfection of every art, to the wealth of nations, to the general comfort and well-being of the community. This principle of division is in some instances pursued so far as to excite the wonder of people to whose notice it is for the first time pointed out. There is no saying to what extent it may not be carried; and the more the powers of each individual are concentrated in one employment, the greater skill and quickness will he naturally display in performing it. But, while he thus contributes more effectually to the accumulation of national wealth, he becomes himself more and more degraded as a rational being. In proportion as his sphere of action is narrowed his mental powers and habits become contracted; and he resembles a subordinate part of some powerful machinery, useful in its place, but insignificant and worthless out of it. If it be necessary, as it is beyond all question necessary, that society should be split into divisions and sub-divisions, in order that its several duties may be well performed, yet we must be careful not to yield up ourselves wholly and exclusively to the guidance of this system; we must observe what its evils are, and we should modify and restrain it by bringing into action other principles, which may serve as a check and counterpoise to the main force.

'There can be no doubt that every art is improved by

confining the professor of it to that single study. But *although the art itself is advanced by this concentration of mind in its service, the individual who is confined to it goes back.* The advantage of the community is nearly in an inverse ratio with his own.

'Society itself requires some other contribution from each individual, besides the particular duties of his profession. And, if no such liberal intercourse be established, it is the common failing of human nature to be engrossed with petty views and interests, to underrate the importance of all in which we are not concerned, and to carry our partial notions into cases where they are inapplicable, to act, in short, as so many unconnected units, displacing and repelling one another.

'In the cultivation of literature is found that common link which, among the higher and middling departments of life, unites the jarring sects and subdivisions into one interest, which supplies common topics, and kindles common feelings, unmixed with those narrow prejudices with which all professions are more or less infected. The knowledge, too, which is thus acquired expands and enlarges the mind, excites its faculties, and calls those limbs and muscles into freer exercise which, by too constant use in one direction, not only acquire an illiberal air, but are apt also to lose somewhat of their native play and energy. And thus, without directly qualifying a man for any of the employments of life, it enriches and ennobles all. Without teaching him the peculiar business of any one office or calling, it enables him to act his part in each of them with better grace and more elevated carriage; and, if happily planned and conducted, is a main ingredient in that complete and generous education which fits a man "to perform justly, skilfully, and magnanimously all the offices, both private and public, of peace and war." '[1]

[1] *Vide* Milton on education.

The view of liberal education advocated in these extracts is expanded by Mr Davison in the essay to which I have already referred. He lays more stress on the 'usefulness' of liberal education in the larger sense of the word than his predecessor in the controversy. Instead of arguing that the utility of knowledge to the individual varies inversely with its utility to the public, he chiefly employs himself on the suggestions contained in Dr Copleston's last sentences. He shows, first, that a liberal education is something far higher, even in the scale of utility, than what is commonly called a useful education, and next that it is necessary or useful for the purposes even of that professional education which commonly engrosses the title of useful. The former of these two theses he recommends to us in an argument from which the following passages are selected:

'It is to take a very contracted view of life,' he says, 'to think with great anxiety how persons may be educated to superior skill in their department, comparatively neglecting or excluding the more liberal and enlarged cultivation. In his (Mr Edgeworth's) system, the value of every attainment is to be measured by its subserviency to a calling. The specific duties of that calling are exalted at the cost of those free and independent tastes and virtues which come in to sustain the common relations of society, and raise the individual in them. In short, a man is to be usurped by his profession. He is to be clothed in its garb from head to foot. His virtues, his science, and his ideas are all to be put into a gown or uniform, and the whole man to be shaped, pressed, and stiffened in the exact mould of his technical character. Any interloping accomplishments, or a faculty which cannot be taken into public pay, if they are to be indulged in him at all, must creep along under the cloak of his more serviceable privileged merits. Such is the state of perfection to which the spirit and general tendency of this system would lead us.

'But the professional character is not the only one which a person engaged in a profession has to support. He is not always upon duty. There are services he owes which are neither parochial, nor forensic, nor military, nor to be described by any such epithet of civil regulation, and yet are in nowise inferior to those that bear these authoritative titles; inferior neither in their intrinsic value, nor their moral import, nor their impression upon society. As a friend, as a companion, as a citizen at large; in the connections of domestic life; in the improvement and embellishment of his leisure, he has a sphere of action, revolving, if you please, within the sphere of his profession, but not clashing with it, in which if he can show none of the advantages of an improved understanding, whatever may be his skill or proficiency in the other, he is no more than an ill-educated man.

'There is a certain faculty in which all nations of any refinement are great practitioners. It is not taught at school or college as a distinct science, though it deserves that what is taught there should be made to have some reference to it; nor is it endowed at all by the public; everybody being obliged to exercise it for himself in person, which he does to the best of his skill. But in nothing is there a greater difference than in the manner of doing it. The advocates of professional learning will smile when we tell them that this same faculty which we would have encouraged is simply that of speaking good sense in English, without fee or reward, in common conversation. They will smile when we lay some stress upon it; but in reality it is no such trifle as they imagine. Look into the huts of savages and see, for there is nothing to listen to, the dismal blank of their stupid hours of silence; their professional avocations of war and hunting are over and, having nothing to do, they have nothing to say. Turn to improved life, and you find conversation in all its forms the medium of something more than an idle pleasure; indeed, a very active agent in circulating and forming the opinions, tastes, and feelings of a whole people. It makes of itself a considerable affair. Its topics are the most promiscuous—all those which do not belong to any particular province. As for its power and influence, we may fairly say that it is of just the same consequence to a man's immediate society how he talks, as how he acts. Now of all those who furnish their share to rational conversation, a mere adept in his own art is universally admitted to be the worst. The sterility and uninstructiveness of such a person's social hours are quite proverbial. Or if he escape being dull, it is only by launching into ill-timed, learned loquacity. We do not desire of him lectures or speeches; and he has nothing else to give. Among benches he may be powerful; but seated on a chair he is quite another person. On the other hand, we may affirm that one of the best companions is a man who, to the accuracy and research of a profession, has joined a free excursive acquaintance with various learning, and caught from it the spirit of general observation.'

Having thus shown that a liberal education is a real benefit to the subjects of it, as members of society, in the various duties and circumstances and accidents of life, he goes on, in the next place, to show that, over and above those direct services which might fairly be expected of it, it actually subserves the discharge of those particular functions, and the pursuit of those particular advantages, which are connected with professional exertion, and to which professional education is directed.

'We admit,' he observes, 'that when a person makes a business of one pursuit, he is in the right way to eminence in it; and that divided attention will rarely give excellence in many. But our assent will go no further. For to think that the way to prepare a person for excelling in any one pursuit (and that is the only point in hand) is to fetter his early studies, and cramp the first development of his mind, by a reference to the exigencies of that pursuit barely, is a very different notion, and one which, we apprehend, deserves to be exploded rather than received. Possibly a few of the abstract, insulated kinds of learning might be approached in that way. The exceptions to be made are very few, and need not be recited. But for the acquisition of professional and practical ability such maxims are death to it. The main ingredients of that ability are requisite knowledge and cultivated faculties; but of the two, the latter is by far the chief. A man of well-improved faculties has the command of another's knowledge. A man without them has not the command of his own.

'Of the intellectual powers, the judgment is that which takes the foremost lead in life. How to form it to the two habits it ought to possess, of exactness and vigour, is the problem. It would be ignorant presumption so much as to hint at any routine of method by which these qualities may with certainty be impaired to every or any understanding. Still, however, we may safely lay it down that they are not to be got "by a gatherer of simples," but are the combined essence and extracts of many different things, drawn from much varied reading and discipline first, and observation afterwards. For if there be a single intelligible point on this head, it is that a man who has been trained to think upon one subject or for one subject only will never be a good judge even in that one: whereas the enlargement of his circle gives him increased knowledge and power in a rapidly increasing ratio. So much do ideas act, not as solitary units, but by grouping and combination; and so clearly do all the things that fall within the proper province of the same faculty of the mind intertwine with and support each other. Judgment lives as it were by comparison and discrimination. Can it be doubted, then, whether the

range and extent of that assemblage of things upon which
it is practised in its first essays are of use to its power?

'To open our way a little further on this matter, we will
define what we mean by the power of judgment, and then
try to ascertain among what kind of studies the improvement of it may be expected at all.

'Judgment does not stand here for a certain homely,
useful quality of intellect, that guards a person from com-
mitting mistakes to the injury of his fortunes or common
reputation; but for that master principle of business,
literature, and talent, which gives him strength in any
subject he chooses to grapple with, and enables him to
seize the strong point in it. Whether this definition be
metaphysically correct or not, it comes home to the substance of our inquiry. It describes the power that everyone desires to possess when he comes to act in a profession,
or elsewhere, and corresponds with our best idea of a
cultivated mind.

'Next, it will not be denied that in order to do any good
to the judgment, the mind must be employed upon such
subjects as come within the cognizance of that faculty, and
give some real exercise to its perceptions. Here we have
a rule of selection by which the different parts of learning
may be classed for our purpose. Those which belong to
the province of the judgment are religion (in its evidences
and interpretation), ethics, history, eloquence, poetry,
theories of general speculation, the fine arts, and works of
wit. Great as the variety of these large divisions of learning may appear, they are all held in union by two capital
principles of connection. First, they are all quarried out
of one and the same great subject of man's moral, social,
and feeling nature. And secondly, they are all under the
control (more or less strict) of the same power of moral
reason.'

If these studies, he continues, 'be such as give a direct

play and exercise to the faculty of the judgment, then they are the true basis of education for the active and inventive powers, whether destined for a profession or any other use. Miscellaneous as the assemblage may appear, of history, eloquence, poetry, ethics, etc., blended together, they will all conspire in a union of effect. They are necessary mutually to explain and interpret each other. The knowledge derived from them all will amalgamate, and the habits of a mind versed and practised in them by turns will join to produce a richer vein of thought, and of more general and practical application, than could be obtained of any single one, as the fusion of the metals into Corinthian brass gave the artist his most ductile and perfect material. Might we venture to imitate an author (whom indeed it is much safer to take as an authority than to attempt to copy), Lord Bacon, in some of his concise illustrations of the comparative utility of the different studies, we should say that history would give fullness, moral philosophy strength, and poetry elevation to the understanding. Such in reality is the natural force and tendency of the studies; but there are few minds susceptible enough to derive from them any sort of virtue adequate to those high expressions. We must be contented therefore to lower our panegyric to this, that a person cannot avoid receiving some infusion and tincture, at least, of those several qualities from that course of diversified reading. One thing is unquestionable, that the elements of general reason are not to be found fully and truly expressed in any one kind of study; and that he who would wish to know her idiom must read it in many books.

'If different studies are useful for aiding, they are still more useful for correcting each other; for as they have their particular merits severally, so they have their defects, and the most extensive acquaintance with one can produce only an intellect either too flashy or too jejune, or infected with some other fault of confined reading. History, for example, shows things as they are, that is, the morals and interests of men disfigured and perverted by all their imperfections of passion, folly, and ambition; philosophy strips the picture too much; poetry adorns it too much; the concentrated lights of the three correct the false peculiar colouring of each, and show us the truth. The right mode of thinking upon it is to be had from them taken all together, as everyone must know who has seen their united contributions of thought and feeling expressed in the masculine sentiment of our immortal statesman, Mr Burke, whose eloquence is inferior only to his more admirable wisdom. If any mind improved like his is to be our instructor, we must go to the fountain-head of things as he did, and study not his works but his method; by the one we may become feeble imitators, by the other arrive at some ability of our own. But, as all biography assures us, he, and every other able thinker, has been formed, not by a parsimonious admeasurement of studies to some definite future object (which is Mr Edgeworth's maxim), but by taking a wide and liberal compass, and thinking a great deal on many subjects with no better end in view than because the exercise was one which made them more rational and intelligent beings.'

But I must bring these extracts to an end. To-day I have confined myself to saying that that training of the intellect, which is best for the individual himself, best enables him to discharge his duties to society. The philosopher, indeed, and the man of the world differ in their very notion, but the methods by which they are respectively formed are pretty much the same. The philosopher has the same command of matters of thought which the true citizen and gentleman has of matters of business and conduct. If then a practical end must be assigned to a university course, I say it is that of training good members of society. Its art is the art of social life, and its end is fitness for the world. It neither confines its views to particular professions on the one hand, nor creates heroes or inspires genius on the other. Works indeed of genius fall under no art; heroic minds come under no rule; a university is not a birth-place of poets or of immortal authors, of founders of schools, leaders of colonies, or conquerors of nations. It does not promise a generation of Aristotles or Newtons, of Napoleons or Washingtons, of Raphaels or Shakespeares, though such miracles of nature it has before now contained within its precincts. Nor is it content on the other hand with forming the critic or the experimentalist, the economist or the engineer, though such too it includes within its scope. But a university training is the great ordinary means to a great but ordinary end; it aims at raising the intellectual tone of society, at cultivating the public mind, at purifying the national taste, at supplying true principles to popular enthusiasm and fixed aims to popular aspiration, at giving enlargement and sobriety to the ideas of the age, at facilitating the exercise of political power, and refining the intercourse of private life. It is the education which gives a man a clear conscious view of his own opinions and judgments, a truth in developing them, an eloquence in expressing them, and a force in urging them. It teaches him to see things as they are, to go right to the point, to disentangle a skein of thought, to detect what is sophistical, and to discard what is irrelevant. It prepares him to fill any post with credit, and to master any subject with facility. It shows him how to accommodate himself to others, how to throw himself into their state of mind, how to bring before them his own, how to influence them, how to come to an understanding with them, how to bear with them. He is at home in any society, he has common ground with every class; he knows when to speak and when to be silent; he is able to converse, he is able to listen; he can ask a question pertinently, and gain a lesson seasonably, when he has nothing to impart himself; he is ever ready, yet never in the way; he is a pleasant companion, and a comrade you can depend upon; he knows when to be serious and when to trifle, and he has a sure tact which enables him to trifle with gracefulness and to be serious with effect. He has the repose of a mind which lives in itself, while it lives in the world, and which has resources for its happiness at home when it cannot go abroad. He has a gift which serves him in public, and supports him in retirement, without which good fortune is but vulgar, and with which failure and disappointment have a charm. The art which tends to make a man all this is in the object which it pursues as useful as the art of wealth or the art of health, though it is less susceptible of method, and less tangible, less certain, less complete in its result.

DISCOURSE VII

LIBERAL KNOWLEDGE VIEWED IN RELATION TO RELIGION

WE shall be brought, gentlemen, to-day to the termination of the investigation which I commenced three discourses back, and which, I was well aware, from its length, if for no other reason, would make demands upon the patience even of indulgent hearers.

First I employed myself in establishing the principle that knowledge is its own reward; and I showed that, when considered in this light, it is called liberal knowledge, and is the scope of academical institutions.

Next, I examined what is meant by knowledge, when it is said to be pursued for its own sake; and I showed that, in order satisfactorily to fulfil this idea, philosophy must be its *form*; or, in other words, that its matter must not be admitted into the mind passively, as so much acquirement, but must be mastered and appropriated as a system consisting of parts, related one to the other, and interpretative of one another in the unity of a whole.

Further, I showed that such a philosophical contemplation of the field of knowledge as a whole, leading as it did to an understanding of its separate departments, and an appreciation of them respectively, might in consequence be rightly called an illumination; also, it was rightly called an enlargement of mind, because it was a distinct location of things one with another, as if in space; while it was moreover its proper cultivation and its best condition, both because it secured to the intellect the sight of things as they are, or of truth, in opposition to fancy, opinion, and theory; and again, because it presupposed and involved the perfection of its various powers.

Such, I said, was that knowledge which deserves to be sought for its own sake, even though it promised no ulterior advantage. But when I had got as far as this I went farther, and observed that, from the nature of the case, what was so good in itself could not but have a number of external uses, though it did not promise them, simply because it *was* good; and that it was necessarily the source of benefits to society, great and diversified in proportion to its own intrinsic excellence. Just as in morals honesty is the best policy, as being profitable in a secular aspect, though such profit is not the measure of its worth, so too as regards what may be called the virtues of the intellect, their very possession indeed is a substantial good, and is enough, yet still that substance has a shadow, inseparable from it, viz. its social and political usefulness. And this was the subject to which I devoted the preceding discourse.

One portion of the subject remains: this intellectual culture, which is so exalted in itself, not only has a bearing upon social and active duties, but upon religion also. The educated mind may be said to be in a certain sense religious; that is, it has what may be considered a religion of its own, independent of Catholicism, partly co-operating with it, partly thwarting it; at once a defence yet a disturbance to the Church in Catholic countries, and in countries beyond her pale, at one time in open warfare with her, at another in defensive alliance. The history of schools and academies, and of literature and science generally, will, I think, justify me in thus speaking. Since, then, my aim in these discourses is to ascertain the function and the action of a university, viewed in itself, and its relations to the various instruments of teaching and training which are round about it, my survey of it would not be complete unless I

attempted, as I now propose to do, to exhibit its general
bearings upon religion.

Right reason, that is, reason rightly exercised, leads the
mind to the Catholic faith, and plants it there, and teaches
it in all its religious speculations to act under its guidance.
But reason, considered as a real agent in the world, and as
an operative principle in man's nature, with an historical
course and with definite results, is far from taking so
straight and satisfactory a direction.   It considers itself
from first to last independent and supreme; it requires no
external authority; it makes a religion for itself.   Even
though it accepts Catholicism, it does not go to sleep; it has
an action and development of its own, as the passions
have, or the moral sentiments, or the principle of self-
interest.   Divine grace, to use the language of theology,
does not by its presence supersede nature; nor is nature
at once brought into simple concurrence and coalition with
grace.   Nature pursues its course, now coincident with that
of grace, now parallel to it, now across, now divergent,
now counter, in proportion to its own imperfection and to
the attraction and influence which grace exerts over it.
And what takes place as regards other principles of our
nature and their developments is found also as regards
the reason.   There is, we know, a religion of enthusiasm,
of superstitious ignorance of statecraft; and each has that
in it which resembles Catholicism, and that again which
contradicts Catholicism.   There is the religion of a war-
like people, and of a pastoral people; there is a religion of
rude times, and in like manner there is a religion of civilized
times, of the cultivated intellect, of the philosopher, scholar,
and gentleman.   This is that religion of reason of which I
speak.   Viewed in itself, however near it comes to Catholicism, it is of course simply distinct from it; for Catholicism
is one whole, and admits of no compromise or modifica-
tion.   Yet this is to view it in the abstract; in matter of

fact, and in reference to individuals, we can have no difficulty in conceiving this philosophical religion present in a Catholic country, as a spirit influencing men to a certain extent, for good or for bad or for both—a spirit of the age, which again may be found, as among Catholics, so with still greater sway and success in a country not Catholic, yet specifically the same in such a country as it exists in a Catholic community. The problem then before us to-day is to set down some portions of the outline, if we can ascertain them, of the religion of civilization, and to determine how they lie relatively to those principles, doctrines, and rules which Heaven has given us in the Catholic Church.

And here again, when I speak of revealed truth, it is scarcely necessary to say that I am not referring to the main articles and prominent points of faith, as contained in the Creed. Had I undertaken to delineate a philosophy which directly interfered with the Creed, I could not have spoken of it as compatible with the profession of Catholicism. The philosophy I speak of, whether it be viewed within or outside the Church, does not necessarily take cognizance of the Creed. Where the country is Catholic, the educated mind takes its articles for granted, by a sort of implicit faith; where it is not, it simply ignores them and the whole subject-matter to which they relate, as not affecting social and political interests. Truths about God's nature, about His dealings towards the human race, about the Economy of Redemption—in the one case it humbly accepts them, and passes on; in the other it passes them over, as matters of simple opinion, which never can be decided, and which can have no power over us to make us morally better or worse. I am not speaking then of belief in the great objects of faith when I speak of Catholicism, but I am contemplating Catholicism chiefly as a system of pastoral instruction and moral duty; and I have to do with its doctrines mainly as

they are subservient to its direction of the conscience and
the conduct. I speak of it, for instance, as teaching the
ruined state of man; his utter inability to gain heaven by
anything he can do himself; the moral certainty of his
losing his soul if left to himself; the simple absence of all
rights and claims on the part of the creature in the presence
of the Creator; the illimitable claims of the Creator on the
service of the creature; the imperative and obligatory
force of the voice of conscience; and the inconceivable evil
of sensuality. I speak of it as teaching that no one gains
heaven except by the free grace of God, or without a
regeneration of nature; that no one can please Him without faith; that the heart is the seat both of sin and of
obedience; that charity is the fulfilling of the Law; and that
incorporation into the Catholic Church is the ordinary
instrument of salvation. These are the lessons which
distinguish Catholicism as a popular religion, and these
are the subjects to which the cultivated intellect will practically be turned: I have to compare and contrast, not the
doctrinal, but the moral and social teaching of philosophy
on the one hand, and Catholicism on the other.

Now on opening the subject, we see at once a momentous
benefit which the philosopher is likely to confer on the
pastors of the Church. It is obvious that the first step
which they have to effect in the conversion of man and the
renovation of his nature is his rescue from that fearful
subjection to sense which is his ordinary state. To be
able to break through the meshes of that thraldom, and to
disentangle and to disengage its ten thousand holds upon
the heart, is to bring it, I might almost say, half-way to
heaven. Here even divine grace, to speak of things
according to their appearances, is ordinarily baffled and
retires, without expedient or resource, before this giant
fascination. Religion seems too high and unearthly
to be able to exert a continued influence upon us: its

effort to rouse the soul, and the soul's effort to co-operate, are too violent to last. It is like holding out the arm at full length, or supporting some great weight, which we manage to do for a time, but soon are exhausted and succumb. Nothing can act beyond its own nature; when then we are called to what is supernatural, though those extraordinary aids from Heaven are given us with which obedience becomes possible, yet even with them it is of transcendent difficulty. We are drawn down to earth every moment with the ease and certainty of a natural gravitation, and it is only by sudden impulses and, as it were, forcible plunges that we attempt to mount upwards. Religion indeed enlightens, terrifies, subdues; it gives faith, it inflicts remorse, it inspires resolutions, it draws tears, it inflames devotion, but only for the occasion. I repeat, it imparts an inward power which ought to effect more than this; I am not forgetting either the real sufficiency of its aids, nor the responsibility of those in whom they fail. I am not discussing theological questions at all, I am looking at phenomena as they lie before me, and I say that, in matter of fact, the sinful spirit repents, and protests it will never sin again, and for a while is protected by disgust and abhorrence from the malice of its foe. But that foe knows too well that such seasons of repentance are wont to have their end: he patiently waits, till nature faints with the effort of resistance, and lies passive and hopeless under the next access of temptation. What we need then is some expedient or instrument which at least will obstruct and stave off the approach of our spiritual enemy, and which is sufficiently congenial and level with our nature to maintain as firm a hold upon us as the inducements of sensual gratification. It will be our wisdom to employ nature against itself. Thus sorrow, sickness, and care are providential antagonists to our inward disorders; they come upon us as years pass on, and generally produce their natural effects on us in proportion as we are subjected to their influence. These, however, are God's instruments, not ours; we need a similar remedy, which we can make our own, the object of some legitimate faculty, or the aim of some natural affection, which is capable of resting on the mind, and taking up its familiar lodging with it, and engrossing it, and which thus becomes a match for the besetting power of sensuality, and a sort of homoeopathic medicine for the disease. Here then I think is the important aid which intellectual cultivation furnishes to us in rescuing the victims of passion and self-will. It does not supply religious motives; it is not the cause or proper antecedent of anything supernatural; it is not meritorious of heavenly aid or reward; but it does a work, at least *materially* good (as theologians speak), whatever be its real and formal character. It expels the excitements of sense by the introduction of those of the intellect.

This then is the *prima facie* advantage of the pursuit of knowledge; it is the drawing the mind off from things which will harm it to subjects which are worthy a rational being; and, though it does not raise it above nature, nor has any tendency to make us pleasing to our Maker, yet is it nothing to substitute what is in itself harmless for what is, to say the least, inexpressibly dangerous? Is it a little thing to exchange a circle of ideas which are certainly sinful for others which are certainly not so? You will say, perhaps, in the words of the Apostle: 'Knowledge puffeth up'; and doubtless this mental cultivation, even when it is successful for the purpose for which I am applying it, may be from the first nothing more than the substitution of pride for sensuality. I grant it, I think I shall have something to say on this point presently; but this is not a necessary result, it is but an incidental evil, a danger which may be realized or may be averted, whereas we may in most cases predicate guilt, and guilt of a heinous kind, where the mind is suffered to run wild and indulge its thoughts without training or law of any kind; and surely to turn away a soul from mortal sin is a good and a gain so far, whatever comes of it.   And therefore, if a friend in need is twice a friend, I conceive that intellectual employments, though they do no more than occupy the mind with objects naturally noble or innocent, have a special claim upon our consideration and gratitude.

Nor is this all: knowledge, the discipline by which it is gained, and the tastes which it forms, have a natural tendency to refine the mind, and to give it an indisposition, simply natural, yet real, nay, more than this, a disgust and abhorrence, towards excesses and enormities of evil, which are often or ordinarily reached at length by those who are not careful from the first to set themselves against what is vicious and criminal.   It generates within the mind a fastidiousness analogous to the delicacy or daintiness which good nurture or a sickly habit induces in respect of food; and this fastidiousness, though arguing no high principle, though no protection in the case of violent temptation, nor sure in its operation, yet will often or generally be lively enough to create an absolute loathing of certain offences, or a detestation and scorn of them as ungentle-manlike, to which ruder natures, nay, such as have far more of real religion in them, are tempted, or even committed. Scarcely can we exaggerate the value, in its place, of a safe-guard such as this, as regards those multitudes who are thrown upon the open field of the world, or are withdrawn from its eye and from the restraint of public opinion.   In many cases, where it exists, sins, familiar to those who are otherwise circumstanced, will not even occur to the mind: in others, the sense of shame and the quickened appre-hension of detection will act as a sufficient obstacle to them, when they do present themselves before it.   Then again, the fastidiousness I am speaking of will create a simple hatred of that miserable tone of conversation which, obtaining as it does in the world, is a constant fuel of evil, heaped up round about the soul: moreover, it will create an irresolution and indecision in doing wrong which will act as a remora till the danger is passed away. And though it has no tendency, I repeat, to mend the heart, or to secure it from the dominion in other shapes of those very evils which it repels in the particular modes of approach by which they prevail over others, yet cases may occur when it gives birth, after sins have been committed, to so keen a remorse and so intense a self-hatred as are even sufficient to cure the particular moral disorder, and to prevent its accesses ever afterwards; as the spendthrift in the story, who, after gazing on his lost acres from the summit of an eminence, came down a miser, and remained a miser to the end of his days.

And all this holds good in a special way in an age such as ours, when, although pain of body and mind may be rife as heretofore, yet other counteractions of evil, of a penal character, which at other times are present, are away. In rude and semi-barbarous periods, at least in a climate such as our own, it is the daily, nay, the principal business of the senses to convey feelings of discomfort to the mind, as far as they convey feelings at all. Exposure to the elements, social disorder and lawlessness, the tyranny of the powerful, and the inroads of enemies are a stern discipline, allowing brief intervals, or awarding a sharp penance, to sloth and sensuality. The rude food, the scanty clothing, the violent exercise, the vagrant life, the military constraint, the imperfect pharmacy, which now are the trials of only particular classes of the community, were once the lot more or less of all. In the deep woods or the wild solitudes of the medieval era, feelings of religion or superstition were naturally present to the population, which in various ways cooperated with the missionary or pastor in retaining it in a noble simplicity of manners. But when in the advancement of society men congregate in towns, and multiply in contracted spaces, and law gives them security, and art gives them comforts, and good government robs them of courage and manliness, and monotony of life throws them back upon themselves, who does not see that diversion or protection from evil they have none, that vice is the mere reaction of unhealthy toil, and sensual excess the holiday of resourceless ignorance? This is so well understood by the practical benevolence of the day, that it has especially busied itself in plans for supplying the masses of our town population with intellectual and honourable recreations. Cheap literature, libraries of useful and entertaining knowledge, scientific lectureships, museums, zoological collections, buildings and gardens to please the eye and to give repose to the feelings, external objects of whatever kind, which may take the mind off itself, and expand and elevate it in liberal contemplations, these are the human means, wisely suggested, and good as far as they go, for at least parrying the assaults of moral evil, and keeping at bay the enemies, not only of the individual soul, but of society at large.

Such are the instruments by which an age of advanced civilization combats those moral disorders which reason as well as revelation denounces; and I have not been backward to express my sense of their serviceableness to religion. Moreover, they are but the foremost of a series of influences which intellectual culture exerts upon our moral nature, and all upon the type of Christianity, manifesting themselves in veracity, probity, equity, fairness, gentleness, benevolence, and amiableness; so much so that a character more noble to look at, more beautiful, more winning in the various relations of life and in personal duties is hardly conceivable than may, or might be, its result when that culture is bestowed upon a soil naturally adapted to virtue. If you would obtain a picture for contemplation which may seem to fulfil the ideal which the Apostle has delineated under the name of charity, in its sweetness and harmony, its generosity, its courtesy to others, and its depreciation of self, you could not have recourse to a better furnished studio than that of philosophy, or to the specimens of it which with greater or less exactness are scattered through society in a civilized age. It is enough to refer you, gentlemen, to the various biographies and remains of contemporaries and others, which from time to time issue from the press, to see how striking is the action of our intellectual upon our moral nature, where the moral material is rich, and the intellectual cast is perfect. Individuals will occur to all of us who deservedly attract our love and admiration, and whom the world almost worships as the work of its own hands. Religious principle, indeed—that is, faith—is, to all appearance, simply away; the work is as certainly not supernatural as it is certainly noble and beautiful. This must be insisted on, that the intellect may have its due; but it also must be insisted on for the sake of conclusions to which I wish to conduct our investigation. The radical difference indeed of this mental refinement from genuine religion, in spite of its seeming relationship, is the very cardinal point on which my present discussion turns; yet on the other hand, such refinement may readily be assigned to a Christian origin by hasty or distant observers, or those who view it in a particular light. And as this is the case, I think it advisable, before proceeding with the delineation of its characteristic features, to point out to you distinctly the elementary principles on which its morality is based.

You will bear in mind then, gentlemen, that I spoke just now of the scorn and hatred which a cultivated mind feels for some kinds of vice, and the utter disgust and profound humiliation which may come over it, if it should happen in any degree to be betrayed into them. Now this feeling may have its root in faith and love, but it may not; there is nothing really religious in it, considered by itself. Conscience indeed is implanted in the breast by nature, but it inflicts upon us fear as well as shame; when the mind is simply angry with itself and nothing more, surely the true import of the voice of nature and the depth of its intimations have been forgotten, and a false philosophy has misinterpreted emotions which ought to lead to God. Fear implies the transgression of a law, and a law implies a lawgiver and judge; but the tendency of intellectual culture is to swallow up the fear in the self-reproach, and self-reproach is directed and limited to our mere sense of what is fitting and becoming. Fear carries us out of ourselves, shame confines us within the round of our own thoughts. Such, I say, is the danger which awaits a civilized age; such is its besetting sin (not inevitable, God forbid! or we must abandon the use of God's own gifts), but still the ordinary sin of the intellect; conscience becomes what is called a moral sense; the command of duty is a sort of taste; sin is not an offence against God, but against human nature.

The less amiable specimens of this spurious religion are those which we meet not unfrequently in my own country. I can use with all my heart the poet's words:

> England, with all thy faults, I love thee still,

but to those faults no Catholic can be blind. We find there men possessed of many virtues, but proud, bashful, fastidious, and reserved. Why is this? It is because they think and act as if there were really nothing objective in their religion; it is because conscience to them is not the word of a lawgiver, as it ought to be, but the dictate of their own minds and nothing more; it is because they do not look out of themselves, because they do not look through and beyond their own minds to their Maker, but are engrossed in notions of what is due to themselves, to their own dignity and their own consistency. Their conscience has become a mere self-respect. Instead of doing one thing and then another, as each is called for, in faith and obedience careless of what may be called the *keeping* of deed with deed, and leaving Him who gives the command to blend the portions of their conduct into a whole, their one object, however unconscious to themselves, is to paint a smooth and perfect surface, and to be able to say to themselves that they have done their duty. When they do wrong they feel, not contrition, of which God is the object, but remorse, and a sense of degradation. They call themselves fools, not sinners; they are angry and impatient, not humble. They shut themselves up in themselves; it is misery to them to think or to speak of their own feelings; it is misery to suppose that others see them, and their shyness and sensitiveness often become morbid. As to confession, which is so natural to the Catholic, to them it is impossible; unless indeed, in cases where they have been guilty, an apology is due to their own character, is expected of them, and will be satisfactory to look back upon. They are victims of an intense self-contemplation.

There are, however, far more pleasing and interesting forms of this moral malady than that which I have been depicting: I have spoken of the effect of intellectual culture on proud natures; but it will show to greater advantage, yet with as little approximation to religious faith, in amiable and unaffected minds. Observe, gentlemen, the heresy, as it may be called, of which I speak is the substitution of a moral sense or taste for conscience in the true sense of the word; now this error may be the foundation of a character of far more elasticity and grace than ever adorned the persons whom I have been describing. It is especially congenial to men of an imaginative and poetical cast of mind, who will readily accept the notion that virtue is nothing more than the graceful in conduct. Such persons, far from tolerating fear as a principle in their apprehension of religious and moral truth, will not be slow to call it simply gloom and superstition. Rather a philosopher's, a gentleman's religion, is of a liberal and generous character; it is based upon honour; vice is evil because it is unworthy, despicable, and odious. This was the quarrel of the ancient heathen with Christianity, that, instead of simply fixing the mind on the fair and the pleasant, it intermingled other ideas with them of a sad and painful nature; that it spoke of tears before joy, a cross before a crown; that it laid the foundation of heroism in penance; that it made the soul tremble with the news of purgatory and hell; that it insisted on views and a worship of the Deity which to their minds was nothing else than mean, servile, and cowardly. The notion of an all-perfect, ever-present God, in whose sight we are less than atoms, and who, while He deigns to visit us, can punish as well as bless, was abhorrent to them; they made their own minds their sanctuary, their own ideas their oracle, and conscience in morals was but parallel to genius in art, and wisdom in philosophy.

Had I room for all that might be said upon the subject, I might illustrate this intellectual religion from the history of the Emperor Julian, the apostate from Christian truth, the foe of Christian education. He in whom every Catholic sees the shadow of the future antichrist was all but the pattern man of philosophical virtue. Weak points in his character he had, it is true, even in a merely poetical standard; but, take him all in all, and I can but recognize in him a specious beauty and nobleness of moral deportment, which combines in it the rude greatness of Fabricius or Regulus with the accomplishments of Pliny or Antoninus. His simplicity of manners, his frugality, his austerity of life, his singular disdain of sensual pleasure, his military heroism, his application to business, his literary diligence, his modesty, his clemency, his accomplishments, as I view them, go to make him one of the most eminent specimens of pagan virtue which the world has ever seen.[1] Yet how shallow, how meagre, nay, how unamiable is that virtue after all, when brought upon its critical trial by his sudden summons into the presence of his Judge! His last hours form a *unique* passage in history, both as illustrating the helplessness of philosophy under the stern realities of our being, and as being reported to us on the evidence of an eye-witness. '"Friends and fellow soldiers,"' he said, to use the words of a writer well fitted, both from his literary tastes and from his hatred of Christianity, to be his panegyrist, '"the seasonable period of my departure is now arrived, and I discharge, with the cheerfulness of a ready debtor, the demands of nature. . . . I die without remorse, as I have lived without guilt. I am pleased to reflect on the innocence of my private life; and I can affirm with confidence that the supreme authority, that emanation of the Divine Power, has been preserved in my hands pure and immaculate. . . . I now offer my tribute of gratitude to the Eternal Being, who has not suffered me to perish by the cruelty of a tyrant, by the secret dagger of conspiracy, or by the slow tortures of lingering disease. He has given me, in the midst of an honourable career, a splendid and glorious departure from this world, and I hold it equally absurd, equally base to solicit, or to decline, the stroke of fate. . . ."'

[1] I do not consider I have said above anything inconsistent with the following passage from Cardinal Gerdil, though I have enlarged on the favourable side of Julian's character: 'Du génie, des connaissances, de l'habilité dans le métier de la guerre, du courage et du désintéressement dans le commandement des armées, des actions plutôt que des qualités estimables, mais le plus souvent gâtées par la vanité qui en était le principe, la superstition jointe à l'hypocrisie; un esprit fécond en ressources éclairé, mais susceptible de petitesse; des fautes essentielles dans le gouvernement; des innocens sacrifiés à la vengeance; une haine envenimée contre le Christianisme, qu'il avait abandonné; un attachement passionné aux folies de la Théurgie; tels étaient les traits sous lesquels on nous peignait Julien.'

'He reproved the immoderate grief of the spectators, and conjured them not to disgrace, by unmanly tears, the fate of a prince who in a few moments would be united with heaven and with the stars. The spectators were silent; and Julian entered into a metaphysical argument with the philosophers Priscus and Maximus on the nature of the soul. The efforts which he made, of mind as well as body, most probably hastened his death. His wound began to bleed with great violence; his respiration was embarrassed by the swelling of the veins; he called for a draught of cold water, and as soon as he had drank it expired without pain, about the hour of midnight.'[1] Such, gentlemen, is the final exhibition of the religion of reason: in the insensibility of conscience, in the ignorance of the very idea of sin, in the contemplation of his own moral consistency, in the simple absence of fear, in the cloudless self-confidence, in the serene self-possession, in the cold self-satisfaction, we recognize the philosopher.

Gibbon paints with pleasure what, conformably with the sentiments of a godless intellectualism, was an historical fulfilment of his own idea of moral perfection; Lord Shaftesbury had already drawn out that idea in a theoretical form in his celebrated collection of treatises which he has called 'Characteristics of men, manners, opinions, views'; and it will be a further illustration of the subject before us if you will allow me, gentlemen, to make some extracts from this work.

One of his first attacks is directed against the doctrine of reward and punishment, as if it introduced a notion into religion inconsistent with the true apprehension of the beauty of virtue, and with the liberality and nobleness of spirit in which it should be pursued. 'Men have not been content,' he says, 'to show the natural advantages of honesty and virtue. They have rather lessened these, the better, as they

[1] Gibbon, *Hist.*, Ch. XXIV.

thought, to advance another foundation. They have made virtue so mercenary a thing, and have talked so much of its rewards, that one can hardly tell what there is in it, after all, which can be worth rewarding. For to be *bribed* only or *terrified* into an honest practice bespeaks little of real honesty or worth.' 'If,' he says elsewhere, insinuating what he dare not speak out, 'if through hope merely of reward, or fear of punishment, the creature be inclined to do the good he hates, or restrained from doing the ill to which he is not otherwise in the least degree averse, there is in this case no virtue or goodness whatever. There is no more of rectitude, piety, or sanctity in a creature thus reformed, than there is meekness or gentleness in a tiger strongly chained, or innocence and sobriety in a monkey under the discipline of the whip. . . . While the will is neither gained, nor the inclination wrought upon, but awe alone prevails and forces obedience, the obedience is servile, and all which is done through it merely servile.' That is, he says that Christianity is the enemy of moral virtue, as influencing the mind by fear of God, not by love of good.

The motives then of hope and fear being, to say the least, put far into the background, and nothing being morally good but what springs simply or mainly from a love of virtue for its own sake, this love-inspiring quality in virtue is its beauty, while a bad conscience is not much more than the sort of feeling which makes us shrink from an instrument out of tune. 'Some by mere nature,' he says, 'others by art and practice, are masters of an ear in music, an eye in painting, a fancy in the ordinary things of orna-ment and grace, a judgment in proportions of all kinds, and a general good taste in most of those subjects which make the amusement and delight of the ingenious people of the world. Let such gentlemen as these be as extravagant as they please, or as irregular in their morals, they must at the same time discover their *inconsistency*, live at *variance* with themselves, and in *contradiction* to that principle on which they ground their highest pleasure and entertainment. Of all other *beauties* which virtuosos pursue, poets celebrate, musicians sing, and architects or artistes of whatever kind describe or form, the most delightful, the most engaging and pathetic, is that which is drawn from real life and from the passions. Nothing affects the heart like that which is purely from itself, and of its own nature: such as the beauty of sentiments, the grace of actions, the turn of characters, and the *proportions and features* of a human mind. This lesson of philosophy even a romance, a poem, or a play may teach us. . . . Let poets or the men of harmony deny, if they can, this force of nature, or withstand this *moral magic*. . . . Everyone is a virtuoso of a higher or lower degree; everyone pursues a grace . . . of one kind or other. The *venustum*, the *honestum*, the *decorum* of things will force its way. . . . The most natural beauty in the world is honesty and moral truth; for all beauty is truth.'

Accordingly, virtue being only one kind of beauty, the principle which determines what is virtuous is, not conscience, but *taste*. 'Could we once convince ourselves,' he says, 'of what is in itself so evident, viz. that in the very nature of things there must of necessity be the foundation of a right and wrong *taste*, as well in respect of inward character of features as of outward person, behaviour, and action, we should be far more ashamed of ignorance and wrong judgment in the former than in the latter of these subjects. . . . One who aspires to the character of a man of breeding and politeness is careful to form his judgment of arts and sciences upon right models of perfection. . . . He takes particular care to turn his eye from everything which is gaudy, luscious, and of false taste. Nor is he less careful to turn his ear from every sort of music besides that which is of the best manner and truest harmony. 'Twere to be wished we had the same regard to a *right taste in life and manners*. . . . If civility and humanity be a taste; if brutality, insolence, riot, be in the same manner a taste . . . who would not endeavour to force nature as well in this respect as in what relates to a taste or judgment in other arts and sciences?'

Sometimes he distinctly contrasts this taste with principle and conscience, and gives it the preference over them. 'After all,' he says, "*tis not merely what we call principle*, but *a taste*, which governs men. They may think for certain: "This is right" or "that wrong," they may believe: "This is a virtue" or "that a sin," "This is punishable by man" or "that by God"; yet if the savour of things lies cross to honesty, if the fancy be florid, and the appetite high towards the subaltern beauties and lower orders of worldly symmetries and proportions, the conduct will infallibly turn this latter way.' Thus, somewhat like a Jansenist, he makes the superior pleasure infallibly conquer, and implies that, neglecting principle, we have but to train the taste to a kind of beauty higher than sensual. He adds: '*Even conscience*, I fear, such as is owing to religious discipline, will make but a slight figure when this taste is set amiss.'

And hence the well-known doctrine of this author that ridicule is the test of truth; for truth and virtue being beauty, and falsehood and vice deformity, and the feeling inspired by deformity being that of derision, as that inspired by beauty is admiration, it follows that vice is not a thing to weep about, but to laugh at. 'Nothing is ridiculous,' he says, 'but what is deformed; nor is anything proof against raillery but what is handsome and just. And therefore 'tis the hardest thing in the world to deny fair honesty the use of this weapon, which can never bear an edge against herself, and bears against everything contrary.'

And hence again conscience, which intimates a lawgiver,

being superseded by a moral taste or sentiment, which has no sanction beyond the constitution of our nature, it follows that our great rule is to contemplate ourselves, if we would gain a standard of life and morals. Thus he has entitled one of his treatises a 'Soliloquy,' with the motto: 'Nec te quaesiveris extra'; and he observes: 'The chief interest of ambition, avarice, corruption, and every sly insinuating vice is to prevent this interview and familiarity of discourse which is consequent upon close retirement and inward recess. 'Tis the grand artifice of villainy and lewdness, *as well as of superstition and bigotry*, to put us upon terms of greater distance and formality with ourselves, and evade our *proving* method of soliloquy. . . . A passionate lover, whatever solitude he may affect, can never be truly by himself. . . . 'Tis the same reason which keeps the imaginary saint or mystic from being capable of this entertainment. Instead of looking narrowly into his own nature and mind, that he may be no longer a mystery to himself, he is taken up with *the contemplation of other mysterious natures*, which he never can explain or comprehend.'

Taking these passages as specimens of what I call the religion of philosophy, it is obvious to observe that there is no doctrine contained in them which is not in a certain sense true; yet on the other hand, that almost every statement is perverted and made false, because it is not the whole truth. They are exhibitions of truth under one aspect, and therefore insufficient; conscience is most certainly a moral sense, but it is more; vice again is a deformity, but it is worse. Lord Shaftesbury may insist, if he will, that simple and solitary fear cannot effect a moral conversion, and we are not concerned to answer him; but he will have a difficulty in proving that any real conversion follows from a doctrine which makes virtue a mere point of good taste, and vice vulgar and ungentlemanlike.

Such a doctrine is essentially superficial, and such will

be its effects. It has no better measure of right and wrong than that of visible beauty and tangible fitness. Conscience indeed inflicts an acute pang, but that pang, forsooth, is irrational, and to reverence it is an illiberal superstition. But, if we will make light of what is deepest within us, nothing is left but to pay homage to what is more upon the surface. To *seem* becomes to *be*; what looks fair will be good, what causes offence will be evil; virtue will be what pleases, vice what pains. As well may we measure virtue by utility as by such a rule. Nor is this an imaginary apprehension; we all must recollect the celebrated sentiment into which a great and wise man was betrayed, in the glowing eloquence of his valediction to the spirit of chivalry. 'It is gone,' cries Mr Burke; 'that sensibility of principle, that chastity of honour which felt a stain like a wound; which inspired courage, while it mitigated ferocity; which ennobled whatever it touched, and under which *vice lost half its evil by losing all its grossness*.' In the last clause of this beautiful sentence we have too apt an illustration of the ethical temperament of a civilized age. It is detection, not the sin, which is the crime; private life is sacred, and inquiry into it is intolerable; and decency is virtue. Scandals, vulgarities, whatever shocks, whatever disgusts, are offences of the first order. Drinking and swearing, squalid poverty, improvidence, laziness, slovenly disorder, make up the idea of profligacy: poets may say anything, however wicked, with impunity; works of genius may be read without danger or shame, whatever their principles; fashion, celebrity, the beautiful, the heroic, will suffice to force any evil upon the community. The splendours of a court, and the charms of good society, wit, imagination, taste, and high breeding, the *prestige* of rank, and the resources of wealth, are a screen, an instrument, and an apology for vice and irreligion. And thus at length we find, surprising as the change may be, that that very refinement of intellectualism, which began by repelling sensuality, ends by excusing it. Under the shadow indeed of the Church, and in its due development, philosophy does service to the cause of morality; but, when it is strong enough to have a will of its own, and is lifted up with an idea of its own importance, and attempts to form a theory, and to lay down a principle, and to carry out a system of ethics, and undertakes the moral education of the man, then it does but abet evils to which at first it seemed instinctively opposed. True religion is slow in growth, and when once planted is difficult of dislodgment; but its intellectual counterfeit has no root in itself: it springs up suddenly, it suddenly withers. It appeals to what is in nature, and it falls under the dominion of the old Adam. Then, like dethroned princes, it keeps up a state and majesty when it has lost the real power. Deformity is its abhorrence; accordingly, since it cannot dissuade men from vice, therefore in order to escape the sight of its deformity it embellishes it. It 'skins and films the ulcerous place,' which it cannot probe or heal,

> While rank corruption, mining all within,
> Infects unseen.

And from this shallowness of philosophical religion it comes to pass that it seems able to fulfil certain precepts of Christianity more readily and exactly than Christians themselves. St Paul, as I have said, gives us a pattern of evangelical perfection; he draws the Christian character in its most graceful form, and its most beautiful hues. He discourses of that charity which is patient and meek, humble and single-minded, disinterested, contented, and persevering. He tells us to prefer each other before ourselves, to give way to each other, to abstain from rude words and evil speech, to avoid self-conceit, to be calm and grave, to be cheerful and happy, to observe peace with all men, truth and justice, courtesy and gentleness, all that is modest, amiable, virtuous, and of good repute. Such is St Paul's exemplar of the Christian in his external relations; and, I repeat, the school of the world seems to send out living copies of this typical excellence with greater success than the Church. At this day the 'gentleman' is the creation, not of Christianity, but of civilization. But the reason is obvious. The world is content with setting right the surface of things; the Church aims at regenerating the very depths of the heart. She ever begins with the beginning; and, as regards the multitude of her children, is never able to get beyond the beginning, but is continually employed in laying the foundation. She is engaged with what is essential, as previous and as introductory to the ornamental and the attractive. She is curing men and keeping them clear of mortal sin; she is 'treating of justice and chastity, and the judgment to come': she is insisting on faith and hope, and devotion, and honesty, and the elements of charity; and has so much to do with precept that she almost leaves it to inspirations from Heaven to suggest what is of counsel and perfection. She aims at what is necessary rather than at what is desirable. She is for the many as well as for the few. She is putting souls in the way of salvation, that they may then be in a condition, if they shall be called upon, to aspire to the heroic, and to attain the substance, as well as the semblance, of the beautiful.

Such is the method, or the policy (so to call it), of the Church; but philosophy looks at the matter from a very different point of view: what have philosophers to do with the terror of judgment or the saving of the soul? Lord Shaftesbury calls the former a sort of 'panic fear.' Of the latter he scoffingly complains that 'the saving of souls is now the heroic passion of exalted spirits.' Of course he is at liberty, on his principles, to pick and choose out of Christianity what he will; he discards the theological, the mysterious, the spiritual; he makes selection of the morally or aesthetically beautiful. To him it matters not at all that he begins his teaching where he should end it; it matters not that, instead of planting the tree, he merely crops its flowers for his banquet; he only aims at the present life, his philosophy dies with him; if his flowers do but last to the end of his revel, he has nothing more to seek. When night comes, the withered leaves may be mingled with his own ashes; he and they will have done their work, he and they will be no more. Certainly it costs little to make men virtuous on conditions such as these; it is like teaching them a language or an accomplishment, to write Latin or to play on an instrument— the profession of an artist, not the commission of an Apostle.

This embellishment of the exterior is almost the beginning and the end of philosophical morality. This is why it aims at being modest rather than humble; this is how it can be proud at the very time that it is unassuming. To humility indeed it does not even aspire; humility is one of the most difficult of virtues both to attain and to ascertain. It lies close upon the heart itself, and its tests are exceedingly delicate and subtle. Its counterfeits abound; however, we are little concerned with them here, for, I repeat, it is hardly professed even by name in the code of ethics which we are reviewing. As has been often observed, ancient civilization had not the idea, and had no word to express it: or rather it had the idea, and considered it a defect of mind, not a virtue, so that the word which denoted it conveyed a reproach. As to the modern world, you may gather its ignorance of it by its perversion of the somewhat parallel term condescension. Humility or condescension, viewed as a virtue of conduct, may be said to consist, as in other things, so in our placing ourselves in our thoughts on a level with our inferiors; it is not only a voluntary relinquishment of the privileges of our own station, but an actual participation or assumption of the condition of those to whom we stoop. This is true humility, to feel and to behave as if we were low; not to cherish a notion of our importance, while we affect a low position. Such was St Paul's humility, when he called himself 'the least of the saints'; such the humility of those many holy men who have considered themselves the greatest of sinners. It is an abdication, as far as their own thoughts are concerned, of those prerogatives or privileges to which others deem them entitled. Now it is not a little instructive to contrast with this idea, gentlemen—with this theological meaning of the word condescension—its proper English sense; put them in juxtaposition, and you will at once see the difference between the world's humility and the humility of the Gospel. As the world uses the word, condescension is a stooping indeed of the person, but a bending forward, unattended with any the slightest effort to leave by a single inch the seat in which it is so firmly established. It is the act of a superior, who protests to himself, while he commits it, that he is superior still, and that he is doing nothing else but an act of grace towards those on whose level, in theory, he is placing himself. And this is the nearest idea which the philosopher can form of the virtue of self-abasement; to do more than this is to his mind a meanness or an hypocrisy, and at once excites his suspicion and disgust. What the world is, such it has ever been; we know the contempt which the educated pagans had for the martyrs and confessors of the Church; and it is shared by the anti-Catholic bodies of this day.

Such are the ethics of philosophy, when faithfully represented; but an age like this, not pagan but professedly Christian, cannot venture to reprobate humility in set terms, or to make a boast of pride. Accordingly, it looks out for some expedient by which it may blind itself to the real state of the case. Humility, with its grave and self-denying attributes, it cannot love; but what is more beautiful, what more winning, than modesty? What virtue, at first sight, simulates humility so well? Though what in fact is more radically distinct from it? In truth, great as is its charm, modesty is not the deepest or the most religious of virtues. Rather it is the advanced guard or sentinel of the soul militant, and watches continually over its nascent intercouse with the world about it. It goes the round of the senses; it mounts up into the countenance; it protects the eye and ear; it reigns in the voice and gesture. Its province is the outward deportment, as other virtues have relation to matters theological, others to society, and others to the mind itself. And being more superficial than other virtues, it is more easily disjoined from their company; it admits of being associated with principles or qualities naturally foreign to it, and is often made the cloak of feelings or ends for which it was never given to us. So little is it the necessary index of humility that it is even compatible with pride. The better for the purpose of philosophy; humble it cannot be, so forthwith modesty becomes its humility.

Pride, under such training, instead of running to waste in the education of the mind, is turned to account; it gets a new name: it is called self-respect; and ceases to be the disagreeable, uncompanionable quality which it is in itself. Though it be the motive principle of the soul, it seldom comes to view; and when it shows itself, then delicacy and gentleness are its attire, and good sense and sense of honour direct its motions. It is no longer a restless agent, without definite aim; it has a large field of exertion assigned to it, and it subserves those social interests which it would naturally trouble. It is directed into the channel of industry, frugality, honesty, and obedience; and it becomes the very staple of the religion and morality held in honour in a day like our own.   It becomes the safeguard of chastity, the guarantee of veracity, in high and low; it is the very household god of society, as at present constituted, inspiring neatness and decency in the servant-girl, propriety of carriage and refined manners in her mistress, uprightness, manliness, and generosity in the head of the family.   It diffuses a light over town and country; it covers the soil with handsome edifices and smiling gardens; it tills the field, it stocks and embellishes the shop.   It is the stimulating principle of providence on the one hand, and of free expenditure on the other; of an honourable ambition, and of elegant enjoyment.   It breathes upon the face of the community, and the hollow sepulchre is forthwith beautiful to look upon.

Refined by the civilization which has brought it into activity, this self-respect infuses into the mind an intense horror of exposure, and a keen sensitiveness of notoriety and ridicule.   It becomes the enemy of extravagances of any kind; it shrinks from what are called scenes; it has no mercy on the mock-heroic, on pretence or egotism, on verbosity in language, or what is called prosiness in manner. It detests gross adulation; not that it tends at all to the eradication of the appetite to which the flatterer ministers, but it sees the absurdity of indulging it, it understands the annoyance thereby given to others, and if a tribute must be paid to the wealthy or the powerful, it demands greater subtlety and art in the preparation.   Thus vanity is changed into a more dangerous self-conceit, as being checked in its natural eruption.   It teaches men to suppress their feelings, and to control their tempers, and to mitigate both the severity and the tone of their judgments.   As Lord Shaftesbury would desire, it prefers playful wit and satire in putting down what is objectionable, as a more refined and good-natured, as well as a more effectual method, than the expedient which is natural to uneducated minds.   It is from this impatience of the tragic and the bombastic that it is now quietly but energetically opposing itself to the unchristian practice of duelling, which it brands as simply out of taste, and as the remnant of a barbarous age; and certainly it seems likely to effect what religion has aimed at abolishing in vain.

Hence it is that it is almost a definition of a gentleman to say he is one who never inflicts pain. This description is both refined and, as far as it goes, accurate. He is mainly occupied in merely removing the obstacles which hinder the free and unembarrassed action of those about him; and he concurs with their movements rather than takes the initiative himself. His benefits may be considered as parallel to what are called comforts or conveniences in arrangements of a personal nature: like an easy-chair or a good fire, which do their part in dispelling cold and fatigue, though nature provides both means of rest and animal heat without them. The true gentleman in like manner carefully avoids whatever may cause a jar or a jolt in the minds of those with whom he is cast—all clashing of opinion, or collision of feeling, all restraint, or suspicion, or gloom, or resentment; his great concern being to make everyone at their ease and at home. He has his eyes on all his company; he is tender towards the bashful, gentle towards the distant, and merciful towards the absurd; he can recollect to whom he is speaking; he guards against unseasonable allusions, or topics which may irritate; he is seldom prominent in conversation, and never wearisome. He makes light of favours while he does them, and seems to be receiving when he is conferring. He never speaks of himself except when compelled, never defends himself by a mere retort, he has no ears for slander or gossip, is scrupulous in imputing motives to those who interfere with him, and interprets everything for the best. He is never mean or little in his disputes, never takes unfair advantage, never mistakes personalities or sharp sayings for arguments, or insinuates evil which he dare not say out. From a long-sighted prudence, he observes the maxim of the ancient sage, that we should ever conduct ourselves towards our enemy as if he were one day to be our friend. He has too much good sense to be affronted at insults, he is too well employed to remember injuries and too indolent to bear malice. He is patient, forbearing, and resigned, on philosophical principles; he submits to pain because it is inevitable, to bereavement because it is irreparable, and to death because it is his destiny. If he engages in controversy of any kind, his disciplined intellect preserves him from the blundering discourtesy of better, though less educated minds; who, like blunt weapons, tear and hack instead of cutting clean, who mistake the point in argument, waste their strength on trifles, misconceive their adversary, and leave the question more involved than they find it. He may be right or wrong in his opinion, but he is too clear-headed to be unjust; he is as simple as he is forcible, and as brief as he is decisive. Nowhere shall we find greater candour, consideration, indulgence: he throws himself into the minds of his opponents, he accounts for their mistakes. He knows the weakness of human reason as well as its strength, its province, and its limits. If he be an unbeliever, he will be too profound and large-minded to ridicule religion or to act against it; he is too wise to be a dogmatist or fanatic in his infidelity. He respects piety and devotion; he even supports institutions as venerable, beautiful, or useful to which he does not assent; he honours the ministers of religion, and he is contented to decline its mysteries without assailing or denouncing them. He is a friend of religious toleration, and that not only because his philosophy has taught him to look on all forms of faith with an impartial eye, but also from the gentleness and effeminacy of feeling which is the attendant on civilization.

Not that he may not hold a religion too, in his own way, even when he is not a Christian. In that case his religion is one of imagination and sentiment; it is the embodiment of those ideas of the sublime, majestic, and beautiful without which there can be no large philosophy. Sometimes he acknowledges the being of God, sometimes he invests an unknown principle or quality with the attributes of perfection. And this deduction of his reason, or creation of his fancy, he makes the occasion of such excellent thoughts, and the starting-point of so varied and systematic a teaching, that he even seems like a disciple of Christianity itself. From the very accuracy and steadiness of his logical powers, he is able to see what sentiments are consistent in those who hold any religious doctrine at all, and he appears to others to feel and to hold a whole circle of theological truths which exist in his mind no otherwise than as a number of deductions.

Such are some of the lineaments of the ethical character which the cultivated intellect will form apart from religious principle. They are seen within the pale of the Church and without it, in holy men and in profligate; they form the beau ideal of the world; they partly assist and partly distort the development of the Catholic. They may subserve the education of a St Francis de Sales or a Cardinal Pole; they may be the limits of the virtue of a Shaftesbury or a Gibbon. Basil and Julian were fellow students at the schools of Athens; and one became the saint and doctor of the church, the other her scoffing and relentless foe.

DISCOURSE VIII

DUTIES OF THE CHURCH TOWARDS LIBERAL
KNOWLEDGE

I HAVE to congratulate myself, gentlemen, that at length I have accomplished, with whatever success, the difficult and anxious undertaking to which I have been immediately addressing myself. Difficult and anxious it has been in truth, though the main subject of university education has been so often and so ably discussed already; for I have attempted to follow out a line of thought more familiar to Protestants just now than to Catholics, upon Catholic grounds. I declared my intention, when I opened the subject, of treating it as a philosophical and practical, rather than as a theological question, with an appeal to common sense, not to ecclesiastical rules; and for this very reason, while my argument has been less ambitious, it has been deprived of the lights and supports which another mode of handling it would have secured.

No anxiety, no effort of mind, is more severe than his, who in a difficult matter has it seriously at heart to investigate without error and to instruct without obscurity; as to myself, if the past discussion has at any time tried the patience of the kind persons who have given it their attention, I can assure them that on no one can it have inflicted so great labour and fatigue as on myself. Happy they who are engaged in provinces of thought so familiarly traversed and so thoroughly explored that they see everywhere the footprints, the paths, the landmarks, and the remains of former travellers, and can never step wrong; but for myself, gentlemen, I have felt like a navigator on a strange sea, who is out of sight of land, is surprised by night, and has to trust mainly to the rules and instruments of his science for reaching the port. The everlasting mountains, the high majestic cliffs of the opposite coast, radiant in the sunlight, which are our ordinary guides, fail us in an excursion such as this; the lessons of antiquity, the determinations of authority, are here rather the needle, chart, and plummet than great objects, with distinct and continuous outline and completed details, which stand up and confront and occupy our gaze, and relieve us from the tension and suspense of our personal observation. And thus, in spite of the pains we may take to consult others and avoid mistakes, it is not till the morning comes and the shore greets us, and we see our vessel making straight for harbour, that we relax our jealous watch, and consider anxiety irrational. Such in a measure has been my feeling in the foregoing inquiry; in which indeed I have been in want neither of authoritative principles nor distinct precedents, but of treatises *in extenso* on the subject on which I have written—the finished work of writers who, by their acknowledged judgment and erudition, might furnish me for my private guidance with a running instruction on each point which successively came under review.

I have spoken of the arduousness of my 'immediate' undertaking, because what I have been attempting has been of a preliminary nature, not contemplating the duties of the Church towards a university, nor the characteristics of a university which is Catholic, but inquiring what a university is, what is its aim, what its nature, what its bearings. I have accordingly laid down, first, that all branches of knowledge are, at least implicitly, the subject-matter of its teaching; that these branches are not isolated and independent one of another, but form together a whole or system; that they run into each other, and complete each other, and that in proportion to our view of them as a whole is the exactness and trustworthiness of the knowledge which they separately convey; that the process of imparting knowledge to the intellect in this philosophical way is its true culture; that such culture is a good in itself; that the knowledge which is both its instrument and result is called liberal knowledge; that such culture, together with the knowledge which effects it, may fitly be sought for its own sake; that it is, however, in addition, of great secular utility, as constituting the best and highest formation of the intellect for social and political life; and lastly that, considered in a religious aspect, it concurs with Christianity a certain way, and then diverges from it; and consequently proves in the event, sometimes its serviceable ally, sometimes, from its very resemblance to it, an insidious and dangerous foe.

Though, however, these discourses have only professed to be preliminary, being directed to the investigation of the object and nature of the education which a university professes to impart, at the same time I do not like to conclude without making some remarks upon the duties of the Church towards it, or rather on the ground of those duties. If the Catholic faith is true, a university cannot exist externally to the Catholic pale, for it cannot teach universal knowledge if it does not teach Catholic theology. This is certain; but still, though it had ever so many theological chairs, that would not suffice to make it a Catholic university; for theology would be included in its teaching only as a branch of knowledge, only as one out of many constituent portions, however important a one, of what I have called philosophy. Hence a direct and active jurisdiction of the Church over it and in it is necessary, lest it should become the rival of the Church with the community at large in those theological matters which to the Church are exclusively committed—acting as the representative of the intellect, as the Church is the representative of the religious principle.   The illustration of this proposition shall be the subject of my concluding discourse.

I say then that, even though the case could be so that the whole system of Catholicism was recognized and professed, without the direct presence of the Church, still this would not at once make such a university a Catholic institution, nor be sufficient to secure the due weight of religious considerations in its philosophical studies.   For it may easily happen that a particular bias or drift may characterize an institution, which no rules can reach, nor officers remedy, nor professions or promises counteract. We have an instance of such a case in the Spanish Inquisition; here was a purely Catholic establishment, devoted to the maintenance, or rather the ascendancy of Catholicism, keenly zealous for theological truth, the stern foe of every anti-Catholic idea, and administered by Catholic theologians; yet it in no proper sense belonged to the Church.   It was simply and entirely a State institution, it was an expression of that very Church-and-king spirit which has prevailed in these islands; nay, it was an instrument of the State, according to the confession of the acutest Protestant historians, in its warfare against the Holy See. Considered *materially*, it was nothing but Catholic; but its spirit and form were earthly and secular, in spite of whatever faith and zeal and sanctity and charity were to be found in the individuals who from time to time had a share in its administration.   And in like manner, it is no sufficient security for the Catholicity of a university even that the whole of Catholic theology should be professed in it, unless the Church breathes her own pure and unearthly spirit into it, and fashions and moulds its organization, and watches over its teaching, and knits together its pupils, and superintends its action.   The Spanish Inquisition came into collision with the supreme Catholic authority, from the circumstance that its immediate end was of a secular character; and for the same reason, whereas academical institutions (as I have been so long engaged in showing) are in their very nature directed to social, national, temporal objects in the first instance, and since they are living and energizing bodies if they deserve the name of university at all, and of necessity have some one formal and definite ethical character, good or bad, and do of a certainty imprint that character on the individuals who direct and who frequent them, it cannot but be that, if left to themselves, they will, in spite of their profession of Catholic truth, work out results more or less prejudicial to its interests.

Nor is this all: such institutions may become hostile to revealed truth, in consequence of the circumstances of their teaching as well as of their end. They are employed in the pursuit of liberal knowledge, and liberal knowledge has a special tendency, not necessary or rightful, but a tendency in fact, when cultivated by beings such as we are, to impress us with a mere philosophical theory of life and conduct, in the place of revelation. I have said much on this subject already. Truth has two attributes—beauty and power; and while useful knowledge is the possession of truth as powerful, liberal knowledge is the apprehension of it as beautiful. Pursue it, either as beauty or as power, to its furthest extent and its true limit, and you are led by either road to the eternal and infinite, to the intimations of conscience and the announcements of the Church. Satisfy yourself with what is only visibly or intelligibly excellent, as you are likely to do, and you will make present utility and natural beauty the practical test of truth, and the sufficient object of the intellect. It is not that you will at once reject Catholicism, but you will measure and proportion it by an earthly standard. You will throw its highest and most momentous disclosures into the background, you will deny its principles, explain away its doctrines, rearrange its precepts, and make light of its practices, even while you profess it. Knowledge, viewed as knowledge, exerts a subtle influence in throwing us back on ourselves, and making us our own centre, and our minds the measure of all things. This then is the tendency of that liberal education of which a university is the school, viz. to view revealed religion from an aspect of its own—to fuse and recast it—to tune it, as it were, to a different key, and to reset its harmonies—to circumscribe it by a circle which unwarrantably amputates here, and unduly develops there; and all under the notion, conscious or unconscious, that the human intellect, self-educated and self-supported, is more true and perfect in its ideas and judgments than that of prophets and apostles to whom the sights and sounds of heaven were immediately conveyed. A sense of propriety, order, consistency, and completeness gives birth to a rebellious stirring against miracle and mystery, against the severe and the terrible.

First and chiefly this intellectualism comes into collision with precept, then with doctrine, then with the very principle of dogmatism. A perception of the beautiful becomes the substitute for faith. In a country which does not profess the faith, it at once runs, if allowed, into scepticism or infidelity; but even within the pale of the Church, and with the most unqualified profession of her Creed, it acts, if left to itself, as an element of corruption and debility. Catholicism, as it has come down to us from the first, seems to be mean and illiberal; it is a mere popular religion; it is the religion of illiterate ages or servile populations or barbarian warriors; it must be treated with discrimination and delicacy, corrected, softened, improved, if it is to satisfy an enlightened generation. It must be stereotyped as the patron of arts, or the pupil of speculation, or the protégé of science; it must play the literary academician, or the empirical philanthropist, or the political partisan; it must keep up with the age; some or other expedient it must devise in order to explain away, or to hide, tenets under which the intellect labours and of which it is ashamed —its doctrine, for instance, of grace, its mystery of the God-head, its preaching of the Cross, its devotion to the Queen of Saints, or its loyalty to the Apostolic See. Let this spirit be freely evolved out of that philosophical condition of mind which in former discourses I have so highly, so justly extolled, and it is impossible but, first indifference, then laxity of belief, then even heresy will be the successive results.

Here then are two injuries which revelation is likely to sustain at the hands of the masters of human reason unless the Church, as in duty bound, protects the sacred treasure which is in jeopardy. The first is a simple ignoring of theological truth altogether, under the pretence of not recognizing differences of religious opinion, which will only take place in countries or under governments which have abjured Catholicism. The second, which is of a more subtle character, is a recognition indeed of Catholicism, but (as if in pretended mercy to it) an adulteration of its spirit. I will now proceed to describe the dangers I speak of more distinctly, by a reference to the general subject-matter of instruction which a university undertakes.

There are three great subjects on which human reason employs itself: God, nature, and man: and theology being put aside in the present argument, the physical and social worlds remain. These, when respectively subjected to human reason, form two books: the book of nature is called science, the book of man is called literature. Literature and science, thus considered, nearly constitute the subject-matter of liberal education; and while science is made to subserve the former of the two injuries which revealed truth sustains—its exclusion, literature subserves the latter—its corruption. Let us consider the influence of each upon religion separately.

1. As to physical science, of course there can be no real collision between it and Catholicism. Nature and grace, reason and revelation, come from the same Divine Author, whose works cannot contradict each other. Nevertheless, it cannot be denied that, in matter of fact, there always has been a sort of jealousy and hostility between religion and physical philosophers. The name of Galileo reminds us of it at once. Not content with investigating and reasoning in his own province, he went out of his way directly to insult the received interpretation of Scripture; theologians repelled an attack which was wanton and arrogant; and science, affronted in her minister, has taken its full revenge upon theology since. A vast multitude of its teachers, I fear it must be said, have been either unbelievers or sceptics or at least have denied to Christianity any teaching, distinctive or special, over the religion of nature. There have indeed been most illustrious exceptions; some men protected by their greatness of mind, some by their religious profession, some by the fear of public opinion; but I suppose the run of experimentalists, external to the Catholic Church, have more or less inherited the positive or negative unbelief of Laplace, Buffon, Franklin, Priestley, Cuvier, and Humboldt. I do not of course mean to say that there need be in every case a resentful and virulent opposition made to religion on the part of scientific men; but their emphatic silence or phlegmatic inadvertence as to its claims have implied, more eloquently than any words, that in their opinion it had no voice at all in the subject-matter which they had appropriated to themselves. The same antagonism shows itself in the Middle Ages. Friar Bacon was popularly regarded with suspicion as a dealer in unlawful arts; Pope Sylvester II has been accused of magic for his knowledge of natural secrets; and the geographical ideas of St Virgil, Bishop of Salzburg, were regarded with anxiety by the great St Boniface, the

glory of England, the martyr-apostle of Germany. I suppose, in matter of fact, magical superstition and physical knowledge did commonly go together in those ages: however, the hostility between experimental science and theology is far older than Christianity. Lord Bacon traces it to an era prior to Socrates; he tells us that, among the Greeks, the atheistic was the philosophy most favourable to physical discoveries, and he does not hesitate to imply that the rise of the religious schools was the ruin of science.[1]

Now, if we would investigate the reason of this opposition between theology and physics, I suppose we must first take into account Lord Bacon's own explanation of it. It is common in judicial inquiries to caution the parties on whom the verdict depends to put out of their minds whatever they have heard out of court on the subject to which their attention is to be directed. They are to judge by the evidence; and this is a rule which holds in other investigations as far as this, that nothing of an adventitious nature ought to be introduced into the process. In like manner, from religious investigations, as such, physics must be excluded, and from physical, as such, religion; and if we mix them, we shall spoil both. The theologian, speaking of divine omnipotence, for the time simply ignores the laws of nature as existing restraints upon its exercise; and the physical philosopher, on the other hand, in his experiments upon natural phenomena, is simply ascertaining those laws, putting aside the question of that omnipotence. If the theologian, in tracing the ways of Providence, were stopped with objections grounded on the impossibility of physical miracles, he would justly protest against the interruption; and were the philosopher, who was determining the motion of the heavenly bodies, to

---

[1] *Vide* Hallam's *Literature of Europe*, Macaulay's essay, and the author's Oxford University Sermons, IX.

be questioned about their final or their first cause, he too would suffer an illogical interruption. The latter asks the cause of volcanoes, and is impatient at being told it is 'the divine vengeance'; the former asks the cause of the overthrow of the guilty cities, and is preposterously referred to the volcanic action still visible in their neighbourhood. The inquiry into final causes for the moment passes over the existence of established laws; the inquiry into physical passes over for the moment the existence of God. In other words, physical science is in a certain sense atheistic, for the very reason it is not theology.

This is Lord Bacon's justification, and an intelligible one, for considering that the fall of atheistic philosophy in ancient times was a blight upon the hopes of physical science. 'Aristotle,' he says, 'Galen, and others frequently introduce such causes as these: the hairs of the eyelids are for a fence to the sight; the bones for pillars whence to build the bodies of animals; the leaves of trees are to defend the fruit from the sun and wind; the clouds are designed for watering the earth. All which are properly alleged in metaphysics; but in physics are impertinent, and as remoras to the ship, that hinder the sciences from holding on their course of improvement, and introducing a neglect of searching after physical causes.'[1] Here then is one reason for the prejudice of physical philosophers against theology: on the one hand, their deep satisfaction in the laws of nature indisposes them towards the thoughts of a Moral Governor, and makes them sceptical of His interposition; on the other hand, the occasional interference of religious writers in a province not religious has made them sore, suspicious, and resentful.

Another reason of a kindred nature is to be found in the difference of method by which truths are gained in theology and in physical science. Induction is the instrument of

[1] *In Augment.*, 5.

physics, and deduction only is the instrument of theology. There the simple question is: What is revealed? All doctrinal knowledge flows from one fountain-head. If we are able to enlarge our view and multiply our propositions, it must be merely by the comparison and adjustment of existing truths; if we would solve new questions, it must be by consulting old answers. The notion of doctrinal knowledge absolutely novel, and of simple addition from without, is intolerable to our ears, and never was entertained by anyone who was even approaching to an understanding of our creed. Revelation is all in all in doctrine; the Apostles its sole depository, the inferential method its sole instrument, and ecclesiastical authority its sole sanction. The Divine Voice has spoken once for all, and the only question is about its meaning. Now this process, as far as it was reasoning, was the very mode of reasoning which, as regards physical knowledge, the school of Bacon has superseded by the inductive method: no wonder, then, that that school should be irritated and indignant to find that a subject-matter remains still in which their favourite instrument has no office; no wonder that they rise up against this memorial of an antiquated system as an eyesore and an insult; and no wonder that the very force and dazzling success of their own method in its own departments should sway or bias unduly the religious sentiments of any persons who come under its influence. They assert that no new truth can be gained by deduction; Catholics assent, but add that, as regards religious truth, they have not to seek at all, for they have it already. Christian truth is purely of revelation; that revelation we can but explain, we cannot increase, except relatively to our own apprehensions; without it we should have known nothing of its contents, with it we know just as much as its contents, and nothing more. And, as it was a divine act independent of man, so will it remain in spite of man. Niebuhr may revolutionize

history, Lavoisier chemistry, Newton astronomy; but God
Himself is the author as well as the subject of theology.
When truth can change, its revelation can change; when
human reason can outreason the Omniscient, then may it
supersede His work.

Avowals such as these fall strange upon the ear of men
whose first principle is the search after truth, and whose
starting-points of search are things material and sensible.
They scorn any process of inquiry not founded on experiment; the mathematics indeed they endure, because that
science deals with ideas, not with facts, and leads to conclusions hypothetical rather than real; metaphysics they
even use as a byword of reproach; and ethics they admit
only on condition that it gives up conscience as its scientific
ground, and bases itself on tangible utility; but as to
theology, they cannot deal with it, they cannot master it,
and so they simply outlaw it and ignore it. Catholicism,
forsooth, 'confines the intellect,' because it holds that
God's intellect is greater than theirs, and that what He has
done man cannot improve. And what in some sort
justifies them to themselves in this extravagance is the
circumstance that there is a religion close at their doors
which, discarding so severe a tone, has actually adopted
their own principle of inquiry. Protestantism treats Scripture just as they deal with nature; it takes the sacred text
as a large collection of phenomena from which, by an
inductive process, each individual Christian may arrive at
just those religious conclusions which approve themselves
to his own judgment. It considers faith a mere modifi-
cation of reason, as being an acquiescence in certain
probable conclusions till better are found. Sympathy,
then, if no other reason, throws experimental philosophers
into alliance with the enemies of Catholicism.

I have another consideration to add, not less important
than any I have hitherto adduced. The physical sciences,

astronomy, chemistry, and the rest, are doubtless engaged upon divine works, and cannot issue in untrue religious conclusions. But at the same time it must be recollected that revelation has reference to circumstances which did not arise till after the heavens and the earth were made. They were made before the introduction of moral evil into the world: whereas the Catholic Church is the instrument of a remedial dispensation to meet that introduction. No wonder then that her teaching is simply distinct, though not divergent, from the theology which physical science suggests to its followers. She sets before us a number of attributes and acts on the part of the Divine Being, for which the material and animal creation gives no scope; power, wisdom, goodness, are the burden of the physical world, but it does not and could not speak of mercy, long-suffering, and the economy of human redemption, and but partially of the moral law and moral goodness. 'Sacred theology,' says Lord Bacon, 'must be drawn from the words and the oracles of God: not from the light of nature or the dictates of reason. It is written that "the heavens declare the glory of God"; but we nowhere find it that the heavens declare the will of God; which is pronounced a law and a testimony, that men should do according to it. Nor does this hold only in the great mysteries of the Godhead, of the creation, of the redemption. ... We cannot doubt that a large part of the moral law is too sublime to be attained by the light of nature; though it is still certain that men, even with the light and law of nature, have some notions of virtue, vice, justice, wrong, good, and evil.'[1] That the new and further manifestations of the Almighty, made by revelation, are in perfect harmony with the teaching of the natural world forms indeed one subject of the profound work of the Protestant Bishop Butler; but they cannot in any sense be gathered from nature, and the silence

[1] *De Augm.*, § 28.

of nature concerning them may easily seduce the imagination, though it has no force to persuade the reason, to
revolt from doctrines which have not been authenticated
by facts, but are enforced by authority. In a scientific
age, then, there will naturally be a parade of what is called
natural theology, a widespread profession of the Unitarian
creed, an impatience of mystery, and a scepticism about
miracles.

And to all this must be added the ample opportunity
which physical science gives to the indulgence of those
sentiments of beauty, order, and congruity, of which I
have said so much, as the ensigns and colours (as they
may be called) of a civilized age in its warfare against
Catholicism.

It being considered, then, that Catholicism differs from
physical science, in drift, in method of proof, and in
subject-matter, how can it fail to meet with unfair usage
from the philosophers of any institution in which there is
no one to take its part? That physical science itself will be
ultimately the loser by such ill treatment of theology I have
insisted on at great length in the first three of these discourses; for to depress unduly, to encroach upon any
science, and much more on an important one, is to do an
injury to all. However, this is not the concern of the
Church; the Church has no call to watch over and protect
science; but towards theology she has a distinct duty: it
is one of the special trusts committed to her keeping.
Where theology is, there she must be; and if a university
cannot fulfil its name and office without the recognition of
revealed truth, she must be there to see that it is a bona
fide recognition, sincerely made and consistently acted on.

2. And if the interposition of the Church is necessary
in the schools of science, still more imperatively is it
demanded in the other main constituent portion of the
subject-matter of liberal education—literature. Literature

stands related to man as science stands to nature; it is history. Man is composed of body and soul; he thinks and he acts; he has appetites, passions, affections, motives, designs; he has within him the lifelong struggle of duty with inclination; he has an intellect fertile and capacious; he is formed for society, and society multiplies and diversifies in endless combinations his personal characteristics, moral and intellectual. All this constitutes his life; of all this literature is the expression; so that literature is to man in some sort what autobiography is to the individual; it is his life and remains. Moreover, he is this sentient, intelligent, creative, and operative being quite independent of any extraordinary aid from Heaven, or any definite religious belief; and *as* such, as he is in himself, does literature represent him; it is the life and remains of the *natural* man, or man *in purâ naturâ*. I do not mean to say that it is impossible in its very notion that literature should be tinctured by a religious spirit; Hebrew literature, as far as it can be called literature, certainly is simply theological, and has a character imprinted on it which is above nature; but I am speaking of what is to be expected without any extraordinary dispensation; and I say that, in matter of fact, as science is the reflection of nature, so is literature also—the one of nature physical, the other of nature moral and social. Circumstances such as locality, period, language, seem to make little or no difference in the character of literature as such; on the whole, all literatures are one; they are the voices of the natural man.

I wish this were all that had to be said to the disadvantage of literature; but while nature physical remains fixed in its own laws, nature moral and social has a will of its own, is self-governed, and never remains any long while in that state from which it started into action. Man will never continue in a mere state of innocence; he is sure to sin, and his literature will be the expression of his sin, and this whether he be heathen or Christian. Christianity has thrown gleams of light on him and his literature; but as it has not converted him, but only certain choice specimens of him, so it has not changed the characters of his mind or of his history; his literature is either what it was, or worse than what it was, in proportion as there has been an abuse of knowledge granted and a rejection of truth. On the whole, then, I think it will be found, and ever found, as a matter of course, that literature, as such, no matter of what nation, is the science or history, partly and at best of the natural man, partly of man fallen.

Here then, I say, you are involved in a difficulty greater than that which besets the cultivation of science; for, if physical science be dangerous, I have said it is dangerous because it necessarily ignores the idea of moral evil; but literature is open to the more grievous imputation of recognizing and understanding it too well. Someone will say to me perhaps: 'Our youth shall not be corrupted. We will dispense with all general or national literature whatever, if it be so exceptionable; we will have a Christian literature of our own, as pure, as true, as the Jewish.' You cannot have it: I do not say you cannot form a select literature for the young, or for the middle or lower classes; this is another matter altogether: I am speaking of university education, which implies an extended range of reading, which has to deal with standard works of genius. or what are called the *classics* of a language: and I say, from the nature of the case, if literature is to be made a study of human nature, you cannot have a Christian literature. It is a contradiction in terms to attempt a sinless literature of sinful man. You may gather together something very great and high, something higher than any literature ever was; and when you have done so, you will find that it is not literature at all. You will have simply left the delineation of man, as such, and have substituted for it, as far as you have had anything to substitute, that of man, as he is or might be, under certain special advantages. Give up the study of man, as such, if so it must be; but say you do so. Do not say you are studying him, his history, his mind, and his heart, when you are studying something else. Man is a being of genius, passion, intellect, conscience, power. He exercises these various gifts in various ways, in great deeds, in great thoughts, in heroic acts, in hateful crimes. He founds states, he fights battles, he builds cities, he ploughs the forest, he subdues the elements, he rules his kind. He creates vast ideas, and influences many generations. He takes a thousand shapes, and undergoes a thousand fortunes. Literature records them all to the life:

> Quicquid agunt homines, votum, timor, ira, voluptas,
> Gaudia, discursus.

He pours out his fervid soul in poetry; he sways to and fro, he soars, he dives in his restless speculations; his lips drop eloquence; he touches the canvas, and it glows with beauty; he sweeps the strings, and they thrill with an ecstatic meaning. He looks back into himself, and he reads his own thoughts, and notes them down; he looks out into the universe, and tells over and celebrates the elements and principles of which it is the product.

Such is man: put him aside, keep him before you; but, whatever you do, do not take him for what he is not, for something more divine and sacred, for man regenerate. Nay, beware of showing God's grace and its work at such disadvantage as to make the few whom it has thoroughly influenced compete in intellect with the vast multitude who either have it not, or use it ill. The elect are few to choose out of, and the world is inexhaustible. From the first, Jabal and Tubalcain, Nimrod 'the stout hunter,' the learning of the Pharaohs, and the wisdom of the East country are of the world. Every now and then they are rivalled by a Solomon or a Beseleel, but the habitat of natural gifts is the natural man. The Church may use them, she cannot at her will originate them. Not till the whole human race is regenerate will its literature be pure and true. Possible of course it is in idea, for nature, inspired by heavenly grace, to exhibit itself on a large scale, in an originality of thought or action, even far beyond what the world's literature has recorded or exemplified; but if you would in fact have a literature of saints, first of all have a nation of them.

What is a clearer proof of the truth of all this than the structure of the Inspired Word itself? It is undeniably *not* the reflection or picture of the many, but of the few; it is no picture of life, but an anticipation of death and judgment. Human literature is about all things, grave or gay, painful or pleasant; but the Inspired Word views them only in one aspect, and as they tend to one scope. It gives us little insight into the fertile developments of mind; it has no terms in its vocabulary to express with exactness the intellect and its separate faculties: it knows nothing of genius, fancy, wit, invention, presence of mind, resource. It does not discourse of empire, commerce, enterprise, learning, philosophy, or the fine arts. Slightly too does it touch on the more simple and innocent courses of nature and their reward. Little does it say[1] of those temporal blessings which rest upon our worldly occupations, and make them easy; of the blessings which we derive from the sunshine day and the serene night, from the succession of the seasons, and the produce of the earth. Little about our recreations and our daily domestic comforts; little about the ordinary occasions of festivity and mirth which sweeten human life; and nothing at all about various pursuits or amusements which it would be going too much into detail to mention. We read indeed of the feast when Isaac was weaned, and of Jacob's courtship, and of the religious

[1] *Vide* the author's Oxford Sermons, vol. i.

merrymakings of holy Job; but exceptions such as these do but remind us what might be in Scripture, and is not. If then by literature is meant the manifestation of human nature in human language, you will seek for it in vain except in the world. Put up with it as it is, or do not pretend to cultivate it; take things as they are, not as you could wish them.

Nay, I am obliged to go further still; even if we could, still we should be shrinking from our plain duty, gentlemen, did we leave out literature from education. For why do we educate, except to prepare for the world? Why do we cultivate the intellect of the many beyond the first elements of knowledge, except for this world? Will it be much matter in the world to come whether our bodily health or whether our intellectual strength was more or less, except of course as this world is in all its circumstances a trial for the next? If then a university is a direct preparation for this world, let it be what it professes. It is not a convent, it is not a seminary; it is a place to fit men of the world for the world. We cannot possibly keep them from plunging into the world, with all its ways and principles and maxims, when their time comes; but we can prepare them against what is inevitable; and it is not the way to learn to swim in troubled waters, never to have gone into them. Proscribe (I do not merely say particular authors, particular works, particular passages), but secular literature as such; cut out from your class books all broad manifestations of the natural man; and those manifestations are waiting for your pupil's benefit at the very doors of your lecture room in living and breathing substance. They will meet him there in all the charm of novelty, and all the fascination of genius or of amiableness. To-day a pupil, to-morrow a member of the great world: to-day confined to the *Lives of the Saints*, to-morrow thrown upon babel; thrown on babel, without the honest indulgence of wit and humour and imagination ever permitted to him, without any fastidiousness of taste wrought into him, without any rule given him for discriminating 'the precious from the vile,' beauty from sin, the truth from the sophistry of nature, what is innocent from what is poison. You have refused him the masters of human thought, who would in some sense have educated him because of their incidental corruption: you have shut up from him those whose thoughts strike home to our hearts, whose words are proverbs, whose names are indigenous to all the world, the standard of their mother tongue, and the pride and boast of their countrymen, Homer, Ariosto, Cervantes, Shakespeare, because the old Adam smelt rank in them; and for what have you reserved him? You have given him 'a liberty unto' the multitudinous blasphemy of his day; you have made him free of its newspapers, its reviews, its magazines, its novels, its controversial pamphlets, of its Parliamentary debates, its law proceedings, its platform speeches, its songs, its drama, its theatre, of its enveloping, stifling atmosphere of death. You have succeeded but in this—in making the world his university.

Difficult then as the question may be, and much as it may try the judgments and even divide the opinions of zealous and religious Catholics, I cannot feel any doubt myself, gentlemen, that the Church's true policy is not to aim at the exclusion of literature from secular schools, but her own admission into them. Let her do for literature in one way what she does for science in another; each has its imperfection, and she supplies it for each. She fears no knowledge, but she purifies all; she represses no element of our nature, but cultivates the whole. Science is grave, methodical, logical; with science then she argues, and opposes reason to reason. Literature does not argue, but declaims and insinuates; it is multiform and versatile: it persuades instead of convincing, it seduces, it carries captive; it appeals to the sense of honour, or to the imagination, or to the stimulus of curiosity; it makes its way by means of gaiety, satire, romance, the beautiful, the pleasurable. Is it wonderful that with an agent like this the Church should claim to deal with a vigour corresponding to its restlessness, to interfere in its proceedings with a higher hand, and to wield an authority in the choice of its studies and of its books which would be tyrannical, if reason and fact were the only instruments of its conclusions? But anyhow, her principle is one and the same throughout: not to prohibit truth of any kind, but to see that no doctrines pass under the name of truth but those which claim it rightfully.

Such at least is the lesson which I am taught by all the thought which I have been able to bestow upon the subject: such is the lesson which I have gained from the history of my own special father and patron, St Philip Neri. He lived in an age as traitorous to the interests of Catholicism as any that preceded it, or can follow it. He lived at a time when pride mounted high, and the senses held rule; a time when kings and nobles never had more of state and homage, and never less of personal responsibility and peril; when medieval winter was receding, and the summer sun of civilization was bringing into leaf and flower a thousand forms of luxurious enjoyment; when a new world of thought and beauty had opened upon the human mind, in the discovery of the treasures of classic literature and art. He saw the great and the gifted dazzled by the enchantress, and drinking in the magic of her song; he saw the high and the wise, the student and the artist, painting, and poetry, and sculpture, and music, and architecture drawn within her range, and circling round the abyss: he saw heathen forms mounting thence, and forming in the thick air: all this he saw, and he perceived that the mischief was to be met, not with argument, not with science, not with protests and warnings, not by the recluse or the preacher, but by means of the great counter-fascination of purity and truth. He was raised up to do a work almost peculiar in the Church—not to be a Jerome Savonarola, though Philip had a true devotion towards him and a tender memory of his Florentine house; not to be a St Carlo, though in his beaming countenance Philip has recognized the aureola of a saint; not to be a St Ignatius, wrestling with the foe, though Philip was termed the society's bell of call, so many subjects did he send to it; not to be a St Francis Xavier, though Philip had longed to shed his blood for Christ in India with him; not to be a St Caietan, or hunter of souls, for Philip preferred, as he expressed it, tranquilly to cast in his net to gain them; he preferred to yield to the stream, and direct the current which he could not stop, of science, literature, art, and fashion, and to sweeten and to sanctify what God had made very good and man had spoilt.

And so he contemplated as the idea of his mission, not the propagation of the faith, nor the exposition of doctrine, nor the catechetical schools; whatever was exact and systematic pleased him not; he put from him monastic rule and authoritative speech, as David refused the armour of his king. No; he would be but an ordinary individual priest as others: and his weapons should be but unaffected humility and unpretending love. All he did was to be done by the light, and fervour, and convincing eloquence of his personal character and his easy conversation. He came to the Eternal City and he sat himself down there, and his home and his family gradually grew up around him, by the spontaneous accession of materials from without. He did not so much seek his own as draw them to him. He sat in his small room, and they in their gay worldly dresses, the rich and the well-born, as well as the simple and the illiterate, crowded into it. In the mid-heats of summer, in the

frosts of winter, still was he in that low and narrow cell at
San Girolamo, reading the hearts of those who came to him,
and curing their souls' maladies by the very touch of his
hand. It was a vision of the Magi worshipping the infant
Saviour, so pure and innocent, so sweet and beautiful was
he; and so loyal and so dear to the gracious Virgin Mother.
And they who came remained gazing and listening, till at
length first one and then another threw off their bravery,
and took his poor cassock and girdle instead: or, if they
kept it, it was to put haircloth under it, or to take on them
a rule of life, while to the world they looked as before.

In the words of his biographer, 'he was all things to all
men. He suited himself to noble and ignoble, young and
old, subjects and prelates, learned and ignorant; and received those who were strangers to him with singular
benignity, and embraced them with as much love and
charity as if he had been a long while expecting them.
When he was called upon to be merry he was so; if there
was a demand upon his sympathy he was equally ready.
He gave the same welcome to all: caressing the poor equally
with the rich, and wearying himself to assist all to the utmost
limits of his power. In consequence of his being so accessible and willing to receive all comers, many went to
him every day, and some continued for the space of thirty,
nay forty years to visit him very often both morning and
evening, so that his room went by the agreeable nickname of
the home of Christian mirth. Nay, people came to him,
not only from all parts of Italy, but from France, Spain,
Germany, and all Christendom; and even the infidels and
Jews, who had ever any communication with him, revered
him as a holy man.'[1] The first families of Rome, the
Massimi, the Aldobrandini, the Colonna, the Altieri, the
Vitelleschi, were his friends and his penitents. Nobles of
Poland, grandees of Spain, knights of Malta, could not

[1] *Bacci*, vol. i, p. 192; ii, p. 98.

leave Rome without coming to him. Cardinals, arch-
bishops, and bishops were his intimates; Federigo Borromeo haunted his room and got the name of 'Father
Philip's soul.' The Cardinal-Archbishops of Verona and
Bologna wrote books in his honour. Pope Pius IV died
in his arms. Lawyers, painters, musicians, physicians, it
was the same too with them. Baronius, Zazzara, and
Ricci left the law at his bidding and joined his congregation,
to do its work, to write the annals of the Church, and
to die in the odour of sanctity. Palestrina had Father
Philip's ministrations in his last moments. Animuccia
hung about him during life, sent him a message after death,
and was conducted by him through purgatory to heaven.
And who was he, I say, all the while, but a humble priest, a
stranger in Rome, with no distinction of family or letters, no
claim of station or of office, great simply in the attraction
with which a Divine Power had gifted him? and yet thus
humble, thus unennobled, thus empty-handed, he has
achieved the glorious title of Apostle of Rome.

Well were it for his clients and children, gentlemen, if
they could promise themselves the very shadow of his
special power, or could hope to do a miserable fraction of
the sort of work in which he was pre-eminently skilled. But
so far at least they may attempt—to take his position, and
to use his method, and to cultivate the arts of which he was
so bright a pattern. For me, if it be God's blessed will that
in the years now coming I am to have a share in the great
undertaking which has been the occasion and the subject
of these discourses, so far I can say for certain that, whether
or not I can do anything at all in St Philip's way, at least I
can do nothing in any other. Neither by my habits of
life, nor by vigour of age, am I fitted for the task of authority
or of rule, or of initiation. I do but aspire, if strength is
given me, to be your minister in a work which must employ
younger minds and stronger lives than mine. I am but

fit to bear my witness, to proffer my suggestions, to express my sentiments, as has in fact been my occupation in these discussions; to throw such light upon general questions, upon the choice of objects, upon the import of principles, upon the tendency of measures, as past reflection and experience enable me to contribute. I shall have to make appeals to your consideration, your friendliness, your confidence, of which I have had so many instances, on which I so tranquilly repose; and after all, neither you nor I must ever be surprised should it so happen that the hand of Him with whom are the springs of life and death weighs heavy on me, and makes me unequal to anticipations in which you have been too kind, and to hopes in which I may have been too sanguine.

CHRISTIANITY AND SCIENTIFIC
INVESTIGATION

A LECTURE[1]

THIS is a time, gentlemen, when not only the classics, but much more the sciences, in the largest sense of the word, are looked upon with anxiety, not altogether ungrounded, by religious men, and whereas a university such as ours professes to embrace all departments and exercises of the intellect, and since I for my part wish to stand on good terms with all kinds of knowledge, and have no intention of quarrelling with any, and would open my heart, if not my intellect (for that is beyond me) to the whole circle of truth, and would tender at least a recognition and hospitality even to those studies which are strangers to me, and would speed them on their way; therefore, as I have been making overtures of reconciliation, first between polite literature and religion, and next between physics and theology, so I would now say a word by way of deprecating and protesting against the needless antagonism which sometimes exists in fact between divines and the cultivators of the sciences generally.

Here I am led at once to expatiate on the grandeur of an institution which is comprehensive enough to admit the discussion of a subject such as this. Among the objects of human enterprise—I may say it surely without extravagance, gentlemen—none higher or nobler can be named than that which is contemplated in the erection of a university. To set on foot and to maintain in life and vigour

[1] This lecture, which was never delivered, is addressed to the School of Science.

209

a real university is confessedly, as soon as the word university is understood, one of those greatest works, great in their difficulty and their importance, on which are deservedly expended the rarest intellects and the most varied endowments. For, first of all, it professes to teach whatever has to be taught in any whatever department of human knowledge, and it embraces in its scope the loftiest subjects of human thought, and the richest fields of human inquiry. Nothing is too vast, nothing too subtle, nothing too distant, nothing too minute, nothing too discursive, nothing too exact, to engage its attention.

This, however, is not why I claim for it so sovereign a position; for to bring schools of all knowledge under one name, and call them a university, may be fairly said to be a mere generalization; and to proclaim that the prosecution of all kinds of knowledge to their utmost limits demands the fullest reach and range of our intellectual faculties is but a truism. My reason for speaking of a university in the terms on which I have ventured is, not that it occupies the whole territory of knowledge merely, but that it is the very realm; that it professes much more than to take in and to lodge as in a caravanserai all art and science, all history and philosophy. In truth, it professes to assign to each study which it receives its own proper place and its just boundaries; to define the rights, to establish the mutual relations, and to effect the intercommunion of one and all; to keep in check the ambitious and encroaching, and to succour and maintain those which from time to time are succumbing under the more popular or the more fortunately circumstanced; to keep the peace between them all, and to convert their mutual differences and contrarieties into the common good. This, gentlemen, is why I say that to erect a university is at once so arduous and beneficial an undertaking, viz. because it is pledged to admit without fear, without prejudice, without compromise, all comers, if they come in the name of truth; to adjust views, and experiences, and habits of mind the most independent and dissimilar; and to give full play of thought and erudition in their most original forms, and their most intense expressions, and in their most ample circuit. Thus to draw many things into one is its special function; and it learns to do it, not by rules reducible to writing, but by sagacity, wisdom, and forbearance, acting upon a profound insight into the subject-matter of knowledge, and a vigilant repression of aggression or bigotry in any quarter.

We count it a great thing, and justly so, to plan and carry out a wide political organization. To bring under one yoke, after the manner of old Rome, a hundred discordant peoples to maintain each of them in its own privileges within its legitimate range of action; to allow them severally the indulgence of national feelings, and the stimulus of rival interests; and yet withal to blend them into one great social establishment, and to pledge them to the perpetuity of the one imperial power—this is an achievement which carries with it the unequivocal token of genius in the race which effects it.

Tu regere imperio populos, Romane, memento.

This was the special boast, as the poet considered it, of the Roman; a boast as high in its own line as that other boast, proper to the Greek nation, of literary pre-eminence, of exuberance of thought, and of skill and refinement in expressing it.

What an empire is in political history, such is a university in the sphere of philosophy and science. It is, as I have said, the high protecting power of all knowledge and science, of fact and principle, of inquiry and discovery, of experiment and speculation; it maps out the territory of the intellect, and sees that the boundaries of each province are religiously respected, and that there is neither encroachment nor surrender on any side. It acts as umpire between truth and truth, and, taking into account the nature and importance of each, assigns to all their due order and precedence. It maintains no one department of thought exclusively, however ample and noble; and it sacrifices none. It is deferential and loyal, according to their respective weight, to the claims of literature, of physical research, of history, of metaphysics, of theological science. It is impartial towards them all, and promotes each on its own place and for its own object. It is ancillary, certainly, and of necessity, to the Catholic Church; but in the same way that one of the Queen's judges is an officer of the Queen's, and nevertheless determines certain legal proceedings between the Queen and her subjects. It is ministrative to the Catholic Church, first, because truth of any kind can but minister to truth; and next, still more, because nature ever will pay homage to grace, and reason cannot but illustrate and defend revelation; and thirdly, because the Church has a sovereign authority, and when she speaks *ex cathedra* must be obeyed. But this is the remote end of a university; its immediate end (with which alone we have here to do) is to secure the due disposition, according to one sovereign order, and the cultivation in that order, of all the provinces and methods of thought which the human intellect has created.

In this point of view, its several professors are like the representatives of various political powers at one court or conference. They represent their respective sciences, and attend to their private interests respectively; and, should dispute arise between those sciences, they are the persons to talk over and arrange it, without risk of extravagant pretensions on any side, of angry collision, or of popular commotion. A liberal philosophy becomes the habit of minds thus exercised; a spaciousness of thought in which lines, seemingly parallel, may converge at leisure, and principles recognized as incommeasurable may be safely antagonistic.

And here, gentlemen, we recognize the special character of the philosophy I am speaking of, if philosophy it is to be called, in contrast with the method of a strict science or system. Its teaching is not founded on one idea, or reducible to certain formulae. Newton might discover the great law of motion in the physical world, and the key to ten thousand phenomena; and a similar resolution of complex facts into simple principles may be possible in other departments of nature; but the great universe itself, moral and material, sensible and supernatural, cannot be gauged and meted by even the greatest of human intellects, and its constituent parts admit indeed of comparison and adjustment, but not of fusion. This is the point which bears directly on the subject which I set before me when I began, and towards which I am moving in all I have said or shall be saying. I observe then, and ask you, gentlemen, to bear in mind, that the philosophy of an imperial intellect, for such I am considering a university to be, is based not so much on simplification as on discrimination. Its true representative defines rather than analyses. He aims at no complete catalogue or interpretation of the subjects of knowledge, but at following out, as far as man can, what in its fullness is mysterious and unfathomable. Taking into its charge all sciences, methods, collections of facts, principles, doctrines, truths, which are the reflections of the universe upon the human intellect, he admits them all, he disregards none, and, as disregarding none, he allows none to exceed or encroach. His watchword is live and let live. He takes things as they are; he submits to them all, as far as they go; he recognizes the insuperable lines of demarcation which run between subject and subject; he observes how separate truths lie relatively to each other, where they concur, where they part company, and where, being carried too far, they cease to be truths at all. It is his office to determine how much can be known in each province of thought; when we must be contented not to know; in what direction inquiry is hopeless, or on the other hand full of promise; where it gathers into coils insoluble by reason, where it is absorbed in mysteries, or runs into the abyss. It will be his care to be familiar with the signs of real and apparent difficulties, with the methods proper to particular subject-matters, what in each particular case are the limits of a rational scepticism, and what the claims of a peremptory faith. If he has one cardinal maxim in his philosophy, it is that truth cannot be contrary to truth; if he has a second, it is that truth often *seems* contrary to truth; and if a third, it is the practical conclusion that we must be patient with such appearances, and not be hasty to pronounce them to be really of a more formidable character.

It is the very immensity of the system of things, the human record of which he has in charge, which is the reason of this patience and caution; for that immensity suggests to him that the contrarieties and mysteries which meet him in the various sciences may be simply the consequence of our necessarily defective comprehension. There is but one thought greater than the universe, and that is the thought of its Maker. If, gentlemen, for one single instant, leaving my proper train of thought, I allude to our knowledge of the Supreme Being, it is in order to deduce an illustration bearing upon it. He, though One, is a sort of world of worlds in Himself, giving birth in our minds to an indefinite number of distinct truths, each ineffably more mysterious than anything that is found in this universe of space and time. Any one of His attributes, considered by itself, is the object of an inexhaustible science; and the attempt to reconcile any two or three of them together—love, power, justice, sanctity, truth, wisdom—affords matter for an everlasting controversy. We are able to apprehend and receive each divine attribute in its elementary form, but still we are not able to accept them in their infinity, either in themselves or in union with each other. Yet we do not deny the first because it cannot be perfectly reconciled with the second, nor the second because it is in apparent contrariety with the first and the third. The case is the same in its degree with His creation, material and moral. It is the highest wisdom to accept truth of whatever kind, wherever it is clearly ascertained to be such, though there be difficulty in adjusting it with other known truth.

Instances are easily producible of that extreme contrariety of ideas which the contemplation of the universe inflicts upon us, such as to make it clear to us that there is nothing irrational in submitting to apparent incompatibilities in that teaching which we have no thought on that account of denying. Such for instance is the contemplation of space, the existence of which we cannot deny, though its idea is able, in no sort of posture, to seat itself (if I may so speak) in our minds; for we find it impossible to say that it comes to a stop anywhere; and it is incomprehensible to say that it runs out infinitely; and it seems to be unmeaning if we say that it does not exist till bodies come into it, and thus is enlarged according to the accident.

And so again in the instance of time. We cannot place a beginning to it without asking ourselves what was before it; yet that there should be no beginning at all, put it as far off as we will, is simply incomprehensible. Here again, as in the case of space, we never dream of denying the existence of what we have no means of understanding.

And, passing from this high region of thought (which, high as it may be, is the subject even of a child's contemplations), when we come to consider the mutual action of soul and body we are specially perplexed by incompatibilities which we can neither reject nor explain. How it is that the will can act on the muscles is a question of which even a child may feel the force, but which no experimentalist can answer.

Further, when we contrast the physical with the social laws under which man finds himself here below, we must grant that physiology and social science are in collision. Man is both a physical and a social being; yet he cannot at once pursue to the full his physical end and his social end, his physical duties (if I may so speak) and his social duties, but is forced to sacrifice in part one or the other. If we were wild enough to fancy that there were two creators, one of whom was the author of our animal frames, the other of society, then indeed we might understand how it comes to pass that labour of mind and body, the useful arts, the duties of a statesman, government, and the like, which are required by the social system, are so destructive of health, enjoyment, and life. That is, in other words, we cannot adequately account for existing and undeniable truths except on the hypothesis of what we feel to be an absurdity.

And so in mathematical science, as has been often insisted on, the philosopher has patiently to endure the presence of truths which are not the less true for being irreconcilable with each other. He is told of the existence of an infinite number of curves, which are able to divide a space, into which no straight line, though it be length without breadth, can even enter. He is told too of certain lines which approach to each other continually, with a finite distance between them, yet never meet; and these apparent contrarieties he must bear as he best can, without attempting to deny the existence of the truths which constitute them in the science in question.

Now, let me call your attention, gentlemen, to what I would infer from these familiar facts. It is, to urge you with an argument *a fortiori*, viz. that, as you exercise so much exemplary patience in the case of the inexplicable truths which surround so many departments of knowledge, human and divine, viewed in themselves; as you are not at once indignant, censorious, suspicious, difficult of belief, on finding that in the secular sciences one truth is incompatible (according to our human intellect) with another or inconsistent with itself; so you should not think it very hard to be told that there exists, here and there, not an inextricable difficulty, not an astounding contrariety, not (much less) a contradiction as to clear facts, between revelation and nature; but a hitch, an obscurity, a divergence of tendency, a temporary antagonism, a difference of tone between the two—that is, between Catholic opinion on the one hand and astronomy, or geology, or physiology, or ethnology, or political economy, or history, or antiquities on the other. I say that, as we admit, because we are Catholics, that the Divine Unity contains in it attributes which, to our finite minds, appear in partial contrariety with each other; as we admit that, in His revealed Nature, are things which, though not opposed to reason, are infinitely strange to the imagination; as in His works we can neither reject nor admit the ideas of space, and of time, and the necessary properties of lines, without intellectual distress; really, gentlemen, I am making no outrageous request when, in the name of a university, I ask religious writers, jurists, economists, physiologists, chemists, geologists, and historians to go on quietly, and in a neighbourly way, in their own respective lines of speculation, research, and experiment, with full faith in the consistency of that multiform truth which they share between them, in a generous confidence that they will be consistent, one and all, in their combined results, though there may be momentary collisions, awkward appearances, and many forebodings and prophecies of contrariety, and at all times things hard to the imagination, though not, I repeat, to the reason.

It surely needs no great boldness to beg of them—since they are forced to admit mysteries, even in the actual issue itself, in the truths of revelation, taken by themselves, and in the truths of reason, taken by themselves—to beg of them, I say, to keep the peace, to live in goodwill, and to exercise equanimity if, when nature and revelation are compared with each other, there be, as I have said, discrepancies—not in the issue, but in the reasonings, the circumstances, the associations, the anticipations, the accidents, proper to their respective teachings.

It is most necessary to insist seriously and energetically on this point, for the sake of Protestants, for they have very strange notions about us. In spite of the testimony of history the other way, they think that the Church has no other method of putting down error than the arm of force or the prohibition of inquiry. They defy us to set up and carry on a school of science. For their sake, then, I am led to enlarge upon the subject here. I say then, he who believes revelation with that absolute faith which is the prerogative of a Catholic is not the nervous creature who startles at every sudden sound, and is fluttered by every strange or frightful appearance which meets his eyes. He has no sort of apprehension, he laughs at the idea, that anything can be discovered by any other scientific method which can contradict any one of the dogmas of his religion. He knows full well that there is no science but in the course of its extension runs the risk of infringing, without any meaning of offence on its own part, the path of other sciences; and he knows also that, if there be any one science which, from its sovereign and unassailable position, can calmly bear such unintentional collisions on the part of the children of earth, it is theology. He is sure, and nothing shall make him doubt, that, if anything seems to be proved by astronomer, or geologist, or chronologist, or antiquarian, or ethnologist, in contradiction to the dogmas of faith, that point will eventually turn out, first, *not* to be proved, or secondly, not *contradictory*, or thirdly, not contradictory to anything *really revealed*, but to something which has been confused with revelation.   And if at the moment it appears to be contradictory, then he is content to wait, knowing that error is like other delinquents; give it rope enough, and it will be found to have a strong suicidal propensity.   I do not mean to say he will not take his part in encouraging, in helping forward the prospective suicide; he will not only give the error rope enough, but show it how to handle and adjust the rope; he will commit the matter to reason, reflection, sober judgment, common sense; to time, the great interpreter of so many secrets. Instead of being irritated at the momentary triumph of the foes of revelation, if such a feeling of triumph there be, and of hurrying on a forcible solution of the difficulty, which may in the event only reduce the inquiry to an inextricable tangle, he will recollect that, in the order of Providence, our seeming dangers are often our greatest gains; that in the words of the Protestant poet:

> The clouds you so much dread
> Are big with mercy, and shall break
> In blessings on your head.

To one notorious instance indeed it is obvious to allude here.   When the Copernican system first made progress, what religious man would not have been tempted to uneasiness, or at least fear of scandal, from the seeming contradiction which it involved to some authoritative tradition of the Church and the declaration of Scripture? It was generally received, as if the Apostles had expressly delivered it both orally and in writing, that the earth was stationary, and that the sun was fixed in a solid firmament which whirled round the earth.   After a little time, however, and on full consideration, it was found that the Church had decided next to nothing on questions such as these, and that physical science might range in this sphere of thought almost at will, without fear of encountering the decisions of ecclesiastical authority. Now, besides the relief which it afforded to Catholics to find that they were to be spared this addition, on the side of cosmology, to their many controversies already existing, there is something of an argument in this circumstance in behalf of the divinity of their religion. For it surely is a very remarkable fact, considering how widely and how long one certain interpretation of these physical statements in Scripture had been received by Catholics, that the Church should not have formally acknowledged it. Looking at the matter in a human point of view, it was inevitable that she should have made that opinion her own. But now we find, on ascertaining where we stand in the face of the new sciences of these latter times, that, in spite of the bountiful comments which from the first she has ever been making on the sacred text, as it is her duty and her right to do, nevertheless she has never been led formally to explain the texts in question, or to give them an authoritative sense which modern science may question.

Nor was this escape a mere accident, or what will more religiously be called a providential event, as is shown by a passage of history in the dark age itself. When the glorious St Boniface, Apostle of Germany, great in sanctity, though not in secular knowledge, complained to the Holy See that St Virgilius taught the existence of the antipodes, the Holy See apparently evaded the question, not indeed siding with the Irish philosopher, which would have been going out of its place, but passing over, in a matter not revealed, a philosophical opinion.

Time went on; a new state of things, intellectual and social, came in; the Church was girt with temporal power; the preachers of St Dominic were in the ascendant: now at

length we may ask with curious interest, did the Church
alter her ancient rule of action, and proscribe intellectual
activity? Just the contrary; this is the very age of universities; it is the classical period of the schoolmen; it is the
splendid and palmary instance of the wise policy and large
liberality of the Church as regards philosophical inquiry.
If there ever was a time when the intellect went wild, and
had a licentious revel, it was at the date I speak of. When
was there ever a more curious, more meddling, bolder,
keener, more penetrating, more rationalistic exercise of the
reason than at that time? What class of questions did
that subtle, metaphysical spirit not scrutinize? What
premiss was allowed without examination? What principle was not traced to its first origin, and exhibited in its
most naked shape? What whole was not analysed?
What complex idea was not elaborately traced out, and,
as it were, finely painted for the contemplation of the mind,
till it was spread out in all its minutest portions as perfectly
and delicately as a frog's foot shows under the intense
scrutiny of the microscope? Well, I repeat, here was something which came somewhat nearer to theology than physical research comes; Aristotle was a somewhat more
serious foe then, beyond all mistake, than Bacon has been
since. Did the Church take a high hand with philosophy
then? No, not though it was metaphysical. It was a time
when she had temporal power, and could have exter-
minated the spirit of inquiry with fire and sword; but she
determined to put it down by *argument*; she said: 'Two
can play at that, and my argument is the better.' She
sent her controversialists into the philosophical arena.
It was the Dominican and Franciscan doctors, the greatest
of them being St Thomas, who in those medieval universities fought the battle of revelation with the weapons of
heathenism. It was no matter whose the weapon was;
truth was truth all the world over. With the jaw-bone of

an ass, with the skeleton philosophy of pagan Greece, did the Samson of the schools put to flight his thousand Philistines.

Here, gentlemen, observe the contrast exhibited by the Church herself, who has the gift of wisdom, and even the ablest, or wisest, or holiest of her children. As St Boniface had been jealous of physical speculations, so had the early fathers shown an extreme aversion to the great heathen philosopher whom I just now named, Aristotle. I do not know who of them could endure him; and, when there arose those in the middle age who would take his part, especially since their intentions were of a suspicious character, a strenuous effort was made to banish him out of Christendom. The Church the while had kept silence; she had as little denounced heathen philosophy in the mass as she had pronounced upon the meaning of certain texts of Scripture of a cosmological character. From Tertullian and Caius to the two Gregories of Cappadocia, from them to Anastasius Sinaita, from him to the school of Paris, Aristotle was a word of offence; at length St Thomas made him a hewer of wood and drawer of water to the Church. A strong slave he is; and the Church herself has given her sanction to the use in theology of the ideas and terms of his philosophy.

Now while this free discussion is, to say the least, so safe for religion, or rather so expedient, it is on the other hand simply necessary for progress in science; and I shall now go on to insist on this side of the subject. I say then that it is a matter of primary importance, in the cultivation of those sciences in which truth is discoverable by the human intellect, that the investigator should be free, independent, unshackled in his movements; that he should be allowed and enabled, without impediment, to fix his mind intently, nay exclusively, on his special object, without the risk of being distracted every other minute in the process and progress of his inquiry by charges of temerariousness, or by warnings against extravagance or scandal. But in thus speaking I must premise several explanations, lest I be mistaken.

First then, gentlemen, as to the fundamental principles of religion and morals, and again as to the fundamental principles of Christianity, or what are called the *dogmas* of faith—as to this double creed, natural and revealed—we, none of us, should say that it is any shackle at all upon the intellect to maintain these inviolate. Indeed, a Catholic cannot help having regard to them; and they as little impede the movements of his intellect as the laws of physics impede his bodily movements. The habitual apprehension of them has become a second nature with him, as the laws of optics, hydrostatics, motion, dynamics, are latent conditions which he takes for granted in the use of his corporeal organs. I am not supposing any collision with dogma, I am but speaking of opinions of divines, or of the multitude, parallel to those in former times of the sun going round the earth, or of the last day being close at hand, or of St Dionysius the Areopagite being the author of the works which bear his name.

Nor, secondly, even as regards such opinions am I supposing any direct intrusion into the province of religion, or of a teacher of science actually laying down the law *in a matter of religion*; but of such unintentional collisions as are incidental to a discussion pursued on some subject of his own. It would be a great mistake in such a one to propose his philosophical or historical conclusions as the formal interpretation of the sacred text, as Galileo is said to have done, instead of being content to hold his doctrine of the motion of the earth as a scientific conclusion, and leaving it to those whom it really concerned to compare it with Scripture. And, it must be confessed, gentlemen, not a few instances occur of this mistake at the present day, on the part, not indeed of men of science, but of religious men, who, from a nervous impatience lest Scripture should not one moment seem inconsistent with the results of some speculation of the hour, are ever proposing geological or ethnological comments upon it, which they have to alter or obliterate before the ink is well dry, from changes in the progressive science which they have so officiously brought to its aid.

And thirdly, I observe that, when I advocate the independence of philosophical thought, I am not speaking of any *formal teaching* at all, but of investigations, speculations, and discussions. I am far indeed from allowing, in any matter which even borders on religion, what an eminent Protestant divine has advocated on the most sacred subjects: I mean 'the liberty of prophesying.' I have no wish to degrade the professors of science, who ought to be prophets of the truth, into mere advertisers of crude fancies or notorious absurdities. I am not pleading that they should at random shower down upon their hearers ingenuities and novelties; or that they should teach even what has a basis of truth in it, in a brilliant, offhand way, to a collection of youths, who may not perhaps hear them, for six consecutive lectures, and who will carry away with them into the country a misty idea of the half-created theories of some ambitious intellect.

Once more, as the last sentence suggests, there must be great care taken to avoid *scandal*, or of shocking the popular mind, or of unsettling the weak; the association between truth and error being so strong in particular minds that it is impossible to weed them of the error, without rooting up the wheat with it. If then there is the chance of any current religious opinion being in any way compromised in the course of a scientific investigation, this would be a reason for conducting it, not in light ephemeral publications, which come into the hands of the careless or ignorant, but in works of a grave and business-like character, answering to the medieval schools of philosophical disputation which, removed as they were from the region of popular thought and feeling, have, by their vigorous restlessness of inquiry, in spite of their extravagances, done so much for theological precision.

I am not then supposing the scientific investigator to be *coming into collision with dogma*; nor venturing, by means of his investigations, upon any interpretation of Scripture or upon other *conclusion in the matter of religion*; nor *teaching* even in his own science, instead of investigating; nor to be careless of *scandalizing the weak*; but, these explanations being made, I still say that a scientific speculator or inquirer is not bound, in the course of his researches, to be every moment adjusting his course by the maxims of the schools or by popular traditions, or by those of any other science distinct from his own, or to be ever narrowly watching what those external sciences have to say to him; being confident, from a generous faith, that, however his line of investigation may swerve now and then, and vary to and fro in its course, or threaten momentary collision or embarrassment with any other department of knowledge, theological or not, yet, if he lets it alone, it will be sure to come home, because truth never can really be contrary to truth, and because often what at first sight is an *exceptio*, in the event most emphatically *probat regulam*.

This is a point of serious importance to him.   Unless he is at liberty to investigate on the basis, and according to the peculiarities, of his science, he cannot investigate at all. It is the very law of the human mind, in its inquiry after and acquisition of truth, to make its advances by a process which consists of many stages, and is circuitous.   There are no short cuts to knowledge; nor does the road to it always lie in the direction in which it terminates, nor are we able to see the end on starting.   It may often seem to be diverging from a goal into which it will soon run without effort, if we are but patient and resolute in following it out; and, as we are told in ethics to gain the mean merely by receding from both extremes, so in scientific researches error may be said, without a paradox, to be in some instances the way to truth and the only way. Moreover, it is not often the fortune of any one man to live through an investigation; the process is one of not only many stages, but of many minds. What one begins, another finishes; and a true conclusion is at length worked out by the cooperation of independent schools and the perseverance of successive generations. This being the case, we are obliged, under circumstances, to bear for a while with what we feel to be error, in consideration of the truth in which it is eventually to issue.

The analogy of locomotion is most pertinent here. No one can go straight up a mountain; no sailing-vessel makes for its port without tacking. And so, applying the illustration, we can indeed, if we will, refuse to allow of investigation or research altogether; but, if we invite reason to take its place in our schools, we must let reason have fair and full play. If we reason, we must submit to the conditions of reason. We cannot use it by halves; we must use it as proceeding from Him who has also given us revelation; and to be ever interrupting its processes, and diverting its attention by objections brought from a higher knowledge, is parallel to a landsman's dismay at the changes in the course of a vessel on which he has deliberately embarked, and argues surely some distrust either in the powers of reason on the one hand, or the certainty of revealed truth on the other. The passenger should not have embarked at all if he did not reckon on the chance of a rough sea, of currents, of wind and tide, of rocks and shoals; and we should act more wisely in discountenancing altogether the exercise of reason, than in being alarmed and impatient under the suspense, delay, and anxiety which, from the nature of the case, may be found to attach to it. Let us eschew secular history and science and philosophy for good and all, if we are not allowed to be sure that revelation is so true that the altercations and perplexities of human opinion cannot really or eventually injure its authority. That is no intellectual triumph of any truth of religion which has not been preceded by a full statement of what can be said against it; it is but the *ego vapulando, ille verberando*, of the comedy.

Great minds need elbow-room, not indeed in the domain of faith, but of thought. And so indeed do lesser minds, and all minds. There are many persons in the world who are called, and with a great deal of truth, geniuses. They have been gifted by nature with some particular faculty or capacity; and, while vehemently excited and imperiously ruled by it, they are blind to everything else. They are enthusiasts in their own line, and are simply dead to the beauty of any line *except* their own. Accordingly, they think their own line the only line in the whole world worth pursuing, and they feel a sort of contempt for such studies as move upon any other line. Now these men may be, and often are, very good Catholics, and have not a dream of anything but affection and deference towards Catholicity, nay perhaps are zealous in its interests. Yet if you insist that in their speculations, researches, or conclusions in their particular science it is not enough that they should submit to the Church generally, and acknowledge its dogmas, but that they must get up all that divines have said, or the multitude believed upon religious matters, you simply crush and stamp out the flame within them, and they can do nothing at all.

This is the case of men of genius: now one word on the contrary in behalf of master minds, gifted with a broad philosophical view of things, and a creative power, and a versatility capable of accommodating itself to various provinces of thought. These persons, perhaps, like those I have already spoken of, take up some idea and are intent upon it; some deep, prolific, eventful idea, which grows upon them, till they develop it into a great system. Now if any such thinker starts from radically unsound principles, or aims at directly false conclusions, if he be a Hobbes, or a Shaftesbury, or a Hume, or a Bentham, then, of course, there is an end of the whole matter. He is an opponent of revealed truth, and he means to be so; nothing more need be said. But perhaps it is not so; perhaps his errors are those which are inseparable accidents of his system or of his mind, and are spontaneously evolved, not pertinaciously defended. Every human system, every human writer, is open to just criticism. Make him shut up his portfolio; good! and then perhaps you lose what, on the whole and in spite of incidental mistakes, would have been one of the ablest defences of revealed truth (directly or indirectly, according to his subject) ever given to the world.

This is how I should account for a circumstance which has sometimes caused surprise, that so many great Catholic thinkers have in some points or other incurred the criticism or animadversion of theologians or of ecclesiastical authority. It must be so in the nature of things; there is indeed an animadversion which implies a condemnation of the author; but there is another which means not much more than the *piè legendum* written against passages in the fathers. The author may not be to blame; yet the ecclesiastical authority would be to blame if it did not give notice of his imperfections. I do not know what Catholic would not hold the name of Malebranche in veneration; but he may have accidentally come into collision with theologians, or made temerarious assertions, notwithstanding. The practical question is, whether he had not much better have written as he has written, than not have written at all. And so fully is the Holy See accustomed to enter into this view of the matter that it has allowed of its application, not only to philosophical, but even to theological and ecclesiastical authors, who do not come within the range of these remarks. I believe I am right in saying that, in the case of three great names, in various departments of learning, Cardinal Noris, Bossuet, and Muratori, while not concealing its sense of their each having propounded what might have been said better, nevertheless it has considered that their services to religion were on the whole far too important to allow of their being molested by critical observation in detail.

And now, gentlemen, I bring these remarks to a conclusion. What I would urge upon everyone, whatever may be his particular line of research—what I would urge upon men of science in their thoughts of theology—what I would venture to recommend to theologians, when their attention is drawn to the subject of scientific investigations —is a great and firm belief in the sovereignty of truth. Error may flourish for a time, but truth will prevail in the end. The only effect of error ultimately is to promote truth. Theories, speculations, hypotheses, are started; perhaps they are to die, still not before they have suggested ideas better than themselves. These better ideas are taken up in turn by other men and, if they do not yet lead to truth, nevertheless they lead to what is still nearer to truth than themselves; and thus knowledge on the whole makes progress. The errors of some minds in scientific investigation are more fruitful than the truths of others. A science seems making no progress, but to abound in failures, yet imperceptibly all the time it is advancing, and it is of course a gain to truth even to have learned what is not true, if nothing more.

On the other hand, it must be of course remembered, gentlemen, that I am supposing all along good faith, honest intentions, a loyal Catholic spirit, and a deep sense of responsibility. I am supposing, in the scientific inquirer, a due fear of giving scandal, of seeming to countenance views which he does not really countenance, and of siding with parties from whom he heartily differs. I am supposing that he is fully alive to the existence and the power of the infidelity of the age; that he keeps in mind the moral weakness and the intellectual confusion of the majority of men; and that he has no wish at all that any one soul should get harm from certain speculations to-day, though he may have the satisfaction of being sure that those speculations will, as far as they are erroneous or misunderstood, be corrected in the course of the next half-century.

INDEX

Abelard, 77
Academies, xxxii f., 188
Adam, the old, 203
Addison, J., 53
Alexander, 101
Alfred, 131
Alma Mater, 122
Analogy of Religion, 81
Anatomy, comparative, 33, 67
Anaxagoras, 95
Andes, 114
Angels, 15
Animuccia, 207
Anthropology, 40
Antichrist, 167
Antiquarian Society, 57
Antoninus, 167
Apollinaris, 6
Apologia, x, xv, xvii, xx
Apostles, 194, 219
Apostolic See, 190. *See* Holy
See
Aquila, 6
Aquinas, St Thomas, 112, 221 f.
Arcesilas, 81
Architecture, 64. *See* Gothic
Areopagus, xl
Arians, 76
Ariosto, 203
Aristotle, xxxiii, 6, 38–40, 61,
81, 87, 89 f., 112, 138, 193,
221 f.

Arnold, Dr, vi
Arts, fine, 61–5
Astronomy, 33
Athanasian Creed, 12
Athens, 95, 183; Northern A.,
130
Attributes, divine, 214 f.
Authority, x, xii f., xx; ecclesi-
astical, 228

Bacon, Friar, xxxiii, 191
Bacon, Lord, xxxiii, 52, 60, 72,
89, 97 f., 149, 192 ff., 196, 221
Balaam, 50
Bannockburn, 131
Baronius, 207
Baxter, 53
Bentham, 77, 228
Bentley, 137
Berkeley, 52, 64
Beseleel, 201
Beveridge, 6
Bible, 55
Bibliography, xxiii
Bigots, 60
Boniface VIII, 131
Borromeo, Frederigo, 207
Bossuet, 6, 229
Boswell, xxxix
British Association, xxxii
Brougham, 18 f.

231